P9-DBY-735

ADAM JASINSKI
Winner of the CBS Reality Show *Big Brother*

# MY KID'S ON DRUGS, NOW WHAT?

The Only Complete Resource for Dealing With the Devastating Disease of Addiction

*My Kid's on Drugs, Now What?*

*The Only Complete Resource for Dealing With the Devastating Disease of Addiction*

 Published in the United States by Adam Jasinski.

Printed in the United States of America by Ingram Content Group.

ISBN: 978-0-9989906-2-0

1 2 3 4 5 6 7 8 9 0

# CONTENTS

# INTRODUCTION

WHAT WERE YOU DOING LAST night?

Were you pacing the living room? Were you sitting at the kitchen table, watching the clock on the microwave with your hands clasped in a silent prayer? Were you wondering where your son was? Were you worried something had happened to your daughter? Did you wait and watch as 10:00 p.m. turned into 3 a.m.?

If you spent last night or any number of nights doing this, you may have an ugly suspicion growing in the pit of your stomach. Something has changed, but what? Is your daughter coming home at all hours, not herself, out of it? Is your son sneaking out of school? Are his grades slipping? Have you noticed dilated pupils, slurred speech?

When the worry is eating at your nerves as you're staring at that clock, the idea that your child is using drugs has probably popped into your head. But it's such an ugly thought, so when your child makes it home and the worry abates, you shove it aside. It's just teen angst. It's just how kids are. It's a phase. Right?

But if you've cracked open this book, it probably means that the suspicion is still there, jabbing at you every now and then, just when you've started to forget it's there.

Maybe you picked up this book to try and figure out if your child is really doing drugs. I can help you do that.

Maybe you opened it because you can't deny it anymore. Maybe you found a pipe or a stash. Maybe your kid got picked up by the cops and is facing jail time. Now you're thinking, "My kid's on drugs. Now what?" "What's next?" "How do I fix this?" "How does rehab work?" I can help you with all that and much more.

So who exactly am I and why am I so confident that I can help?

My name is Adam Jasinski. You may have heard of me due to my win on the reality show *Big Brother*. If you remember that, you may remember that not long after my face hit the news for my win, it hit the screens again due to my arrest for drug possession and distribution. My addiction didn't start after *Big Brother*; it started in my teens, as did the major symptoms of my bipolar disorder.

I've been where your child is at right now. I've felt both the rush and the helplessness of being hooked on drugs. I know how an addict thinks. I know what can break through the fog and make an addict own up to their addiction. I know which elements of the recovery process work and which ones you need to watch out for. I also know what it's like to struggle with mental illness, which is a very common cause of drug addiction.

I have been sober for eight years. I came out of addiction alive. I gained the upper hand, and I've held onto it. I work as a consultant for facilities that treat drug-addicted youth, and I've recently helped my mother create a recovery center for addicts and those suffering from both addiction and primary mental health disorders, called Oceans Medical Centers. I have the know-how and the first-hand experience, but more importantly, I have a strong desire to help parents who have been where mine have been, and teach them how to pull their children out of the same dark pit that I dug myself out of.

I don't ever want another mother to sit at her kitchen table, staring into space, worried sick that her baby isn't coming home this time. That's why this book will seek to lay out each and every step of the recovery process. Within these pages, I have used my own personal experience as both a former addict and as a professional consultant who works with addicted kids on a daily basis. I've seen or experienced all the problems. I know them, and I know how to overcome them. I've seen what works and what doesn't.

I am able to provide a unique perspective because I get what it's like to be an addicted kid. I haven't forgotten. My ability to get into their heads allows me to translate the motivations, the fears, and the cries for help into something that parents can understand and work through. My connection with addicted youth has earned me many, many success stories. I have testimonials from both parents and addicts promising that what I do in the field works. You can find those at adamjasinski.org.

The information I will provide in this book is both relevant and current. Many books that cover addiction are dated or do not focus on youths. Others are written based on old memories. A lot are written by PhDs or doctors who have never experienced addiction in the real world. While I will share my memories with you, I will also be speaking from current experience as a seasoned professional in the field of rehabilitation and recovery.

This book's focus is not narrow—it covers the whole process, from figuring out if and what your child is using to long-term sobriety after treatment—but it is extremely detailed. Most books that cover the larger picture leave out the specific details and leave the reader thinking, "Well that's a great idea, but how do I actually go about it?" I'm going to lay out the step-by-step processes in a way that no one has before.

In these pages, I'll first walk you through how to know for sure if your child is using and, if so, what he is using. I'll help you understand how your daughter is getting these drugs. I'll teach you how to approach your son about the problem and how to rid yourself of unnecessary and unwarranted self-blame, guilt, denial, and embarrassment.

Next, we'll move on to beginning the treatment process. There is a false belief among the public that addiction can't really be treated, that addicts just gather some clean time here and there, a few years or months at a time, and that they always slip back up. While this does occur—and serves to fuel such rumors—I'm here to tell you that treatment does work. Now, can an addict ever be "cured?" Not really, but there are treatment options that work. Addicts *can* remain sober for the rest of their lives. Unfortunately, 90% of addicts never receive treatment, perhaps thanks to the false notion that addiction treatment is ineffectual.

In this book, I'm going to explain how you can get successful treatment for your child. I'll walk you through how to stage a compelling intervention. I'll walk you through finding insurance plans and picking out the right rehab center for your child. I don't want you to ever be in the dark about any stage of the treatment process, so I'm going to let you know exactly what your child will experience in a detox facility and a rehabilitation center. I'll explain what goes on in group therapies, and all of the different things it can uncover about the core reasons why your child started using. I'll even provide you with a rough daily schedule for rehab activities. You'll know who's involved with what stages of the process so that you know which professional to call for any situation.

I don't want to leave you hanging after treatment is over, because rehab is not the end. Not even close. I'm going to take things much further and walk you through aftercare, as well. First, I'll walk you through selecting a sober home and an outpatient program that will help your child transition slowly into an independent, sober life. By the end, you'll know what sort of rent these facilities require, their rules, and how you can make those rules work for you if your child should need to come live with you for a while after completing aftercare.

It's also important that you understand what challenges life can bring recovering addicts even after rehab is complete and they've moved out of a sober home, gotten a job, and are living independently (That sounds great in and of itself, doesn't it?). I'll let you know the warning signs you need to look out for that could signal relapse. I'll let you know what circumstances, like a bad dating relationship, you should try to steer your child away from.

The purpose of this book is not to provide quick fixes or half-formed solutions. It's about reaching out a hand to guide you through a rarely talked about world and to provide step-by-step solutions to rarely talked about problems so that you can watch your child succeed again. Right now you may feel like you've lost your son or daughter. You haven't lost your child; your baby is still there, just lost in a fog with drugs leading the way, deeper and deeper into the mist. But you can use this book to start fanning away the fog. I'm going to help you understand the steps that will help your child.

Even though this book is addressed to you, the parents, my job is to help both you and your kid. I'm like a realtor trying to create a satisfactory deal for both the buyer and the seller. I understand troubled kids, so I can impart to you the best ways to connect with them. In fact, I've even included a chapter on my secrets for a drug-free life that I recommend you let your child read directly when the time is right.

By the time you reach the back cover, you will feel both prepared and empowered. You will feel you know what steps to take. You will finally have an achievable plan of action. Every situation is different, though, so you may still have specific questions that pertain directly to your unique situation. If that's the case, please know that my desire to help does not end with this book. There are a number of ways to contact me or find specific articles or blog posts of mine that delve into minute detail on specific subjects and situations. You can find links to all of those resources in the appendix. Please, get in touch. I'm here to help.

At this moment, you probably feel helpless to change the course of your child's life. I'm sure you've tried, but it doesn't matter how hard you try if you don't know what you're doing. The reason people with addicted loved ones feel helpless is because they've never been taught what to do. There is a stigma around drugs that keeps people from talking about them, sharing their experiences with others in the same boat, or asking for help. This is potentially deadly.

The only way you're going to help your child is if you educate yourself on the subject of recovery first. An educated parent doesn't have to wonder what to do next. An educated parent doesn't have to second guess decisions on which rehab facility to use or what to do when rehab is over. An educated parent has confidence because he or she is following a strategic game plan with solid reasoning behind every step.

By reading this introduction, you're taking the first step toward educating yourself on the who, when, where, why, and how of addiction and recovery. If you continue to read on, by the end you can confidently take the helm and steer your child out of stormy, thrashing, deadly waters and into the sun. Your child is not gone, but he does need your help. An addict cannot see clearly. An addict cannot find his way out of the mist without a powerful beam of light and a helping hand.

No more feeling helpless to change anything. No more despair. No more worry and long nights. I'm going to help you take control. I'm going to help you reach out into the fog and find your child's hand so that you can guide him or her back home.

# CHAPTER 1:
# ADDICTION 101: THE MAKING OF AN ADDICT

IT IS ESTIMATED THAT 1 in 12 Americans over the age of 12 are addicted to drugs. Drug prevention programs ought to be targeting middle schoolers and elementary students, not just teenagers. By the time a child reaches 14, it's often too late. By 18, three out of four children have tried drugs.

Parents, though, like to believe that only children subjected to terrible home lives and poverty succumb to addiction, but that just isn't true. Addiction is a disease, and it does not discriminate. A middle class child can come across these dangerous substances just as easily as an abused child living well below the poverty line. If you have a suspicion that your child is using, one of the best ways to confirm or deny that suspicion is to take the time to understand what addiction is. In peeling back the layers of addiction, you will find patterns and signs that are common to all substance abusers because they are connected to the very nature of addiction.

If you have already caught your child using, the need to understand addiction is even stronger. If you want to free your child from addiction's grip, you must understand the beast you're fighting. You must also understand what your child is going through in order to make the necessary connection with your son or daughter that will allow you to convince him or her to seek out treatment.

So without further ado, let's examine what addiction actually is.

## Addiction and the Brain

According to the National Institute on Drug Abuse, addiction is "a chronic relapsing brain disease that is characterized by compulsive drug seeking and use, despite harmful consequences." Addiction is not only a disease, but an epidemic, with experts estimating that one in ten people are addicts. Contrary to the popular belief that's developed over previous years that addiction is a just a selfish choice made by weak, undisciplined losers who could easily decide to stop at any time if they really wanted, science has defined addiction as a disease of the brain. Yes, an addict makes a conscious choice to try drugs, make no mistake about that. However, once true addiction sets in, it actually physically alters the brain's structure and function so that it has an insatiable desire for a specific substance. That desire becomes part of the addict's physical makeup and is extremely hard to deny or overcome.

People are drawn to the effects of drugs because they make the body feel good, and we humans are designed to seek out pleasure. Most illegal drugs trigger the release of dopamine in the brain. This is the neurotransmitter found in the midbrain (the region that controls emotion, motivation, and pleasure) that makes us feel happy. Drugs overload the dopamine circuits and create a sense of euphoria. This is what alters an addict's brain.

See, dopamine is our body's reward system. When you do something good for your body, like exercise, the brain releases dopamine to reward you for good behavior, like giving a dog a treat for doing a trick. This reward system conditions the brain to view the drugs as good, desirable, and even critical. This is what makes addiction a disease. The mind actually begins to scream out and demand more drugs. The mind is a powerful thing that controls a person's every action. The battle against addiction is a battle against the mind. And not the logical mind, either.

In the 1960s, a neuroscientist named Paul MacLean proposed the Triune Brain Theory. This theory stated that the brain was made of three parts: the reptilian brain that guided primitive behaviors, the limbic system that controlled emotion, and the neocortex that controlled logic and reasoning. Now, modern scientists don't really follow this model anymore because it is way too oversimplified to accurately define the brain, but for the purposes of explaining addiction, it works just fine. Addiction triggers the reptilian brain through its dopamine reward system. The reptilian brain is responsible for compulsive behaviors, and because of the overload of dopamine, seeking out drugs becomes a compulsion. Drug use reinforces the reptilian brain, rewards it for compulsive behavior, and essentially makes it the prominent "brain." An addict's neocortex tells him drugs are ruining his life; they've made him lose his job; they've made him lose a great girl. The neocortex begs the addict to see reason and quit. The addict hears the neocortex, but the reptilian brain is louder. It wrestles control away from the neocortex and pushes the addict to pick up the needle or sniff another line.

Drugs mess with MacLean's limbic system as well. Drugs force the brain to produce unnaturally high amounts of dopamine. The brain adapts to the added levels by stopping natural dopamine production. The brain is tricked into thinking that more than enough dopamine has already been produced, but really it just produced all of it in one short burst. After the high wears off, the brain doesn't give the addict any more dopamine boosts. So, that happy feeling entirely goes away once the drugs wear off. If the addict wants to feel that euphoria, he must use again. When the drugs wear off, there's no euphoric or happy feeling. This is what leads to severe mood swings in most addicts.

It also sucks the joy out of things the addict once loved. Things that once brought him joy now seem boring, irrelevant, or even unpleasant because he can no longer get that happy rush from participating in those things because his brain can't produce dopamine on its own. Has your son or daughter lost interest in something he or she once loved?

Eventually the body becomes entirely dependent on the substance to just feel normal. To get that high—the extreme euphoria—the addict must take more and more drugs. This is called building up a tolerance, and it is extremely dangerous because it leads to overdoses and dependence. Eventually, the amount of drugs needed to produce the high will be too much for the body to withstand.

When I first started using cocaine, one or two bumps every now and then was sufficient to keep me happy. But near the end, when things began to get really bad, I had to have an 8-ball (3.5 grams or an eighth of an ounce) in my pocket at all times just to function.

This utter dependence on the drugs for the body to function "normally" is what leads to nasty withdrawal symptoms if an addict tries to quit on his own. It's like when someone who drinks coffee everyday gets a headache because he skipped a cup, but on a much, much larger scale. The brain has been rewarding the addict for using, and when he stops, his body punishes him.

That is what makes addiction so frightening and so hard to overcome. The addict is fighting his own brain, his own body. It's a battle with oneself, which is always the hardest sort to win.

## Addiction and Genetics

Some people are actually predisposed to addiction from birth. It's unfair, but true. My mother's father was an abusive alcoholic who eventually drank himself to death. My uncle abused meth, and on top of that, there is history of addiction on my father's side, too.

From the moment I was born, my risk for becoming an addict was extremely high. Experts believe that addiction is 60% genetic and 40% environmental. There is an addiction gene. Families can pass along a gene that predisposes a person to compulsive, addictive behavior just like they can pass on a gene that predisposes a person to be very good at math or have athletic prowess. However, that gene must be activated, if you will. Something environmental (a traumatic experience, the death of a loved one, or just extreme peer pressure from a classmate) has to trigger that gene.

The addiction gene can lay dormant for many, many years, unbeknownst to the carrier and his or her loved ones. For some, the gene is never triggered, but that person can still pass it on to his or her child. For others, the gene is activated, but the person doesn't attach the behavior to drugs. For instance, my mother most definitely has an addiction gene, but she throws it all into her work. She does not stop. She has been able to direct that potentially destructive predisposition toward something positive that allows her to be productive.

A stressor or trigger for the gene can be just about anything, from things as simple as puberty or going to the wrong party, to things like extreme stress, physical abuse, or depression.

## Addiction is Patient but Not Kind

Because the gene can lay dormant potentially forever, addiction is like a patient mythical creature brooding in its lair, just waiting quietly for a victim to pass close enough to the lip of its cave. Mental illness works much the same way. Mental disorders can be passed down genetically, as well, and many of them don't develop until at least late teens or early twenties. When that addiction switch is flipped on, however, it's easy to accidentally hit another switch right next to it that activates a dormant mental illness gene. Early drug use can lead to psychosis and other psychological issues in teens. Without the drug use, that mental illness might never have been activated or at least wouldn't have been as severe.

Mental illness is perhaps even sneakier than addiction because it can disguise itself as other things. I have dealt with mental illness for much of my life, but I was not accurately diagnosed as bipolar until my 30s. All throughout high school and my twenties, my parents and I were told I had ADD.

Addiction, however, is a very progressive disease. A person may not develop into an alcoholic until later in life, even if the gene was actually triggered years earlier. Sometimes addiction explodes and settles in rapidly after the first use, but many times, it slowly creeps up and peeks out its head on its own sweet time.

It can strike anybody. It can hit Hardworking Hank, who pulled himself up by his bootstraps, paid his own way through college and law school, and quickly climbed the ranks at a stellar firm. Hank falls into a routine, and he's always out at social functions where alcohol is readily available. He partakes after a hard day's work, but he's able to control himself. Suddenly, when Hank hits 50, he's a full blown alcoholic. He can't stop anymore, can't regulate his intake. He looks around at his newly shattered life through the bottom of his bottle and wonders, "How did this happen to me?"

It may seem to Hank that it happened all of a sudden, out of nowhere, but the truth is that it happened very slowly. It was one extra drink before heading home. It was having one extra nightcap before heading to bed. Then it became two extra drinks at the bar just on Saturdays. Then Fridays and Sundays, too. And ever so slowly, addiction took hold.

Hank probably started drinking somewhat regularly

on the weekends in his teens. That is when the trigger is activated for most addicts. As a general rule, if someone hasn't used a substance by the time they are 21, they probably never will. This is why postponing and preventing your child's experimentation as long possible is so vital. Addiction is triggered in the formative years, and not everyone feels it creep up slowly like Hank. Kids who are using hard drugs like cocaine and heroin will fall harder and faster, and the addiction will be even more difficult to shake. The scary thing is that, thanks to the pill pushing epidemic and the growing accessibility and trendiness of hard drugs like heroin, kids are getting their hands on the heavy stuff far earlier than ever before. This escalation to hard drugs puts kids on hyper speed from use to abuse, and treatment centers are having a harder and harder time helping these kids. It is not that treatment doesn't work; it's that the cases that flood through center doors are becoming more and more severe. Recovery is harder to achieve and takes longer. The brain and body are still developing in the teenage years, and exposing a developing brain to addictive substances essentially hard wires the habit into the system. Someone who tries cocaine in their twenties or later is far less likely to develop a habit than someone who first tried it at 15, though it does happen. When it does, though, the problem is never as severe and is easier to overcome. An older brain is capable of more rational decision making and has already developed free of addictive habits, so it's easier for an older person to walk away.

## Is Addiction a Choice?

There is a difference between addiction and the choice to use drugs. Even someone predisposed for addiction has a choice initially. When the gene is triggered, drugs are not the only option, as I explained with my own mother. Now there is such a thing as a workaholic, and it still isn't the healthiest of choices. There are also people who become addicted to working out or losing weight. All of those things have to be addressed in their own way. However, those things don't have the same brain-altering effect as drugs (unless the athlete is using performance enhancing substances). Yes, things like working out produce dopamine, but they don't overload the circuits. Likewise, there is no physical, debilitating withdrawal from cutting back on time at the office.

The choice to turn to drugs as the solution to an underlying problem—such as someone suffering from depression seeking the thrilling high of cocaine to forget the pain—is a conscious choice that only the user is responsible for, even if someone else hands them the drugs. However, once addiction sets in, choice is squashed by desire and need. Overcoming addiction is not about strength of character or will power to fight your way through the urges. Once it sets in, things can go nowhere but down because addiction is progressive and completely overrides the brain. On their own, addicts can only fall deeper into addiction.

I cannot count how many times I've heard an addict say, "I never thought I would get to this point." When the addiction first starts, it's small, and the addict convinces herself that she has boundaries, that she's still in control. She'll tell herself, "I'll never use a needle," or, "I'll never smoke crack, I'll just snort the powder," or, "I'll stay away from hard liquor and stick to wine." For a while, she'll abide by those rules, but then the disease progresses. Decision making is gone. It feels impossible; shooting heroin, smoking crack, or drinking liquor becomes instinct, as normal and necessary as breathing.

This is hard for a non-addict to understand, but I assure you that your addicted loved one has moments when he or she desperately wants to stop but simply cannot—it's a physical impossibility. To those who say getting clean and quitting cold turkey is a choice, I ask, "Can you choose away cancer or multiple sclerosis?" Addiction, once in place, is a disease with debilitating symptoms that must be treated by medical professionals, like any other.

Yes, it is actually possible for an addict to not pick up the needle and stop for a while. It will be extremely painful, but it's possible. However, if the underlying causes aren't actually treated, the disease *will* come back, again and again. The four most common issues behind the most extreme addiction cases are incredible stress, some sort of trauma, genetic predisposition, and mental illness. Addicts will not address these real issues on their own, because they can't admit the depth of their problem. They tell themselves they are in control of their choices and behaviors because admitting the truth is too frightening. And without acceptance of the truth and professional treatment, they cannot hope to be cured.

## Addiction Symptoms

Every drug has its own set of physical symptoms, and I am going to address them a little later on in another chapter. What I want to talk about now, however, are the overarching symptoms that affect addicts of every substance. These take the form not of specific physical ailments but of consequences.

The physical symptoms like the shakes, aches, and pains of withdrawal or the hyperactive high of cocaine are the surface level of the biological consequences. However, there are long-term negative effects of substance abuse. Alcoholics destroy their liver and kidneys. Meth addicts rot away their teeth and their bodies. If carried on for too long, the symptoms of addiction can become permanent and outlast the addiction itself. Drugs can take a person's life even if they get treatment and kick the habit.

There are also social consequences. If convicted of a drug-related crime, addicts have a much harder time finding a job when they are released, even if they are clean. It can affect the whole course of their life. The stigma of drugs will follow them wherever they go.

Some of the most painful are the emotional and relational consequences. You are probably already feeling some of those effects. Addicts will pull away from loved ones, hurt them, yell at them, and even assault them. They will withdraw from positive influences and align themselves with negative people who only amplify their problems. Sometimes the good relationships are damaged beyond repair.

Lastly, there are spiritual consequences. Addiction is like being dragged behind a galloping horse. The addict has no control over his own life. His identity starts to slip away because he doesn't do the things he once loved. Drugs become his identity. Drugs wrack his brain day in and day out. It becomes damn near torture; it's not much of a way to live. Even after successful treatment, an addict can still feel the aftershocks of this consequence. With his identity stripped, he can feel empty, alone, and lost. If he was addicted for a long time, he may not even know what he likes or even what he believes anymore. To overcome this spiritual emptiness, he will need to reexamine himself and start carving out his unique identity all over again.

## Functioning vs. Nonfunctioning Addicts

Some addicts adopt a "go big or go home" approach to their use. They get real bad real fast. This is the alcoholic who doesn't just get sloppy and impaired every night, he's the sort who can't remember where he's been for the last three days because he's been in and out of blackouts. This is the drug addict who jumps from little stuff like club drugs to meth in a matter of months and starts acting completely out of her mind.

Their use escalates at alarming rates, and they get real pleasure from getting completely fucked up.

As bad as this is, it can potentially be better for them in the long run, because this sort of use is identified very quickly by the addict's loved ones and forces them to spring into action. There is no room for denial or "Maybe she's just going through a phase."

I myself was a functioning addict. I wasn't coked out of my mind all the time. I was still working toward goals, coming up with new business ventures (though I rarely finished any of them). Hell, I got on *Big Brother* and won. I had to stop using once on the show, but I was still an addict, and I picked it back up shortly after the win.

It all eventually caught up with me, as it does with every functioning addict, but it took 25 years of constant use and abuse. I didn't use crazy amounts and go out of my head. I just got buzzed. But I was buzzed almost all the time, and real buzzed at night when I went out partying.

Still, to others, I appeared to have my life together (so I thought). I was a go-getter. I was energetic and fun. People liked to be around me. But, unbeknownst to me or anyone around me, all the while the disease was growing.

No one wants to admit they have a drug problem, and functioning addicts can easily convince themselves they don't. At first, they're still living pretty normally. Nobody seems to notice, so they must be okay, right?

It's all just smoke and mirrors. I masked the level of my problem from both others and myself. I told myself I didn't have a problem, I just liked to party.

Well, like my dad says, all parties come to an end. Mine ended in jail. I got off fairly easy considering that, for many, the end is a fatal overdose. Hopefully, though, you've caught this thing in time that the end of addiction for your child is just rehab.

## The Progression of Addiction

It's important to understand how addiction progresses from a one-time choice to a disease. The first use is probably for social or recreational reasons. However, sometimes it starts with something less pleasant like a traumatic experience.

Next, it becomes a problem, but the addict still has control. He is using because he wants to, and he can decide when and where he wants to use, probably mostly for social reasons still.

However, he begins to like it more and more. He begins to crave it, and then his use becomes regular. He is using much more often, and it isn't just as social events. He's starting to skip out on responsibilities to use, but if something really important is going on, he still has the ability to hold off on his use and get things done.

Slowly, though, the drugs begin to gain ground, and regular use turns into abuse. He's using at inconvenient times. He's showing up to family functions high. His control is slipping. The cravings are coming more frequently, and they're much louder. He's starting to forgo both responsibilities and things he enjoys.

Then comes full-blown addiction. He's using every day. He's showing up for work out of his mind. He doesn't think about much of anything other than when he's going to use next, when he's going to need more, and how he's going to get more.

But the one good thing about most diseases is that, in this day and age of advanced medicine and therapy, they are both preventable and treatable. If your child is already using, you've passed the prevention stage, but all is not lost. This disease can be treated.

In order to assess what level of treatment your child

needs and how urgent your timeline is, you need to figure out where your child is on the progression line.

And that's just what I'm going to help you do, but first, now that you understand what you're up against, I want to talk about you for a bit.

# CHAPTER 2:
# THE POWER OF ADMITTING YOU'RE POWERLESS

DRUGS TAKE. THEY TAKE WITHOUT regard of circumstance or age. They don't just take from the addict either. As the parent of an addict, drugs have taken from you as well. They've taken your peace of mind. They've taken your confidence as a parent. You may feel like they've taken your child from you. But in reality, your child is still yours, and nothing can take that fact away from you.

If you're reading this book, you want to help your child. You've probably already tried, but even your best effort just isn't working. That's why I've written this book: to help you take control of the situation and help your child.

Whether you are reading this after just finding drugs in your child's sock drawer for the first time or whether your child has lost a job or gone to jail for the second or third time due to drug abuse, the method is still the same. The first steps never change. You must let go of the guilt and take control.

Drugs take, and to take back what they've stolen, you have to get past denial and admit to yourself what you've unwittingly given up to them: power.

## The Sobriety Stigma

I took the long road to sobriety. I was under the impression that it just wasn't for me. In fact, I thought it was a load of bullshit. Looking back from where I am today, I know that isn't true. It's possible, and it's a hell of a lot better than I imagined. That's why I'm sharing my story and the knowledge I gathered throughout the course of my addiction and my past eight years of sobriety.

My resistance stemmed from the fact that there is a stigma about sobriety among addicts, just as there is a stigma about addiction within society at large. The feeling among addicts is that rehab means giving up your freedom. A common phrase is, "Rehab is for quitters." The images that come to mind are cold and clinical: white rooms, hospital gowns, a strong anti-bacterial smell from freshly soaped white floors. Rehab also evokes institutional images: bars, guards, and closed doors. It's just not true, if you go to the right place.

During my recovery, I didn't know there were better options. I was doing and selling drugs in the rehab capital, here in Florida, but I ended up in Massachusetts for rehab — not by choice, but because the courts put me there in a state-run program. I went the more traditional route and ended up in a state-run program there. That was more institutional—a big place with lots of patients without much time for individualized care. Then I did my aftercare program at an actual hospital in New Jersey. When I finally got back home to Palm Beach County, Florida, after serving my jail time, I looked around through sober eyes and realized the best help in the country had been right outside my front door, and I'd been too messed up to see it. Most of the centers in Florida are small, privately run businesses that work almost like a family unit. Plenty of time is given to the individual, but it's also like a family of peers all working together toward the same goal. The patients get to know each other, and the center organizes outings and fun activities around town for everyone. It's like a vacation in many ways, the way it can put your world back home into perspective. I couldn't help wondering if I'd admitted my problem earlier and sought help from one of the hundreds of places around me, maybe I could have avoided the hard route and gotten help before things got extra bad.

But there is something else that holds addicts back from seeking sobriety. Most of all, change is scary, and so ego gets in the way to protect the brain from fear. I thought I didn't need rehab. I thought I had my life under control. I thought I could manage my problems by myself. If I had stepped back and looked at my life objectively (a very hard thing to do), I would have realized that my life was about as far from manageable as you can get.

And the addiction doesn't just make the *addict's* life unmanageable. It affects you, the parent, too. You begin to try and manage your child's life as well as your own. You take on the life of an addict secondhand as you try to juggle your own responsibilities while trying to impose strict responsibility upon your child's life.

## In the Grip of Drugs:

Drugs are a murderer. Drugs are a wrecking ball. Drugs are a sugar-high two-year-old on a toddling rampage, leaving a trail of spilled grape juice all over the white rug and permanent marker scribbles all over the white walls. Nothing is left untouched by the influence of drugs in the life of an addict. You, the parent, feel the fallout, too.

When I was sixteen, all of the money I received, tucked neatly into Christmas cards, went toward buying crack. My mom had to come break me out of a crack house on Christmas. Christmas will always bear a stain in her memory now.

Have you ever found yourself hesitating to slip a few bills into your child's Christmas card? If so, it's time for a change.

I used to shovel snow out of driveways with my dad to earn some extra money. After my addiction started, that money went to heroin. What was once a fun bonding experience with my dad is now tainted.

Have any of your family traditions been tainted by your child's addiction? If so, it's time for a change.

I once left my fifteen-year-old little brother alone at Burger King for hours so I could go buy and use crack, heroin, and xanax.

Have you ever hesitated to let another child go out with your addicted child? If so ... well, I think you get the drill by now.

Unless you've been educated on how to fix these problems, the drugs take their toll on everyone involved, and it only gets harder and harder.

## So What Do I Do About It?

First, you must address that feeling of powerlessness you are no doubt feeling somewhere inside. Don't deny it. It's perfectly normal.

You've sat at home at the kitchen table or in your easy-chair not really watching the TV show that's playing out across the screen, wondering if and when your child will walk through the door. You wonder if they will ever be upfront with you about using. You wonder how much danger they are in when they leave your home. Then there are the questions that come in quick succession, each one a razorblade that cuts into you a little deeper each time. What's the matter with me? Why did they choose this? What's the matter with them?

*What did I do wrong?*

This is probably the most heartbreaking question because you look around at how much suffering your child's addiction has caused both you and them, and you blame yourself, even when you know you shouldn't. That blame combined with the feeling of utter powerlessness you feel when you are unsure how to proceed or what steps to take can be overwhelming and can cause you to lose hope in finding a solution.

That is why the first step of AA is to admit you are powerless over drugs and alcohol and that your life has become unmanageable. This also rings true for those who are trying their best to help and support an addict.

Powerlessness comes in the form of staring endlessly at the clock, waiting for your child to come home and wondering if they ever will. You keep calling your kid's cellphone, getting no answer. You don't realize that on the other end of that line, your child isn't comprehending that you are worried sick. The idea isn't crossing his mind. All your child keeps wondering is, "Why won't they leave me the fuck alone?" Unless your child is also a parent, he can't understand the sick-to-your-stomach worry that is eating away at you on his behalf. That worry builds up so high you can hardly contain it, and when your kid finally does come through the front door, while you feel some relief, most of that worry turns to anger that your child put you through that experience. You yell and scold rather than showing the concern you really feel. It's a defense mechanism, but it starts a war, and absolutely no progress is made toward turning things around.

The first step to overcoming that powerless, worried, angry feeling is admitting the reality of the situation, no matter how ugly it may be.

## Avoiding Quick Fixes

Just because an addict stops using for a period of time, doesn't mean the addiction has hit zero. Once they pick back up again, it's like they never quit. Just quitting because of pressure from parents or a lack of means to obtain the drugs or even a sudden desire to get back in control won't fix the root cause, and thus won't be permanent.

In order to take the correct steps, you need to accept that what you are trying at the moment, no matter how much hard effort you have put into it, just isn't making things better. The quick fixes like taking the car keys, grounding, and other forms of "tough love" punishment aren't going to create the change you're praying for. You must understand the *need* for a new approach before you can accept a new approach. No matter how small of a step it seems, the only way to move toward positive progress is to understand and admit that drugs have sent life spinning out of control for everyone involved, not just the addict.

You may think at this point that it can't get much worse, but trust me, it can. The addiction will only progress. Kids are masters at masking the severity of their problems. They aren't the only ones, either. Many parents do this, too, to avoid the pain of the truth. This is called minimizing, and it does no one any good. Don't underestimate the seriousness and the power of addictive substances. Once the line into drugs is crossed, it only gets easier to try harder and harder stuff. Your child will keep actively using while you can only sit at home, watching, waiting, and listening for a sign of what to do, a sign that they are coming back to you. You'll soak in all the lies and the desperate calls begging for money. You'll say you're drawing a line in the sand, that this is the last time, but until you admit that you are powerless to stop your child's addiction on your own, it won't be. It is okay to admit that you're stuck. It's okay to admit that you are powerless at the moment. Only by admitting that powerlessness can you make the correct moves to overcome it and take back the controls.

Don't blame yourself for being powerless. Likewise, don't point the fingers of blame at your spouse or other family members or the people your child hangs out with. This has nothing to do with your social status, your financial situation, or your parenting abilities. Having a nice house, sending your kid to the best school, and giving your child what he or she needs will never guarantee that your kid will avoid drugs.

Don't feel bad for yourself. Admitting powerlessness is not a sign of weakness. You know this feeling isn't your fault, so quit blaming yourself. Stop asking how you got here and start asking what you will do next. Acknowledge that your child is who he/she is, you are where you are, and you just have to take it from there. You have to admit you are powerless in your current situation in order to realize that you can't just put another Band-Aid on it or sweep the ugly reality under the rug one more time, because that clearly isn't working. You have to realize that doing so is only aiding the addict in making the damage worse.

## The Addiction Stigma

You may have sought out the quick fixes in order to quickly sweep away the problem and avoid the embarrassment that comes with the stigma of addiction. It's a natural response, especially if you are an active member of the community or a very private person, but it is a response you need to shove aside. You must embrace your child's problem, accept it as the current reality.

Remember that embarrassment is better than a complete disregard. Many of my drug-addicted friends had parents who simply didn't care, usually because they were addicts themselves or were too busy at work to be bothered.

I was fortunate that my mother never struggled with feeling embarrassed about my addiction (she simply wasn't the type of person to give a damn about what others thought), but she didn't approach my addiction with flippancy. She certainly didn't encourage it, as many of my friends' parents did, knowingly or unknowingly.

If you are feeling embarrassment, know that it is a natural reaction that stems from an overarching parental desire to feel proud of your child. The danger of embarrassment is that it can cause you to deny. Once you know your child has a serious problem and accept that, you aren't going to be worrying about reputation, you're going to be worrying about helping your child. The embarrassment usually comes when you get that first gut feeling that something is wrong. Your mind makes the logical jump to drugs, but the stigma rises up and the feelings of embarrassment come to the surface, and so you shove the idea aside, telling yourself your child couldn't possibly be doing drugs. You raised them better than that.

What you must come to grips with is that your child's addiction doesn't make you a bad parent. You may feel that way, but it simply isn't true. Kids from all walks of life and all ages and all types of upbringings fall into the trap of drug addiction. It has nothing to do with you. It's your child's choice. If you believe that your child's addiction reflects on your parenting, you will probably keep denying the severity of the issue and keep putting on the Band-Aids. Then it's usually too little too late.

Once you toss aside the denial, accept your own powerlessness, and decide to take serious action, the embarrassment about what the PTA or your neighbors think goes away.

But there is another type of embarrassment that comes along with addiction that is sometimes upheld throughout the whole rehabilitation process, and it shouldn't be. Once the problem is brought to light, many parents adopt the "Don't tell Grandma" approach. This is when parents try to hide the problem, or at least the severity of it, from other family members. Sometimes, the hiding even happens within the immediate family unit. Sometimes Mom will catch Johnny with a pipe and decide that she can deal with it herself without telling Dad. He's been so stressed lately, and this would only add more to it, right?

My mom was guilty of this. Even though my dad was aware of my problem, she always hid drug-related issues from him, especially when they involved finances, like hefty court fines. She knew it would only make him angry, so she tried to spare him, but the end result is just a lot of secrets that still remain untold.

This approach is dangerous because it has the potential to inhibit the rehabilitation process. An addict needs to be surrounded by support. Everyone in the family needs to be united in helping the addict. Hiding things from one another can create a rift in the family that is detrimental to the addict's recovery and eventually creates room to pass around blame.

## Moving Forward

You need to admit that the damage is already done, that alone you are powerless to fix it, that quick fixes aren't the answer. It's not easy. By reading this book you will come to understand what you can do. You will get an idea for what your child is thinking and what's really going on in their life and in their head. You will begin to rebuild the bond of trust between yourself and your child. Once trust is rebuilt, you can put the lawyers and the lies and the stories about why they need money behind you.

It's going to take time and hard work, but you will see progress. You will take actionable, preemptive steps with proven results rather than trying to patch up the damage once it's already done. Action is key. Without it, there is no forward movement. Your child will repeat the same behaviors and you will deal with the same issues over and over and over.

You also need to understand that things aren't going to turn out perfect right away. Relapse is a part of being sober, and there is a good chance it will happen along the way to long-term sobriety. The key to being sober is figuring out for yourself that you need to be sober. Your child has to get sober for themselves. Rehab has to be their idea, or it won't take. The process varies for each individual. Some addicts achieve sobriety right away, after only one rehab period. For others, it takes months or years to get completely straight.

The attitude parents need to have is one of preparedness. Don't *expect* your kid to mess up again—because that attitude suggests a lack of faith in your child—but be prepared for it. Preparedness suggests dedication to the process and to your child, and your child will pick up on that.

Understand that successful rehab is about figuring out the why in order to get the how. There is something in your child's personality, experience, or head that has lead them to addiction. Until that thing is identified and dealt with, it will keep driving your child back to drugs. That identification process can take time, and the length of that time will depend on your child's ability to open up. If you can establish trust within a unified family ready to support the addict all the way through the process, it will work to make your child feel more at ease and better able to express and discover the motivations behind his or her drug use.

No matter how hopeless and powerless you feel right now, you can use it to your advantage. Admitting your current powerlessness will actually spur you on to take control and prepare for the upcoming treatment so that you can help your child through the process. I'm going to give you the steps to do that. I'm going to give you the steps to feel powerful again, because you'll know what to do this time, rather than dwelling on it or denying it or praying they will get better on their own.

# CHAPTER 3: GETTING TO THE TRUTH

Dealing with denial and admitting your powerlessness in your current situation is a hard, painful step, but once you've come to grips with the reality that your child is using—or even if you just have a fleeting idea that their use might be getting beyond acceptable—the next step is taking action. What you need is to get real answers, and though the answers may hurt, you should find some comfort in the fact that you are making positive headway in getting help for your child.

## Finding a Balance

One of the things many parents cling to is the idea that all kids experiment. "He's just being a teenager." "Lots of kids try that at her age." "She's only drinking a little every now and then." Never preach moderation to your child. No simpering calls as she heads out the door, saying, "If you have something to drink, make sure it's just one."

It's true that children will probably experiment with different substances as they grow older, but you should never encourage such behavior with the tacked on warning of, "Use responsibly." There really isn't any level of responsible use for teens. But you still have to be aware that it is probably going to happen at least once. If your child comes home smelling of booze or weed once or twice, that is something that should be taken with a grain of salt and attributed to youthful experimentation. It would be unwise to crack down hard on such an instance. However, if it becomes a common thing, or you notice the smell or influence of alcohol while driving, then it's time to get more serious.

Even that first instance of use needs to be addressed, just leave the shouting out of it. Let your kid know you know and that you disapprove, and leave it at that. If your child knows that you disapprove of even the smaller things like smoking pot, they are less likely to do it again. It doesn't mean they won't, but the risk is significantly lowered (believe it or not), especially if you have a healthy, communicative relationship with your child.

You don't want to be the "cool parent." You want to be the firm but fair parent. The child of a firm but fair parents knows that they aren't going to blow up in her face if she goes to a kegger for homecoming, but she also knows it's not okay to get sloppy drunk or bring pot around the house. That whole idea of letting your kid drink and smoke in your house because, "At least I know where she is and that she's safe," is a bunch of bullshit. For one, adult supervision doesn't make it legal (you could get in a lot of trouble, especially if your kid has friends over), and more importantly, it teaches your kid that such things are acceptable. Teens are all about pushing boundaries. If you've already pushed back that boundary line to accept pot and alcohol in the house, what's your child going to do to push the envelope now?

Make your limits clear and enforce them. Expect your teen to have a drink every now and then at a party, but make it clear if he comes home drunk, there are consequences, and always encourage him not to drink at all. Stick to your chosen consequences consistently. Children need structure and boundaries, and remember, the more prevention you do in those early years, the less likely use will become abuse.

## Use vs Abuse

When it comes to more commonplace substances like

alcohol and marijuana, there is an acceptable level of use. Just as you are not an alcoholic for having a glass of wine to unwind at night, your child is not an addict if all he's doing is trying some weed or doing a keg stand at a party. However, for those predisposed for addiction or those who are dealing with hard life circumstances such as eating disorders, bipolar disorder, grief over the death of a loved one, etc., there is a switch lingering in the brain. If that switch is turned on, use becomes abuse. As a general rule of thumb, casual experimentation means trying out a substance and using it less than five times. Abuse is characterized by an insatiable need for the substance. There is nothing occasional about abuse; it's a near daily habit. That habit can range from mild (getting drunk every night around eight o'clock) to severe (smoking through $200 worth of meth a day). Once that habit is developed, many substance abusers gravitate toward a drug of choice. In the beginning, it's just about getting fucked up, but if not stopped in the early phases of abuse, things escalate. More drugs are added to that drug of choice. Well over 50% of people who overdose have around three or more drugs in their system on the toxicology report. Sadly, after the abuse switch is turned on, it can't be turned off. Once the switch is flipped, that person can't go back to just casual use, because it will always turn into something more; they have to stop completely.

There are screening tools available that allow medical professionals to gauge a person's level of addiction. Tests like the National Institute on Drug Abuse's NIDA screening tool and the American Academy of Pediatrics Committee on Substance Abuse's recommended CRAFFT tool are a series of questions your doctor can ask your child. An example question from the CRAFFT test is "Do you ever use alcohol or drugs to relax, feel better about yourself, or fit in?" Based on your child's answers, a medical professional can determine if your child's use is casual experimentation or addiction. Of course, your child has to actually participate. These tools are in their infancy, but they are constantly being improved. You can't keep your child from growing up. If you try, you will only push your son or daughter away. You can't keep your kid from experimenting with things like alcohol and marijuana because those substances are everywhere, and they are widely seen as acceptable amongst your child's peers. While you can't raise your kid in a bubble, you have to be able to notice if that switch is flipped. Don't crucify your son the first time he comes home red-eyed and craving Cheetos. However, if you catch him high as a kite at all hours of the day, if he has no money despite a part-time job, or you start noticing him looking sick on a regular basis, it's time to assume that use has become abuse and to take steps to know for certain.

## The Warning Signs

Not sure how to tell if your child's experimentation has become addiction? Well, addiction is a diseases, so it has observable symptoms. Substance abuse leads to tolerance and dependence. Addicts need more and more of their drugs of choice to stay satisfied. As explained in chapter one, their happiness becomes chemically tied to the drugs' effects, and they physically *cannot* stop using without withdrawal symptoms. Eventually, they stop having fun altogether. Their life is a mess and they feel like hell, but they still can't stop using. As things spiral downward, it gets harder and harder for them to hide the warning signs.

Is money missing from your wallet? Has your child undergone sudden and significant weight loss? These are signs that their use is more than recreational. Drugs have now begun to affect their everyday life, and your wallet. Stealing your money shows a true desperation for more of whatever they are using. The weight loss is a sign of long-term use and abuse that has become serious enough to alter your child's body.

Once you've determined (in your mind) that your child is using, or at least have a deeper pit in your stomach that's telling you it's true, the next step is to determine what type of drug your child is abusing.

## Warning Signs for Specific Drugs

As you go through this brief list, keep in mind the different types of drugs listed here. There are the typical recreational drugs like alcohol and marijuana, but don't let them just slip under your radar because they are more widely accepted. Alcohol withdrawal is one of the most serious and painful withdrawals, and can even lead to death. Though it appears to have some great medical benefits, marijuana is still illegal in many states and can lead to unwanted and unnecessary trouble for your child. Its partial legalization, while wonderful for those who truly need it for medical reasons, is making it even more commonplace and acceptable. However, this means it is more accessible, and that can cause problems. It is still a gateway drug if adopted in the formative teenage or middle school years. There are club drugs like molly and ecstasy that have that "feel good" party effect but aren't as serious when it comes to rehab and withdrawal. There are barbiturates like Xanax and other prescriptions that are often overlooked but can lead to serious addiction. There are uppers like crank and cocaine that leave their mark in the form of jitters and spouting tongue twisters on hyper drive. And finally, there are opiates like heroin and certain pills like Oxycontin, which lead to the most excruciating withdrawals and can be the hardest addictions to shake physically and mentally.

Take a moment to look through the list below just to begin getting an idea of what your child is on. If you're reading this book, odds are that you've noticed at least a few of these signs.

- Alcohol—the smell on their breath, throwing up, missing liquor bottles.
- Marijuana—the odor, finding rolling papers, bowl bong, cigar papers, and of course, tie-dyed shirts and a new appreciation for Bob Marley.
- Prescription pills, Benzos—your pills are missing, badly slurred words, loss of memory, groggy.
- Prescription pills, Opiates—empty or missing pill bottles from a past injury, itching, scratching their nose, pin-point pupils, slow speech.
- Cocaine—sniffling, loss of weight, bags under eyes, wide eyes, no money, up all night, missing for a few days, huge pupils, talkative heightened speech.
- Heroin—finding needles, poor complexion (almost sick looking), wearing long sleeves to cover track marks, vomiting, groggy speech, withdrawal symptoms like shaking.
- PCP—Delusional, breath smells like cleaning fluid, erratic behavior.
- Club drugs—all of a sudden they blast electronic music, want to go to raves, come home telling you they love you, have a hard time sleeping, vomit frequently, look like they are just wasted.
- Designer drugs, Bath salts—Extreme paranoia, insane behavior, strip and run around naked (not kidding).

**For a more detailed list of the different types of drugs as well as their symptoms, duration periods, sources, and cost, flip over to the appendix.*

## The Warning Signs of Withdrawal

Another way to tell how serious your child's substance

use may be getting is to look for the signs of withdrawal. As a teen or even as a young adult in their twenties, your kid isn't going to have unlimited resources ... unless you're the parent of a YouTube star or Justin Bieber. That means there will be times when they can't get the drugs their body now craves, and they will go into withdrawal.

Some general signs of withdrawal to look for are anything from strong mood swings to shaking and demanding money.

Uppers like cocaine won't show as serious signs, as the physical withdrawal from these drugs isn't as bad, and a person can be off them for longer before withdrawal even sets in. Most of the time they will sleep off the physical withdrawal, but the mental withdrawal effects—the overwhelming desire to take another line—last much longer.

Though they don't induce the most dangerous type of withdrawal, opiates like heroin have the worst withdrawal symptoms when it comes to actually feeling the excruciating discomfort, and the signs are hard to miss. A person withdrawing from opiates will look just plain sick. They will shake, appear restless, and they will probably be heading off to the bathroom a lot with diarrhea and vomiting.

## Getting Ahead of the Game

The brief list above ranges from common party substances like alcohol and marijuana, to hard drugs like heroin and cocaine. Hard drugs should never be "experimented" with. They are also harder to talk about, as there is such a stigma around them. That's why, with the more accepted substances like alcohol and marijuana, you should make sure you establish an open dialogue with your child, ideally even before they begin trying them. But, of course, an ideal situation is hard to come by, so don't beat yourself up if you haven't been doing this. Any situation can be turned around.

Firstly, you don't want to be harsh in these conversations.

You want to establish yourself as an open-minded companion. Why? If they fear punishment from you even for having a little alcohol at a party, they will definitely fear talking to you if they begin to struggle with hard drugs. So, they will hide it for as long as possible, not seeking the help they need.

How do you initiate these conversations? If you notice bloodshot eyes or boozy breath, make sure your child knows you noticed. One of the best ways to approach this is in a lighthearted fashion, according to the old adage that most truth is told in a jest. Saying something like "Was it good weed, son?" will let your child know that you noticed (he was probably hoping you wouldn't), but that he isn't going to get raked over the coals for it. It lets your child know he or she isn't going to "get away with it" under Mom or Dad's nose, but it also establishes you as someone they can confide in about the substance use without judgement or punishment.

Now you can ask some more probing questions like "Where did you get it?" and "Is this the first time you've used it?" that help you understand just how often your child is experimenting and who is supplying it for them. If you do this when drugs aren't a problem and hard drugs have never been touched, it is easier to approach your child if you start asking yourself, "Is my child using drugs?" Casual use can turn to dependence and abuse very quickly, so stay ahead of the game and catch it early on.

If you've dabbled in substance use, share your personal history. When you're warning your kid against the dangers of drugs, they're probably going to ask you if you've used anyway. The question, "Mom/Dad, have you ever used drugs?" especially if unprompted, is often a way for your child to gage if you understand the struggle he or she feels, fighting peer pressure to use or fighting your own personal urges to use. They are also probing to find out whether or not you feel a certain level of use is acceptable. If you only ever used alcohol or recreational drugs as a fun, occasional outlet of indulgence, let your child know that you understand that sort of thing. Make it clear you aren't going to punish him or her for doing the same but be sure to warn against the dangers casual use can open up. If you have personal experience with addiction, be open about your struggles and what those substances cost you. Be open and blunt about the realities. My mom once told me, "If you keep this up, you will end up alone in a parking lot somewhere. I know." That little hint that maybe she'd been where I was stuck with me, and when I did in fact find myself alone in a parking lot, it came back full force. It helped me realize she was right, and I was wrong. Making a connection like that can really help. But this is all an ideal scenario, right? Remember, if you're past that point of preemptive dialogues, don't beat yourself up, get motivated instead. You can still begin to establish trust and rapport with your kid about drugs. True, it will be a little tougher, but it's not unreachable. If you've cracked down hard and punished them for smoking weed or drinking in the past (or even for something more serious), the next time you realize your child is high or under some sort of influence, surprise them with a new approach. They will be wary at first, probably assuming it's some kind of ploy, but once they realize they really aren't getting chewed out and aren't going to be, you've crossed a new bridge. Next, try talking to them about their drug use when they aren't under the influence, and remember to approach them as a friend would: gently and without judgement, rather than cracking a whip. Addiction already comes with feelings of alienation, shame, loneliness, helplessness, confusion, and guilt, especially in teens. You don't want to pile on more guilt and shame by dragging your teen through the mud.

## Getting an Honest Answer

If you have laid the groundwork, you can approach your child with more confidence, and your child will be less likely to clam up. However, that doesn't mean you will easily get a "yes" out of them. They won't shut down or run, probably, but telling the truth about hard drugs is hard. This is because a lot of times, your child isn't even able to admit themselves that they have a problem, much less admit it to you. My parents were friendly with me when they began to suspect my problem, but I still lied.

Instincts are your best friend in this situation. If you feel it's getting serious, it probably is, so trust that and don't let up. Tell your child what you have noticed. Don't say it accusingly, but let them know that you've been watching, that you are concerned. Remember, though, that kids think they are invincible. If you tell them what they are doing can kill them, they often brush that off. You can try to get the harsh realities into their head with real world examples (perhaps they know someone who has overdosed, or maybe you do), but they still might have themselves convinced that they are smarter than those other people, that they've got it figured out. Your biggest struggle will be finding a way to get past the "It won't happen to me" mentality. The key that unlocks that door will be slightly different for every child. If you succeed, and they open up and admit their problem, wonderful! That is ideal. If not, there are other ways you can find out.

## Ways to Know for Sure

There are three ways to know for sure that your child is abusing drugs.

The first is a direct confrontation. Ask your child straight to his face if he is using. If you've succeeded with those preemptive dialogues and have earned your child's trust, you may be one of the lucky parents who actually gets a straight answer. But know that this is extremely rare. As I have said before, most addicts can't even admit the problem to themselves. So, instead of asking something like, "Are you addicted to ___?" phrase the question more like, "How often are you using ___?" By asking questions like this, you can potentially lead your child to understanding the issue himself. If your son has to lay out to you exactly what he's on, how often he uses, and what it's costing him ("When was the last time you [insert something your child used to love doing here]?"), the idea that he has a problem may just start to make sense. Don't yell. Show both concern and compassion, but let your child know you expect answers. Start off by thanking your kid for being honest. Something like, "Okay, Johnny. Thanks for telling us. I know it's hard talking about this to us because we're your parents." If you say this instead of shouting, your child will probably be shocked into paying attention. He may even feel some gratitude toward you. Then you press on to the more probing questions that not only give you more information but also force your child to think about the bigger picture of his addiction. Ask things like, "Does your day revolve around using?" and "Are you frustrated that you can't seem to stop?" and "What's important to you? Is it really these drugs?" and "Are you really bored with your life? Why exactly are you doing this?" He may not answer these questions right that moment, and that's okay. He may not know the answers himself or he may just be too embarrassed to tell you, but the key is to get his gears turning about his answers. This will get him a step closer to accepting treatment.

Like I said, though, a direct admission is super rare. So, the second method is to search for evidence yourself. This can be a touchy subject with some parents, but let any guilt go. This is a life or death situation; you need to understand that just as much as your child does. Search through everything in your kid's room. Flip over the mattress, empty drawers, rifle through pockets, and go through her phone. You are looking for paraphernalia (things like pipes, baggies, needles, and the drugs themselves), text messages to dealers, or anything out of the ordinary. Then it's time for a new confrontation. It's a lot harder for your child to deny using when you have actual evidence to show. The same rules for addressing the issue still apply. Keep calm, don't judge, but get to the heart of the matter.

The third method is to obtain an at-home drug test and make your child take it. Again, there will need to be some sort of conversation before you thrust a cup at your kid and tell him to pee in it. You will get serious push-back on this method, especially if your child used recently, but it is the most accurate and sure-fire way to get to the bottom of the use. It will not only tell you if they are using but also what they are using and how much is in their system. However, it's likely your child understands this, too, and that is why he will go to insane lengths to avoid taking the test. I will discuss methods kids use to cheat tests like these and how you can combat that in the next chapter, along with where to get these tests and how they work.

With any of these methods, be prepared for wild, rage-filled reactions from your child. Any sort of confrontation about a problem your child doesn't want to admit to herself is going to lead to a push-back and a possible blow up. You need to understand that some kids run away to avoid admitting the issue to themselves and their parents. They may run off to shack up with a boyfriend or girlfriend, or go crash with some of the friends they get high with. You need to be prepared for this sort of reaction.

Of course, you don't want your child running away. The best way to avoid this is to prepare yourself mentally for the confrontation. Be prepared for the push-back and don't let it get to you. If you fly off the handle, too, things will only escalate. The main reason kids run away is because they don't want to be called out on their problem. If you remain calm and non-judgmental, but rather concerned and in charge (both of the situation *and* your emotions), there is less chance of disaster. Your main goal in these conversations should be to let your child know you aren't crucifying him; you're helping. If your child threatens to leave, say something like, "You'd be running from the drugs, not me. I don't want you to leave. I'm not angry; I'm not forcing you out. I'm trying to make you see what you're running from. I know what's going on here, and you need to admit it to yourself." If you go ahead and call him out, calmly, he doesn't really have anything to run from, because the thing he feared has already happened. If you do it without yelling, he may think, "That wasn't so bad." Crisis averted.

One more thing you need to understand is that if your child is under eighteen, it is much easier to get them to comply with some of these methods because they are your dependent and you can make them comply with your requests. If they are over eighteen, things become more difficult.

Now, if they still live with you and you provide them with money and a roof, that means there are boundaries. Whether those boundaries are spoken or not, they are understood. You child will be more willing to comply because you support them and there is an obligation attached to that, even if they are a legal adult.

But if they are over eighteen and out of the house, that obligation is gone, and you will have a much harder time getting your kid to seek help ... unless you toss the parent persona aside. That parent-child relationship is something you have built with effort and care over the years, so it can be hard to put it away. Your instinctive reaction when your child refuses to take a drug test, for example, may be to "put your foot down." That stern, authoritative approach may have worked on them as a teen, but once they are older they will reject that approach with a scoff and flippant wave of their hand. What you need to do instead is have a sincere talk. Talk to your kid like the adult they are. Cut to the chase and level with them. The parent relationship has to be put aside and substituted for a respected peer relationship.

If your gut is telling you that getting your kid to comply with a test, no matter their age, is going to be like pulling teeth with no Novocain, let me tell you now that you're right. So why go through all the trouble?

Asking them to submit to an at-home drug test brings things to a head. If those results come back positive, denial isn't going to work anymore—for either of you. That positive result will get things moving toward a solution, and that is why it is so important.

There are two major options when it comes to getting your kid tested. One, use the family physician for a blood or urine test. Two—the option that I recommend most highly—is to order an at-home test.

The next chapter will provide you with the details on how and where to get one of these tests, how they work, and how to get your child to actually take one without cheating (because I can pretty much guarantee you that they will try). But for now, just know that you need one, and focus on building/practicing the rapport necessary to talk to your child about their use. If you can do that, the testing will go smoother. Still not butter spread smooth—maybe more like thick jam smooth—but things will definitely go down easier.

## What Not to Do

Don't fall into denial. You may have cast it aside in order to take the next steps of questioning, testing, and finding out for sure that your child is using, but you can slip back into it. Denial is easier, and thus it's a very attractive solution. Fight the urge. Your baby needs you, and ignoring the problem isn't going to help anything.

Don't blame others. My mother always blamed my friends for my drug use. I loved that! It let me off the hook. It is entirely natural for a parent to want to hold onto the idea that their child is an angel, and that if something as serious and dangerous as drug use has snuck into their life, somebody else must have shoved that crap through the doggy door. You have to resist this mindset because it gives them a pass, which is dangerous. It's a way to make you feel better, but it isn't good for your kid. Let go of the "Not my baby" syndrome. It may function as a source of relief for you because it can allow you to blame some other kids' parents for the problems you are facing, but remember that your child's decision to do drugs does *not* reflect on your parenting. The "not my baby" excuse is a way for your kid to divert the conversation and avoid the confrontation. When you start asking them about where they got the drugs and why they started using, your kid will divert to the "Billy gave them to me. I felt pressured," defense because they know it will turn your gaze away from them and onto that no-good Billy. It was your child's decision to do the drugs, nobody else's. If your child is using hard drugs, that's not about having a little fun at a party with friends and doing a keg stand because everybody was cheering their name. Something deeper is going on, and if you toss the blame on others, you aren't going to get to the heart of the matter.

Don't try to lock your kids away from the world. Doing this will only turn you into an enemy rather than a confidant. Kids are more resourceful than adults usually give them credit for; they will find a way around all of your precautions, and resent you to boot.

Don't ever feel guilty. If you truly have your child's best interests at heart, that will show in your concern and will resonate with your child. Ignore that twinge of guilt when you look through jean pockets, nightstands, and cars for drugs and paraphernalia if you have a feeling your child is using. If you find such things, it's a sign of serious personal use, not just casual use in social settings, and signs like that should be caught early on. Also, if your kid knows you feel guilty about such searches, he or she will get comfortable with using in the house, and that is something you definitely don't want, as it just gives your child another avenue and location for drug use. It's also important to note that if your child is leaving you signs around the house in obvious places, it could be more of a cry for attention and love than the thrill of using. Your child could be silently asking you for help. Don't ignore it.

## Conclusion

Remember, no matter how much you want to believe that Johnny or Katie isn't using—and no matter how they scream, kick, and yell—if your gut is telling you something's wrong, it probably is. If you're having the conversation, there's a reason for it. For your sanity and your child's safety, find out. Know for sure.

Establishing a dialogue can not only help you figure out if and what your child is using, but also lays the groundwork for a successful rehabilitation process. If you can establish a rapport that gets you to the truth of what your child is using, that rapport can carry over into figuring out the even more important question of *why* your child is using.

Talk to your kid. Don't yell. That's not to say that you can't be stern and serious when it's necessary, but rather that you should speak conversationally and express understanding. And don't just speak. Listen. If you aren't listening to what they are saying, they aren't going to see a point in talking to you about it.

Your child is going to need you more than ever as you help them move toward sobriety. These are sensitive times in their lives: be their rock, be a parent, be a friend, and be concerned. If they are using a drug you are unfamiliar with, get knowledgeable about it. Don't be afraid to administer a drug test or take them to the doctor. Get ahead of the abuse before it gets ahead of you. No matter how uncomfortable, inconvenient, or heartbreaking it is, please know for sure if your child is using drugs.

# CHAPTER 4:
# PUT IT TO THE TEST

ONCE YOU KNOW OR AT least have a strong feeling that your kid is on drugs and you feel as if you can begin talking to them about it in a productive fashion, it is time to pull out the big guns and quit messing around. Get your child to take a drug test.

Why? Well, just because you know they are on drugs, that doesn't mean they are going to quit denying it. Even if they open up to you a little and admit that they have done drugs before, it is highly unlikely that they will reveal the extent of their addiction unless you no longer allow them to deny it.

You might be asking, "But why would they deny it if I've established myself as a friend they can talk to?" Because they are embarrassed and afraid of how you will react. Plus, they really don't want to admit to using drugs, because they know that you, as a parent, will want them to stop. It's as simple as that. Also, as I've said before, they probably haven't admitted the extent of the problem even to themselves, much less their parents. They may admit to using lesser drugs, such as marijuana, just to get the conversation over with.

A drug test is the wrecking ball that breaks down the last of the denial defenses. Denial is the rubble that has to be completely cleared for you to keep moving down the road to sobriety. Drug tests are also a great deterrent to help keep the addiction from worsening while you try to bring all the pieces together to get your kid into rehab. Bottom line, it puts a stop to the bullshit. Test results don't lie.

But most people don't know much about drug tests, how they work, or how to obtain them. So, let's go ahead and dive into what I believe is the best option—fast, reliable, and affordable—the at-home drug test.

## The At-Home Test Explained

At-home drug tests can be delivered directly to you from services like Exact Drug Test. I had a part in founding the site www.exactdrugtest.com, which is designed to offer the best at-home urine and saliva drug tests at the best possible prices. There is no need to go to Walmart and spend $35 when you can get the same thing for half the price online without dealing with the embarrassment of checking out at the store. We can ship to your office or home in a discreet package. We offer a deeply discounted subscription service and multiple price options to help cut costs. These are hard times, and you're going to need help. We designed Exact Drug Test as a platform apart from other test-delivery services by also providing access to on-call professionals. Having an expert in your corner can provided reassurance and direction after those test results come in, and that is why we go above and beyond to offer that to you.

These can present a moral dilemma because it can be seen as an invasion of your child's privacy. However, remember that knowing that your child is using and knowing what they are on provides the tools, knowledge, and education to not only take this first step in addressing the substance abuse, but to provide a comprehensive resource and forum in which to address addiction and get to the ultimate solution, sobriety. There is also solace in knowing, and though the reality can hurt, it is far better than the constant questioning and panic that comes from being unsure.

I will also tell you that having to pee in a cup in front of my mother definitely curbed my drug use while I was under her roof. This was back when home drug tests were not readily available or deliverable to your door. My mother was a director for one of the top two laboratories in the country, so she made me pee in a cup (embarrassing for both parties involved, believe me) and then took my urine sample to work with her, covered in plastic wrap, and sent it out for testing. I can only imagine how embarrassing that must have been for her. It wasn't a cake walk for me either. In fact, I think this deterrent gave me a leg up over other users I knew, and I was able to finish high school and college as a result of her methods.

Nowadays, with www.exactdrugtest.com in your corner, the testing can be done from the privacy of your own home and you get results instantly with over 95% accuracy. No cringe-worthy store checkout process. No waiting for a lab to test and get back to you with a report. No sitting in medical offices.

The tests come in discrete packaging, right to your house. The most popular test (and the one easiest to administer) is the twelve panel drug test cup. You can also get hair, blood, or saliva tests, but the urine samples are the fastest, most accurate, and most cost effective method. The "twelve panel" part simply means that the urine will be tested for twelve different drugs. A "panel" is simply a type of drug.

Now, there are well over sixty panels that a sample can be tested for, but the twelve tested in these at-home tests are the most common types. You can get similar products from places like Walmart for over $30, but the tests I provide through www.exactdrugtest.com typically beat those prices at under $20. There are also single panel tests available that only test for one specific type of drug, but it is far better to purchase one product that covers all of the bases rather than buying a single panel and crossing your fingers that you've bought the right test that matches what your child is actually on. If your kid is really deep into their use, odds are they will "pop dirty" (meaning come up positive on the test) for multiple drugs. More than three fourths of overdose deaths have more than three types of abusive drugs come back in the toxicology report.

Using the Exact Drug Test twelve panel is simple, too, as the instructions provided are straightforward and walk you through the process step by step. The instructions also list which drugs will be tested for and how to read the results. Of course, after getting the results, you should be far more concerned about large doses of opiates than you should traces of marijuana.

If the test comes back positive for one or more drugs and you would like to know the levels, you can put it in the bio bag that comes with the kit and send it to a lab that will thoroughly analyze it. The lab tests are usually somewhere around $100, and the cost of this is included in some of the higher-priced kits, but honestly, knowing the levels isn't nearly as important as just knowing. The simple at-home test is really what you want. It rips that cat, clawing and mewling, right out of the bag and gets the conversation started and the road to treatment paved.

When you are preparing to administer a test, do keep in mind that drugs filter through the system at different rates, with marijuana staying the longest at up to thirty days, while things like certain opiates pass in and out within just a few hours. Cocaine and heroin usually only last for about three days.

**For more details on the duration of drugs in the system, please refer to the appendix.*

In drug testing, there are regulated cutoff levels, meaning that a positive result will only show if more than a specific amount of the drug is present. The Exact Drug Test tests have some of the lowest possible detection levels to ensure the most accurate results, but still, time is of the essence when it comes to testing.

So, have a test ready and don't hesitate to use it as soon as you think your child is on something.

**The Blood Test Option**

You may remember from the previous chapter that you can also take your child to the doctor for a blood test. The family physician is a safe environment where you don't have to worry about judgement or legal action. Doctors are there to help. The only legal obligation a doctor has in regards to reporting an incident is when there is a threat of self-harm. If your child is in a stable mind-frame, the doctor doesn't have to turn over any information, and they won't. These drug tests are about getting your kid better, not turning them over for corporal punishment. If you play it right, the blood test option can be less stressful. You can have a conversation in advance with the doctor, set your kid up for a "routine" blood test, and have the doctor order a toxicology test on it without your child knowing the real reason for the visit.

## The Drug Test Deterrent

If your child tests positive on that first test, stock up on those cups and let your child know you've done so. As I've already said, this was a real deterrent for me, and it probably will be for your child, too. When you start asking your child to take regular drug tests, it's an eye-opener for them. They know you aren't messing around anymore. It is even more effective if you don't approach them with anger when you present the test, but rather concern. Now, you will still have to be firm, because no one wants to pee in a cup in front of their parent, but don't yell or get angry. This shows your child that you are doing this out of serious concern. It also lets them know that you know they've been lying—that they can't sneak things by you anymore. Also, knowing that at any time they could walk through the door and see a cup waiting on the table will make them think twice before using. Now, just thinking twice won't deter them from using every time, but it will have an impact on the regularity of their use.

## Refusal and Cheating

When my parents first asked me to take a test, I blew my lid. Why? I was pumped full of heroin, cocaine, Xanax, and PCP, and I *did not* want my family to know I was using. I refused the test for days. I refused until my mother was in tears. That was when I relented ... or appeared to. I thought I was real slick. My father had apparently forgotten to flush, so I used the pee left in the toilet.

The crazy part? The test came back positive for marijuana!

I never told on my dad, and I was relieved that my mom didn't find out what I had really been on. But that relief was short lived. My mother wasn't stupid. She had seen the signs and knew that I wasn't just smoking pot (plus I think my brother was sort of her informant). A week later, she started asking again. She asked every single night, and she put blue dye in the toilet tank so that I couldn't pull my old trick.

So what did I do? I got clean pee from a friend, put it in a travel shampoo bottle, heated it up in the defroster in the car on the way back home, put it in my underwear, and snuck it into the cup. When it came back negative, my mother wanted so badly to believe it ... but a mother's instincts don't lie.

She asked again, and this time I let bleach dry on my fingers and dipped them into my pee, which I had already diluted by drinking tons of water. I had also taken multivitamins that gave my pee a bright yellow color instead of a clear, diluted one. There are also drinks like Ready Clean that help mask drugs to aid in the passing of drug tests.

When the test came back, it showed that the sample had

been tampered with. So my mom kept at it. It went on for weeks, and I began to feel terribly guilty about the pain I was causing her. I could see I was breaking her heart and that I was tearing apart my family. That was when I fessed up ... sort of. I waited a few days before I took an honest test so that the hard drugs like heroin and cocaine would be gone.

After that, though, I slowed down. I didn't use nearly as often for the rest of my high school career. I ended up quitting the harder drugs and got back on the right path for the time being. Testing just by itself is a temporary fix, though, because after I left home, I picked back up on my using. However, it can be a very successful deterrent that can slow down your child's use while you find them help.

Be aware that your child will pitch fits and rage at you just for asking them to take a test. Don't let their anger make you raise your voice. They are acting that way because they are scared and they feel guilty. They don't want you to know.

Be persistent and be prepared for the crazy things your child will do to cheat the test. The best way to make absolutely sure you're getting a real sample is to watch them go. As invasive and embarrassing as that sounds, sometimes it's necessary. Even then, your child could have taken a drink like Ready Clean or refused the test until they were sure the drugs were out of their system.

You must dedicate yourself to the testing for it to be effective. Have those cups ready, and your child will begin to picture them sitting on the counter or the kitchen table every time they are tempted to use. It isn't a perfect fix, but it's worth the time and trouble.

## Conclusion

Drug testing is a deterrent, but it is not a solution. Knowing why your kid is using is the real key that unlocks the door to sobriety. Now, don't worry; that is a topic that will be discussed extensively later on. Just know that drug tests are important and are a great tool for slowing the progression of addiction. They are better than the quick fix BandAids we talked about in the first chapter, but they are still only medical tourniquets. They can slow the bleeding and save a life, but eventually they have to be removed and the stitches have to be applied, which is what happens in rehab.

Whatever testing method you choose, a definitive test will steer the conversation from constant denial to, "OK what are we going to do about it next?" And that's exactly where you want to be.

# CHAPTER 5:
# HOW DID WE GET HERE?

WHEN THE TRUTH COMES OUT and you begin to accept it, a whole new box of questions is thrown open. How did this happen? Why did they start using? Finding the answer is one of the major keys needed to unlock healing for yourself and your child. However, it's not easy to get a logical reason or any sort of solid answer from your child to begin with. It is a tough enough task getting straight answers from any young adult, never mind one who is using drugs. If you ask, you'll probably get a lot of shrugging and mumbling, followed by outbursts of angry admonitions to just leave them alone, if you keep pressing. The thing is, in all likelihood, your child doesn't really know the answer yet either.

Sometimes the child, at a loss for a real answer and with an inability to examine his or her own motivations, blames the parents. Your child may lash out and tell you all of this is your fault, and you, like many parents, may latch onto that and take it to heart. It's sometimes easier for parents to lay all the blame on themselves in an attempt to take it off their child. They want to imagine that it wasn't their baby's fault. It's a lie. Plain and simple. There is no way that your actions are the sole reason your child got to this point. You may have fed your son when he was a baby, but by no means did you force-feed him drugs. If you were that type of parent, I'm sure you wouldn't be reading this book! Right now, your child is a shell of his former self because drugs have completely taken hold. That influence is what drives him to hurt you, to blame you. It blinds him to reality and prevents him from seeing the true cause. To truly let go of drugs, he must uncover what lead him to use in the first place, which is no easy task.

So, in the hopes that a little direction can help you and your child begin to work through the underlying causes of the current situation, I'm going to lay out some of the most common reasons people become addicts. There are million variables and combinations that can lead to addiction. Every addict's path is as unique as a snowflake, but there's a good chance that each path is paved with one or more of the following reasons.

## Genetics/Predisposition

We talked about this in Chapter One, but I want to reiterate it here because it is a major cause of addictive behavior. Some people are actually wired for addiction. It's an unfair cause, but it's a very real one. Normally, though, this genetic predisposition lays dormant until it is triggered by one or more of the following other reasons.

## Finances

Money is known for causing problems in many areas of life. This is another. Some people use because they feel serious financial stress. They can't pay the bills. They can't live the way they'd like to. So, they turn to substances to ease the stress and pain. When the late car payments and electric bills mount up on the table, and the landlord calls to say that rent is past due, it all seems like too much to handle. Getting high sounds like the perfect answer to escape it all.

Now, unless your child is older and already living on their own, this probably isn't the case. However, other people use because they have too much extra money on their hands, and they simply can. For years, I sniffed coke with the mega rich. Why do all rock stars and celebs have drug problems? Excess, plain and simple. When I won Big Brother, I had 500 grand in the bank. What did I do with it? Partied hard! Because I had the money to do it, and it was easy.

So, on a smaller scale, if your teenager gets a large allowance and/or has a job but doesn't have to pay for their own gas or their own entertainment, they may start blowing it on things they know you won't buy for them.

## The Glamorous Allure

When celebrities are posting videos on SnapChat of themselves smoking a joint and rappers fill their CDs with rhymes about drinking syrup (liquid codeine), the use of drugs becomes glamorized and mainstream. Kids naturally want to mimic their idols in order to be cool, so they pick up all of that idols habits, both good and bad—drugs included. The problem with celebrity social media showcasing drug use is that kids only get little snippets and impressions. They don't see the ugly side of drugs in those laid-back videos where their favorite actor or rapper is lounging around blowing cool smoke rings and talking about the high life. They see the occasional celebrity drug-related meltdown, but the glamorized version is what hits them on a daily basis. Even the meltdowns are sensationalized and charmed. When was the last time you remember a celebrity serving hard jail time for drug use? It doesn't happen, and it gives kids a false impression that can be extremely dangerous. As a result, teens have more flippant attitudes toward drugs in this era than ever before. In fact, they are often seen as positive influences that make you more artistic, cool, and successful.

## Work Influence

Certain career fields have a higher percentage of drug

use amongst employees than others. Topping the list are construction work and the service industry (such as restaurants and retail businesses). Heroin or meth may have been a foreign thing to your child until everyone on their long weekend shifts was doing it or talking about doing it. Maybe your child's first introduction to coke was by a coworker who asked them to go hang out after work.

My first experience with this sort of influence was at seventeen. I went to work with my uncle, who was a foreman for TGI restaurant remodeling jobs. It was a tough gig, and the workers often had to be alert and on the job for eighteen to twenty hours straight. How did they do it? Crystal meth. What did I say when they offered me some? Yes.

## Emotional Damage

When people hurt, they look for relief. Sometimes drugs rush in and fill that need. Drugs temporarily numb pain, push away bad memories, and provide a false sense of comfort and euphoria. The initial hurt can be anything: a death in the family, a divorce, being cheated on, getting dumped by a first love, or even struggling with gender identity and all the bullying that can ensue as a result, just to name a few. The pain can burn so deep that the only escape is getting fucking wasted. It's hard to cope and open up with new emotions that you can't process yet. Drugs and alcohol are a lot more appealing than having to deal with such hurt or grief.

## Dysfunctional Family Life

This doesn't necessarily have to mean growing up in a terrible home with family members who are abusive or neglectful, although that is a major stressor. This can be something as common as witnessing a truly ugly divorce at an early age or being surrounded by family members who solve problems by shouting and fighting. Sometimes the child's parents or guardians are addicts themselves, and when Mommy or Daddy gets sent off to rehab or worse, the child is bounced around between family members, never feeling stable or totally safe and loved.

## Poverty/High Risk Upbringing

This is the cause everyone turns to. It's the one middle class parents shake their fingers at, not wanting to believe such things will ever touch their child. There's a reason behind these assumptions, though. If a child grows up in an impoverished neighborhood, there is an extremely high likelihood that he or she will be exposed to violence, crime, and drugs at a very early age. If you grow up in the neighborhood where the drug dealers flock to hide from police and service their customers, you're bound to run into them eventually.

## Peer Pressure

As a young adult, the need to fit in and be considered cool is tremendous. It's a constant drive in the back of teens' minds. This is a point in their life where their bodies are changing and they are trying to figure out who they are, what they like, who they like, and what they want to do in life. That desire for identity, confidence, and approval may draw them to the older kids in the neighborhood who already seem so "together" and cool. But maybe those kids smoke pot or abuse alcohol. To fit in, the younger kid feels pressure to do as they do.

It's not always older kids, either. Teens are frequently changing cliques and looking for new people to fit in with if one group doesn't work out. It's easy to fall into a group that abuses substances for fun, and if the new kid perceives this group as cool, he or she will seek to emulate them to be accepted.

The first time I smoked a cigarette, I was trying to impress my brother and our friend, Billy. Not as immediately serious of a substance as, say, heroin—and many teen groups don't go beyond alcohol or pot—but there is always the chance of a child stumbling upon peers who dabble in more dangerous things.

You must teach children how to find an "out" for these situations. My father used to say, "Just get a club soda on ice with a lime, and everyone will think you're drinking." The ideal solution is to teach your kids how to say a flat out no to peer pressure, but many teens struggle to do so, especially when they are the odd man out at a party. Let them know there are ways to slide out of it a little cleaner. If they always bring their own car to parties rather than riding with friends, they have the go-to excuse of "I'm driving." If things get too out of hand, they can drive themselves out of there, claiming they have to get up early. If they aren't old enough for a car, make sure you drive them there and pick them up. Then their excuse of "My mom is driving me home, and if she notices I'm high she's gonna kill me," doubles as a deterrent because it's true.

People who use love having company. It makes them feel like what they're doing is alright, and they will try their best to rope others in. You must teach your child the tools to avoid and say no to these people.

## Life Pressures

Sure, kids don't have to pay bills or worry about a 401K, but what many adults fail to remember is that they deal with their own sets of pressures. Children feel pressure to do well in school so that they succeed in life down the road. When finals role around, both in high school and college, the amphetamine, Adderall, starts making its rounds around the school. It helps the brain stay on task, and it's very popular amongst students who need to cram in a late night study session or keep focused in an exam.

There's also the huge cultural pressure to perform well in sports. Many kids have dreams of full-ride sports scholarships and superstardom. The temptation of steroids is sometimes too great to resist.

## For Simple Enjoyment

It is the standard trademark of a teen to be rebellious, daring, reckless, and impulsive. These attitudes are portrayed in movies and are echoed by grouchy, mumbling adults. Every child picks up drugs of their own free will, but some do it simply out of curiosity and the desire to have some illegal fun. I was one of those kids. I wanted to live the lifestyle, feel the rush and partake in the hustle. It was cool. It was exciting. I liked getting completely messed up on drugs and losing myself to the chaos.

## Nothing Else to Do

Boredom is a diseases that plagues young adults. You probably can't count how many times your child has moaned, "I'm so bored." That boredom springs from a complete lack of responsibilities. If they don't have chores they have to get done or organized activities like clubs and sports that keep them busy, children get into all kinds of trouble. Often it's just simple mischief, doing stupid things with friends. However, it's a big reason why many kids progress to drugs.

The saying about idol hands is true. Too much downtime is dangerous in an age where kids sell drugs to kids and illegal substances can easily pop up at parties.

If a child has nothing they *have* to do, they will grow bored of the same old same old ordinary things they can do (video games, TV, going to the movies, etc.), and they will start looking for new, exciting things that they know they shouldn't do, just to cut through the boredom.

Using illegal substances adds spice to a dull life. Some people cheat on their partner to feel some sort of thrill and find relief from the same routine. Kids will use drugs because they like the idea of being able to get away with it. The forbidden aspect adds an element of excitement to a mundane life. Once they get a taste of that thrill, going out to a movie sounds terribly dull in comparison to getting fucked up.

## Brat Syndrome

Some children are spoiled to the core. All parents want their kid to have everything. That's natural, and there's nothing wrong with it ... so long as it doesn't go so far as to allow a child everything immediately with no responsibility or work required. It's a fine line that is easy to cross. Once it's crossed, the child expects everything they want when they want it as a free handout. However, sometimes the parent grows wise to this and backpedals. Sometimes, the child gets a little older and tries to strike out on their own only to find that life doesn't run on free giveaways. When they don't get what they want, sometimes those extremely spoiled children don't know how to cope, and moving back in with Mom and Dad and chasing an immediate, temporarily satisfactory drug high looks like the more fun option.

## Lack of Life Skills

Children can be spoiled in other ways besides simple monetary handouts and a constant inflow of stuff. I see so many kids who have no concept of simple life skills. I was one of them. My mom and dad never made me do my own laundry, clean up around the house, make my own food, or do my own shopping.

When a child has never had to lift a finger and has no idea how to do the simplest of everyday tasks, life can easily become overwhelming when they move out and start living on their own. Since they've never had to cope with an unpleasant situation, and anything they didn't want to do was handled by Mommy or Daddy, their first response is to sit back and forget about it rather than attacking the problem by themselves. What better way to forgot responsibilities than to go out and get high?

## Living in Bubble Land

Parents are protective of their children, and many times this causes them to rush behind their kids and clean up any mess left in their wake. When the child gets in trouble at school for cheating or fighting, or screws up her car and gets a mark on her record for being the cause of a wreck, Mom or Dad comes to talk to the principle or shells out the money for car repairs.

But if children never clean up their own messes and never fully reap the consequences of bad decisions, they begin to feel that the law does not apply to them. They develop a conscious, or even subconscious, notion that they can get away with things. Then illegal drugs don't seem like a huge risk. What could go wrong in their charmed life? Even if something bad did happen, Mom and Dad would be there to fix it, right?

A lack of understanding about the law and a lack of experience with the stress of handling one's own mess causes illegal drugs to look like a party favor.

## Medicating an Injury

Broken bones and other injuries are a mainstay in the lives of young adults, especially highly active ones. If your son breaks his ankle playing soccer, he may be prescribed

Tylenol #3. What most people don't realize is that just because it has the household name Tylenol on it doesn't mean it's the same thing. Tylenol #3 contains the opiate codeine, which is an addictive substance and can easily be abused if its true nature is not understood. It's easy to take one too many pills a day to get relief from the pain. Codeine produces a sort of high that regular Tylenol does not. Your son may decide he likes that feeling, his body may begin to crave it, and once the prescription runs out, he may seek out street drugs that provide a similar effect. However, pain pills are expensive out on the black market, so many kids decide to give heroin a whirl because it provides more bang for their buck and it's more readily available.

## Self-Medication

Self-medicating is often a result of an undiagnosed mental health concern. Someone developing schizophrenia in their late teens may feel overly paranoid and need to calm down. They may swipe Xanax from Mom's medicine cabinet. Someone suffering from depression may want a pick-me-up and turn to an upper like cocaine or meth. I was bipolar manic and didn't know it for a long time. At first, I just used weed to try and slow myself down, but when that didn't give me the relief I needed, it turned into more and more drugs to just feel normal. It sounds crazy, but to many in AA, it rings true.

## Living up to Expectations

Some kids put way too much pressure on themselves. They have a crippling fear of failure and are afraid to let themselves and their loved ones down. They know their parents want them to land a scholarship to ease the pain of tuition payments. They want to be the best at everything they do. They want to be a winner. Then, when life doesn't go as planned and pressure mounts, they begin to panic. That's when the temptation of drugs steps in.

Sometimes kids do this to themselves, other times the parents unknowingly turn up the pressure by continuously voicing what they would like their child to achieve. It's great to let your kids know that you have high expectations for them because you know they can do whatever they set their minds to, but constantly discussing exactly what you'd like them to achieve instead of letting them choose achievements for themselves can put huge pressure on them. Especially when those expectations are raised sky-high.

Drugs then become a means for escaping the pressure. In a sad reversal, eventually they become a serious crutch that holds back the user from achieving just about anything.

## Conclusion

A good number of the reasons I just listed may sound like everyday experiences that all kids have been facing for decades: taking care of their own mess, dealing with pressure to succeed, coming in contact with bad influences at school and work, etc. Yes, it's true. I'm sure you faced those same challenges as a kid. So you're probably thinking, "Why would a kid turn to drugs to solve those everyday things?" Well, because drugs are more readily available than ever. In the information age, kids know about drugs from a very early age. They stumble upon drug references in the media, and an explanation of those references is just a Google search away. Drugs aren't whispered about in secret amongst the younger generation. Often, they're boasted about. Kids are being exposed to drugs younger and younger. I know twelve-year-olds who smoke crack, and their mommies and daddies are millionaires. When I was growing up, heroin and harder drugs were shunned and looked down on. Now I regularly hear stories about Friday night high school parties where the attraction is no longer kegs of beer, but mounds of dope for everybody to share. Kids are sitting around on couches and living room floors nodding out. When kids are exposed to these substances early in life, they can quickly become addicted to multiple different substances at once.

You might think extreme privilege or even just an upper middle class upbringing can shield a child from drugs. This idea stems from many people's misconception that drugs are a "ghetto" problem or that they only exist in the rough parts of town. I hate to burst your bubble, but the more money a kid has access to, the more downtime they have, and the fewer responsibilities delegated to them, the more likely they are to use.

Many common factors that lead to use stem from immaturity. In order to grow up, a child has to get a taste of adult reality. They need to learn life skills. They need to do the busy work and the chores and the crappy jobs *for themselves.* They need to deal with the consequences of their actions without outside help. They need to understand the value of the dollar and the value of hard work. All of these things keep them motivated and active so that they don't go looking for illegal entertainment, they can wrap their heads around the dangerous consequences of drugs, and they can have the fortitude to withstand social pressures.

There is no one specific answer for why young people use drugs. Each will have their own reasons, and some are more serious than others. Some causes are rooted in boredom, laziness, and immaturity. Others are rooted in pain, distress, and insecurity. Often, there is more than one reason behind every addict's use. However, the most common issue that lurks at the root of the others is stress: stress over financial independence, stress over fitting in, stress over living up to potential, etc. It is so important that, as a parent, you teach your child how to handle stress. Kids can easily wallow in whatever is stressing them out. They obsess over it. You have to teach them to let it go, move away, and approach again from a new angle. Teach them to flush that stress out with a coping mechanism like exercise, heading off to a quiet place, or interacting with something that brings them joy before turning their attention back to the stressful matters at hand. You need to recognize that any new phase in your child's life, such as moving from high school to middle school, getting a boyfriend or girlfriend, moving away to college, getting their own apartment, or starting to pay their own bills can awaken new stressors for your child. The best thing to do is have an open dialogue with your kid about what to expect in this new phase and how to handle it so that they aren't blindsided. Teach them how to write a check for their rent, how to set up automatic payments on a utility bill, how to deal with heartbreak, etc. This can help prevent use from becoming abuse, but if that ship has already sailed, these sorts of conversations will still be extremely helpful after your child gets out of treatment. It's never too late to start the dialogue.

No matter the cause of abuse, experimentation can quickly progress to addiction, and that is when all other aspects of life need to be put temporarily to one side. Instead of brushing off the use, you must address it quickly and cut off the head of the snake before it grows. Instead of screaming, yelling, and blaming yourself or your child, you need to approach the situation with a calm demeanor and a concrete strategy. That's what this book is here to do. In the coming chapters, this book will teach you how to tread the troubled waters of addiction and create an actionable strategy that will pull your child safely out of the storm. Don't waste any more days or let any more time slip by without seeking a solution. Now that you've got idea about the "why," you must move on to how to handle today, tomorrow, and the years to come.

# CHAPTER 6:
# PREPARING AND PAYING FOR REHAB

When you've successfully given your child a drug test and the results have come back positive for drugs (if the test comes back negative and you were vigilant enough during the process to know it wasn't altered, then you can be happy in the knowledge that you were wrong and move on), you should not only stock up on those cups as a deterrent, but also start preparing for the ultimate goal: getting your kid into treatment.

Your mind may be jumping directly to an intervention, but there are a few things you need to do before that. Sadly, the majority of patients who enter treatment never complete it. This is often due to a lack of planning. The addicts are forced against their will into any old facility that is just looking to make some money off them, not really caring if they get better or not. To avoid these issues, you must plan everything out down to the minute details.

Ideally, you want your kid to go straight into treatment right after you have an intervention. (Don't worry, I'll get you through the intervention, as well, but let's first get things in order before you go telling Johnny he's going to rehab and start issuing empty threats.) Now, if your child is still capable of staving off use on her own for a few days at a time or if she isn't using hard, extra dangerous drugs, you have the option to send her to groups like AA and NA or enroll her in an outpatient program where she can stay at home and just go in for therapy a few times a week before considering inpatient rehab. However, it's often very hard to gauge your child's level of addiction on your own because your kid isn't likely to be honest about just how often he or she uses. If you think it isn't too serious yet, you can try one of these less invasive options and see how it goes, but in the meantime, you should be looking into rehab options just in case you notice things continuing to go downhill.

If you have even the slightest inkling your child's use is serious or on the fast track to becoming serious, rehab is the most well-rounded and effective option. But if you want it done right, you have to have a couple of things lined up first.

You need to pull together a medical team (an addiction physician, a therapist, etc.) to help you craft a detox plan. You need to find the best insurance policy you can afford to pay for the treatment. Most importantly, you need to find the proper drug treatment facility for your child.

## Assembling a Medical Team

This step may seem a little premature to you right now. Again, you might be asking, "Shouldn't I be focused on getting my kid into rehab as fast as possible? Why do I have to waste time finding a medical team when I'm going to be sending my kid to a facility that has its own team?" or, "Isn't that what rehab is for?"

Forming a group of medical professionals that you trust and who know your child is an essential part of the road to lasting recovery. You do at some point expect your kid to come home, and this team of professionals will be there when that day comes, but you will also need to get advice, educate yourself, and know what to do and who to call when the intervention happens and it's game on!

At one of the sober houses I consult for, if a kid we're working with gets back a dirty drug test, the staff doesn't waste time accusing that kid of being high and chewing him out right then and there. No, we take the information, keep a set of eyes on him, and begin to form a plan behind the scenes. This involves notifying the emergency contact and the staff of his current program, if he's in one. It's a team decision. We contact the detox or treatment center and arrange transportation. We do all the prep work for readmission before the kid knows we know he is using.

Some are highly compliant and willing to get help, but that's not always the case. They will kick, scream, and deny it to the end most times. However, when they are presented with well thought out options for help and everything goes down seamlessly, there is no room for them to say no.

Once you prepare and decide to do an actual intervention (meaning your son or daughter will be going to rehab immediately afterward or else there will be concrete consequences) and your kid agrees to get help, you want to put them in the car and get them to the facility before they have time to change their mind or start to come up with any more excuses about why they don't need to go. Remember, they are on drugs and *cannot* make rational decisions!

If you've already assembled a group of professionals that know your kid and the situation, then those people can guide you and may even show up to that intervention and help you steer your loved one toward rehab. When your child comes out of rehab, they will return to a group of people who already know and care for them, already have their information, already have an established rapport with them, and will thus help them stay on track.

So, talk to your family doctor or find a local addiction specialist. That way you have a doctor in your corner who could suggest a rehab facility or two that might suit your kid best. You can also use the "Find a Doctor" resource on the American Society of Addiction Medicine's (ASAM) website. Addiction medicine specialists from all around the country apply for membership to this prestigious organization, and you can search their listings by state.

Try to find a local addiction therapist as well. Remember, there is an underlying reason your kid is using drugs, and in order keep your kid clean long term, you have to figure out what that is. That's what therapists do for a living. If you can find one who specializes in helping patients suffering from addiction, even better.

Do some research and find a local hospital within five miles of your house that offers a detox program. Now I'll be honest with you, none of these programs are usually great. These types of places are usually stuffed deep in the hospital next to the psych ward and are full of hard-core users that have been pulled off the street and have nowhere else to go. Now, I'm sure the parent in you is cringing at the thought of your baby being anywhere near a place like this, but you still want to be aware of which hospitals offer detox programs in case of an emergency.

Overdoses do happen, and if it happens to your kid, you want to be able to tell the ambulance exactly where you want your child taken.

Of course, private care is preferred. Some associations offer an OPD (outpatient detox), which is conducted from your own home. You will go to their offices regularly, and they will prescribe medication to help with the withdrawal. These are a good option, but they aren't fast enough in an emergency scenario. That is why you should keep a hospital with a detox center on speed dial. Still, it's a great idea to be aware of who offers those OPD services in your area and familiarize yourself with them. You can find such things by simply googling "addiction specialist" or "outpatient detox specialist" and seeing which physicians near you offer outpatient care.

Another precaution you can take is to inform your family

physician of your situation. Your child may already have an established positive relationship with that doctor through discussing previous concerns. Also if your child suffers medical side effects from use, such as contracting Hep C, this is the best person to talk to. There is always a need for a medical doctor, while specialists are good for just one specialty, so do not keep your kid's regular physical out of the loop.

Another must is to keep Narcan in your home if your child is on heroin or some other opiate—especially since those are some of the most dangerous types. Narcan comes in a shot like an EpiPen or in a nasal spray, and it's what the EMT's will bring with them if your child overdoses. It is an antidote which counteracts the specific effects of opiates. This drug has been out for decades, but with the recent epidemic it is surging in popularity. Put it with the first aid kit or the Band-Aids—somewhere easily accessible but out of the way. Let your kid know it's there in case they have friends over while you're not home and, God forbid, an overdose occurs. With Narcan, they can at least prevent a death. It can be prescribed, and now it's even available at CVS over the counter in select states. Ask your doctor or local pharmacist about getting Narcan so that you can administer a lifesaving dose faster. It's always better safe than sorry.

Now that you've done your research on medical pros, taken precautions, and formed a team, if there is an emergency before you've managed to get your kid to a treatment facility, you will have a plan of action. You will also have a support group to draw on for help and education. When your kid gets out of rehab, that support group will be waiting to help them.

Think of it as leaving a long list of numbers for the babysitter when your kid was little. All the bases are covered. This sort of precaution and preparation also shows that you are not playing games any longer, and this is going to get real. You're here for your child, and you're going to be well versed and prepared to make this journey a success!

## Paying for Rehab

Insurance is now your best friend. You want to make sure you choose your best friend wisely, so you don't get screwed over. You want a best friend who has your back.

Luckily, there have been some recent changes in the healthcare system that make acquiring insurance that covers addiction and mental health much easier. For instance, the Mental Health Parity and Addiction Equality Act (Parity Act for short), put into effect in 2008, dictates that insurance companies must treat addiction just like any other illness. That means they must provide you with the same level of coverage for addiction as they would a chronic physical illness like cancer. Now, the law doesn't mandate that they *have* to actually cover addiction or mental health care; it only means that they must treat it equally should they cover it. However, in light of this law, more insurance companies are fully covering addiction and mental health treatment. You want to make sure the policy you choose has proper coverage for your whole family as well as the addicted member.

Why is insurance so important? A good treatment center can run up a bill of $30,000 a month. Ouch!

Without insurance, getting your child the help they need will leave you with a pile of unpaid medical bills and a credit report that looks like a disaster zone. This takes a toll on everyone. It hurts financially, and it hurts your child's chance of success of moving forward after getting sober.

In the past, a lot of parents had to leave their older children to fend for themselves because insurance only allowed dependents aged eighteen and under. Now you can list your child on your insurance until they are twenty-six.

Insurance is worth it, and I recommend it wholeheartedly. With the right plan, you can get your child the right care for only a few hundred bucks a month rather than thousands.

## Coverage Types

First off, there are government policies such as Medicaid and Medicare, which are available for families with low budget incomes who need help. A lack of funds doesn't have to stand in the way of saving your child. The policies range in name by state, but they all require that you use specific medical facilities and doctors that are within the policy's network. The downside is that mental health facilities are rarely covered under these policies, and the facilities you can go to are limited and not top-of-the-line. These types of policies usually cover more institutionalized, governmental treatment centers and those hospital detox programs we talked about earlier in the chapter. With a Medicaid or Medicare plan, you are usually only covered for a few days of treatment—just long enough to detox and stabilize the addict before sending them back home. While this can save your child's life, it isn't going to do much in the way of correcting the problem long term. Some Medicare policies do cover real rehab (and you should fight to get one that does), but the facilities usually house hardened drug addicts and life-long criminals who have been forced to be there or have nowhere else to go. These aren't the ideal peers you want around your child. The people you put them into rehab with are going to be their example and will shape their attitude about sobriety and getting back on track.

However, while these aren't the best options, they are still better than nothing. These types of facilities will get your child clean; it's just going to be a lot more work once they get out. Without therapy or outside help, it is much easier to relapse. But that is why you assembled a team of helpers, right? The rehab programs are the most costly part of the process, and some of these government plans help get that out of the way and allow you to save your money to go toward things like therapy later.

If you can afford a private health insurance policy, the cheapest option is usually an HMO plan. Once again, though, these plans require you to go to specific doctors and facilities within the network. These facilities aren't usually as institutionalized as a state-run facility, but you still have to go through a list of covered programs to make your choice. Those lists are limited, with only about 10% of the nation's treatment centers and 5% of the nation's independent laboratories and substance abuse doctors accepting an HMO policy. Usually it only covers the big, commercialized centers, and many have waiting lists.

The next option is the EPO. It's the HMO's better looking cousin. The majority of services will still have to come from within the policy's network of providers, but there are options available for certain out-of-network services to be paid for as well.

The best type of plan is the PPO. You don't have to pluck a facility or doctor out of a network of select providers; you have the freedom to choose any medical provider of your liking. You can get around $50,000 worth of treatment coverage a month with these policies, making them top-tier and exactly what you are looking for in an ideal situation. They are nicknamed "Cadillac plans" for good reason.

Now, of course, the better the policy, the more expensive your monthly payment will be, but I can guarantee you that you won't ever get a monthly bill for $50,000 if you have a kick ass insurance plan.

## Some Extra Insurance Pointers

Find a local agent who specializes in personal insurance and healthcare to help you make the decision that is right for you, your kid, and your budget. Explain what your needs are. Let them know that your kid is suffering from drug addiction and that you are looking for the best possible policy to get them the help they need. You cannot be denied coverage due to a pre-existing mental health or substance abuse condition, so never hesitate to tell an agent about your child's problem for fear of being rejected. The only way they can help is if you lay out all the cards.

The first thing you should look at when selecting a policy is the amount of mental health coverage allotted to you. As I've said already, not all of them will offer this type of coverage, but if you have selected one that does, make sure you look at just how many days of treatment the policy covers. The more treatment days you can get, the better chance your child has at achieving a stronger foothold in sobriety. To learn more about mental health policies and the coverage owed to you by law, visit http://www.apa.org/helpcenter/parity-guide.aspx. If you have trouble finding coverage or are concerned about an overly high copay, visit the U.S. Department of Health and Human Services' website, https://www.hhs.gov/mental-health-and-addiction-insurance-help.

Be careful if you've chosen something like Obamacare or the healthcare.gov option. Those healthcare system websites can be harder to navigate than a Prius in a tornado. It's hard to tell exactly what policy you are getting. Make sure you look hard at the deductible. The reason you're looking into something like Obamacare is because your budget is low, so getting roped into a policy with a $6,000 deductible (meaning you have to pay up to $6,000 before the policy will pay anything) is counterintuitive. Many deductibles on the government-subsidized Obamacare plans are not worth a damn thing when it comes to getting into rehab. The $6,000 dollars I mentioned above is on the light side. These days, the deductibles are in the $15-20,000 dollar range. Plus, the payments are subsidized with tax credits, which creates a whole other issue you may come across at tax time. Also, in the Marketplace, as it's called, there is open enrollment from Nov. 1st to Dec. 15th to receive coverage that starts on Jan. 1st. If you pay your first payment after Dec 15th and before Jan. 1st, your coverage will start on Feb. 1st. Most insurance policies work this way; it's not like car insurance, where it is active immediately or at midnight the next day. Your coverage usually won't begin until the following month, so it makes sense to plan ahead. The cost of the Marketplace plan may seem like a great deal when you're paying $150–250 a month for insurance, but it is not worth a damn for anything but basic checkups. There seems to be change looming, however, with the Trump administration. The goal is to open up coverage options nationally. As of now, it's done by state, and in states with high rates of addiction like Florida it is nearly impossible to get an individual plan to cover quality treatment. That's why it's always recommended to get your kids on your work plan because those tend to be better policies. If your child is under 26, she is good to go on your plan, but after that you should help her look into enrolling directly through an agent and avoid the Obamacare plans completely. I am told you cannot even get a PPO policy in many states anymore, as Obama care has gotten progressively worse. I'm not one to take sides, but I see firsthand the hardships addicts are going through to get the proper coverage needed to get quality help. Hopefully change is on the horizon.

Don't get suckered. If you are going to go this route, make sure you are the one getting the policy, not your child. Sometimes it may be better to get it and not tell them they are covered. Many addicts I see here in South Florida use their insurance cards like Visas. They know that they can go out and get fucking messed up anytime, and when the money is gone and they have no place to go, they will use their insurance to check into a rehab, get right, and then *Bang!*

go right back at it. Please be observant of this behavior, and don't hesitate to pull the insurance if they begin to abuse it.

Some addicts may even engage in fraudulent behaviors, so be wary if your child has his own account. I recommend that you, the parent, help handle the process because addicts may ask for the money to pay the premium and actually use it for drugs. Get the log in info and the password to the insurance account and watch what is going on with it. Make sure it's active and paid up to date. See what is being charged to it.

Another thing to watch out for with insurance is doctor shopping. Kids go to multiple doctors and get their fix via prescription. Whether it's for Suboxone, pain meds, or benzos, addicts are resourceful and *will* manipulate the system, so be vigilant with what your son or daughter does with the insurance card, as well. The last thing you need is thousands and thousands of unpaid bills or copays amassing unchecked.

These Obamacare and Marketplace kinds of policies are designed to give you a break based on your income. Even if your kid is managing to hold a job right now, they are going to have to leave it to get into a program, so they won't have a job to keep the policy.

Always go with the highest level of insurance you can afford. This is a worthwhile expense, so put everything you can toward it. Another thing to avoid if your kid is over eighteen is the tough love, "you're an adult; do it yourself" mentality. While this approach can teach a child responsibility in normal situations, it isn't the best idea in this one. In all likelihood, your kid struggles to hold down a job—it's part of addiction. So, you are going to be able to afford the better policy, not your kid.

I got my coverage through a government agency and went to a county facility for my rehab through scholarship programs. To get scholarship money from the state, county, or city, make some calls and explain the situation. Ask if they have grants available. I got a county grant to pay for my treatment. Sometimes the state, county, or city will simply choose a facility and send your kid there for free, but again, it's usually not one of the best places. A grant is what you want.

Rehab facilities sometimes offer scholarships as well. It's just a matter of asking and explaining your financial situation and the needs of your child. Some programs leave a small percentage of their beds available to give away for free. Usually, in these types of situations, you pay for housing only, and they either cover the cost of treatment or base the cost on a sliding scale, meaning they take your income into account and set the price based on what you can afford.

Even with a scholarship or grant, it's hard enough to make you want to just give up. A government institution is cold and impersonal. It's easier to get sober when you are surrounded by peers and people who don't judge or discriminate. I wish my mom had gotten me private insurance instead of making me find and pay for my own.

So forget the "tough love" and get your kid under your policy, and get the best one you can. Don't choose a cheaper policy if you don't have to, but if you simply have no other choice, know that there are options. You can ask your church for help or seek out charity-run rehabs, like the Salvation Army's Adult Rehabilitation Centers. Ask about those scholarships and sliding scale payment plans when you get a rehab center on the phone. Don't mortgage your house. Do what you can to catch a break on the price and then get what you can afford. Just because a rehab facility has fancy bells and whistles doesn't mean it's a surefire center for success. Recovery is an uphill battle wherever your child goes; just do your best to find a center with professionals who care and know what they are doing.

If you are able to choose the best option, the PPO, the silver plan or better is probably going to be the best, most balanced option.

If you can't afford a PPO, the process is going to be a little harder. Take the time to go all the way through the provided network list and pick the absolute best facility that's covered. Know that there will be more work on the back-end because the extra services that help keep your child sober outside of rehab won't be available through your coverage. But that doesn't mean all hope is lost, not by a long shot. A good support group for your kid is worth its weight in gold. You can even look for a therapist yourself that works for cheaper and is willing to work with your budget. It will take a lot of legwork, but it's possible. And if your kid sees all of the effort you are still putting in after rehab, they will have one more motivator to stay sober—and a pretty big one at that.

If for any reason your insurance provider denies your request for rehab coverage, understand that you have the right to appeal that decision. Get your doctor on the phone and connect him or her to your insurance company if you can. Your doctor can better explain the medical necessity of treatment and how dangerous a denial of coverage is for your child.

My final pointer is to fight for inpatient rehab, meaning your child stays at a rehab center full-time with experienced staff around her all day every day. Your insurance provider may push you to put your child in outpatient care, where patients stay at home and just go into the center for therapy sessions and meetings with a physician. They push for this because it's cheaper for them, but you need to fight for inpatient, unless all your child is doing is smoking joints. Inpatient facilities provide the essential structure and supervision necessary to facilitate recovery and healing. It's much easier to maintain clean time in a controlled environment, and the longer your child's brain has to heal before she gets out, the better. Addicts need to have time to know what abstinence and sobriety can feel like; I know I had no clue about any of that before I entered rehab.

You should only consider outpatient care if your child's use isn't serious and you are just trying to steer her back in the right direction before a joint becomes something stronger. You wouldn't want to put a young stoner in with young meth and heroin addicts; that's putting a puppy in a lion's den. Suddenly your son or daughter is around "cool" peers who shoot needles, listening to how they think. You don't want that influence if you can help it; IV drug use is, in my opinion, the strongest line to addiction and the hardest form to break.

## Proceed with Caution

As of right now, there is not much regulation for drug treatment. There is a definite lack of set-in-stone protocols for acceptable practice. As a result, there are plenty of greedy individuals and companies out there ready and willing to exploit addicts and their families. Some rehab centers are basically giant factories, churning through patients solely for the money. When money is the only motivator for those running the facility, practices can easily become unscrupulous. Corners may be cut, patients may be overcharged or billed for services they didn't receive—you name it. Buyer beware, especially online. You need to dig deep to find out if the facility you're looking at on Google is actually a treatment center or a referral service that gets paid to send you to one of those factory-like facilities. They will do whatever they can to pull you in, even posting fake pictures of people smiling in a room that looks like a resort even though their facility looks more like a jail. New laws are coming down the lines. Florida has recently passed a few that try to regulate marketing tactics for treatment centers, but not every state even has that much. So, when faced with extravagant promises about absolute or guaranteed healing that make it sound like you shove an addict through the doors and he pops out a Valedictorian, remember that there are no real promises in addiction recovery. All that we recovery professionals and loved ones like you can do for an addict is to do our best. There are no guarantees.

You also need to be aware that the phrase "addiction treatment" has no standard definition. Treatment can mean anything from heavily medicating patients to psychotherapy. Some centers operate under a boot camp mentality, using overly rigid rules, intimidation, and physical exertion to try and "straighten out" patients. This never works. Addicts need empathy and guidance, not orders and punishment. Other centers use out-of-the-box, trendy (often to the point of being ludicrous) treatments that have no empirical evidence backing them, like healing through massage therapy and trips to the beach. Others try to rely solely on spiritual healing. Yes, faith can give an addict purpose and help them heal emotionally, but there needs to be science, medication, and mental health treatment involved, too.

You need to be very cautious when seeking a rehab center. Examine the facility's website carefully, interact in online forums, make phone calls, and understand the different kinds of legitimate treatment. I'm going to help you with that last part. I also want to give you some pointers on how to find a quality facility.

## Finding the Right Facility

You are searching for two major factors when it comes to picking the facility best suited for your child's needs.

1. A well-structured facility that actually achieves results.
2. A facility where you and your child feel comfortable and are treated with one-on-one attention.

A simple Google search will pull up thousands of results.

The ones near the top of the page are going to be the really large places and the headhunter marketing companies who place people in rehab just to chase fatter paychecks. This industry is booming, and many unscrupulous players have entered the game as a result. Many of the online sites are simply placement services looking to get you and your money into any center. They couldn't care less if it's actually the right fit. They are taking advantage of addicts and their loved ones at their weakest moment. This is why I harp on education and research. Please speak to a center directly. Some of these marketing services may be of help, but if the conversation is strictly about your insurance, hang up and get a new place on the phone. *Do your homework,* and watch out for scam artists! Find the right fit.

The larger programs may have plenty of resources and good physicians, but they are usually packed with patients. As a result, you and your child may end up treated a little bit like cattle, shuttled from one treatment and one doctor to the next with no real explanation or time to understand what's actually going on, simply because everything is on a strict, fast-paced schedule due to the massive volume of patients.

Think of it like a school. Usually, the schools with the best education programs are the smaller, private schools where there are less students vying for the attention of the teachers.

You'll also have to decide whether you want a local facility or one out of state. Many parents are drawn to the local option. It's natural to want to keep your child close, but it can be hard to find a good local facility unless you live in one of the drug recovery meccas like Florida or California. Don't settle for a subpar facility just because it will keep your kid close.

Even if you do find a great facility locally, consider finding someplace just as good out of state. If you keep your kid local, you aren't removing them from their environment. They'll be more likely to sneak out or have friends come pick them up. Familiar surroundings evoke familiar habits. Besides, if you can send them someplace new and nice, like Florida, it will feel more like a vacation and a fresh start, and your kid may be more likely to agree to go and stick with it. Tropical or trendy destinations are way more appealing and less embarrassing than the place a few miles away. For detox, take what you can get, but for the inpatient program, open their horizons; show them there is life beyond Mom and Dad's house!

Make sure all the facilities you're interested in have some sort of mental health track, especially if your kid has already been diagnosed with a mental illness. Mental health issues are one of the most common causes for drug addiction. You need to treat the source. Even if you don't know for sure that your child has a mental illness, make sure there are people and programs at the treatment center that can help you find out.

Once you've narrowed down your options, you should begin making some phone calls. The number provided on a facility's website is most likely going to send you to the admissions department. It's the job of the admissions department staff to get you into the program. They will try to sell it to you, essentially.

If you can bypass them once you get your basic questions asked, do so. You don't need a sales pitch. You need real answers. Try asking to speak to an actual in-house therapist or member of the program's clinical team. The way that therapist or physician speaks to you, and their ability to answer some of your tougher questions, will help you decide if that facility is the right one.

## Asking the Right Questions

So what questions should you be asking once you get somebody on the phone, whether it be admissions or a member of the clinical team?

Here are a few that you absolutely must ask in order to make an educated decision:

- Do you take my insurance?

Rehab costs money, so you want to get this question out of the way quickly so you know the value of your insurance and have the info ready from the start. They will ask you for the name of the company, the policy number, the name and date of birth of your child, and then the name and date of birth of the subscriber, along with the mailing address. They don't need more than that; don't give out your social!

Chances are, if one program accepts your insurance plan, all of them will, or at least the large majority. That's the power of good insurance. Some people think that those programs that are picky about insurances and make you shell out tons of money must the "better" ones, but that just isn't true. Always go with a facility that takes your insurance, and save yourself a massive headache and financial stress.

Once that first facility runs your insurance and tells you you're approved, know that you can begin shopping around because that means many other facilities will accept it, too. So start asking the more probing questions and don't say yes to the first place you call.

- How many beds do you have?

This gives you an idea of the maximum number of patients the facility accepts and how many people are potentially going to be in the program at the same as your kid.

- How many people are currently on your census, and what's your average group size?

This will tell you how many people are currently in the program. If they aren't super busy—with say only forty people in a facility that holds one hundred—this would be a good time to get your child enrolled. But know that they could fill up fast at any time.

- How many clients for each therapist?

The answer should be between eight and ten. If it's any more than that, it probably means each therapist has a large case load, and individual treatment may suffer.

- How many therapists are on staff, and what are their backgrounds?

You're looking for a variety. It gives your child more options to choose from. If they don't click with the therapist they are given and there are no others with open slots, no real therapy will be going on. They need to be able to ask for a new one.

- What areas do you specialize in outside of drug abuse?

Drug abuse affects more of your kid's life than you may realize. Treatment needs to go beyond correcting the use. For starters, your kid is going to need further medical tests. Kids on drugs are far more likely to contract Hepatitis C and other diseases. Ask how often your child will see medical professionals, and if your child has a condition that requires a specialist, make sure they have someone on hand who can help with that.

- Do you have a primary mental health program?

Mental health treatment is a *huge* component. There is going to be a lot rising to the surface when the drugs are out of the equation, so choose a center that can accommodate those needs. Sometimes a severe mental health issue can be a larger problem than the addiction, actually fueling it further. At the very least, the facility you choose needs to address mental health in some way, but a facility that can admit your child solely on the basis of a mental illness (aka a primary mental health program) is ideal. Programs, like Oceans Medical Centers, that give mental health concerns equal weight and levels of care are more balanced than those that address those issues only as a side track during therapy. If you feel your child may benefit from mental health care, accommodate for those needs from the get go or you will get poor results fast.

- What's next? How long is the program?

You're going to want to get your child ongoing therapy after the treatment to help him keep his head in the right place for continued sobriety. You may even want to send him to a halfway house where he can be around likeminded peers helping each other to stay sober. Ask about how the center handles aftercare. What is their usual recommendation after the inpatient residential stay? Do they use a halfway house? Do they offer aftercare of their own? How long is the stay? When should you plan on making that transition from inpatient care to aftercare? These are all great questions to have answers to.

- Do you have any alumni I can speak with that do not work there?

Talking to some outside success stories can clue you in

on some of the ins and outs of a program that a regular staff member won't tell you. I have a long list of successful clients that I can refer people to, and the program you select should too.

- How long have you been in business? Do you have other locations?

Personally, I'm not a fan of the big chain programs that have locations all over the country. The Mom & Pop programs are my preference. They are cozy, and they usually have a good, genuine reason for doing what they do. You want a program with a pulse and a moral compass that is active in the community and delivers proven results.

- Does the program have any accreditation?

There are three major certifications a program can have: CARF, JCAHO, and NCQA. JCAHO is the biggest, and certain insurances require you to choose a JCAHO accredited facility. If a program has received all three of these, it is top tier when it comes to professionalism. Many of those big facilities on the top page of the Google search have these certifications. And that's wonderful. But don't forget to take into consideration the number of patients they handle all at once.

As far as insurance and accreditations go, ask your insurance company. Some may require you stay in-state for any type of treatment. The trend of many insurance companies is to require the program be JACH accredited in order for them to cover the stay. So, call the insurance company and know the parameters of what you can get coverage for before you start the process.

## One Final Tip

These questions can help you make an educated decision, but my final tip to you is to remember that you and your child can choose to leave and go to another treatment center at any time. All of the programs out there will tell you they are the best, but if you don't like anything about the place you chose, don't let them convince you that there is some sort of mandatory length of stay. There is zero commitment! If you aren't happy, start the process over with a better understanding of exactly what you need and find somewhere new. Track your child's eagerness. A good program will produce motivated kids. It's not always the case, but if know how to gauge whether your kid's just bitching vs. truly having a bad, unhelpful experience . The clients at my mom's facility, Oceans Medical Centers, are happy, excited, and enjoy coming to group and to the center—at least for the most part—because the staff treat them as clients and not as cattle.

## Conclusion

Finding a group of professionals can mean the difference between life and death in an emergency situation. They also provide a circle of support that will help keep you and your child upright throughout the whole, weary process.

Finding the right insurance plan is essential and can mean the difference between long-term success and short-lived sobriety. Get the very best one you can afford, and put tough love aside.

Finding the best treatment facility for your child's needs can take a lot of hunting, but effective treatment is the root of success and lasting sobriety. Take your time with the selection process; you have every reason to be picky.

Once you do all three of these things—here comes the hard part—you are ready for an intervention.

# CHAPTER 7: INTERVENTION

Here it is. That last big step to getting your son or daughter into rehab. Now that you've done your prep work— assembling a medical team, selecting your insurance, and hunting down the right facility—it's time for the intervention.

After all the suffering and the massive amount of leg work on your part up to this point, here is the first big step toward change, toward your child getting clean and reversing the course of their life—not to mention easing the strain on yours.

You've put the lies and denials behind you, let your loved one know you're serious about getting them help, and set all of the ducks in a row to make it happen. You're ready now for the last hoorah that will hopefully end with your child walking through the doors of the facility you've chosen.

## What Exactly Is an Intervention?

There are two types of interventions: formal and informal. The formal intervention is the method popularized by reality shows, and it's the method you should try first because if it is successful, your child gets into rehab that same day.

In the simplest terms, a formal intervention is a scheduled, structured environment where the addict is not so much confronted, but rather presented with the opportunity to get clean in the most appealing, seamless, and painless way possible. Get the idea of confrontation out of your mind. An intervention isn't about forcing someone into rehab. A forced rehab stint will not produce results, because the addict then feels no desire to actually make the change. Instead, an intervention is about showing your loved one the light and letting them see the possibilities that rehab will open up.

When done correctly, an intervention is very detail oriented. You will need to do some prep work with all of the people you're inviting to the intervention. If you don't, you may end up with a terribly awkward situation in which you say something like, "Honey, it's time to get help. We all have a few things to say to you," and then everyone in your group sort of looks at you with wide, glassy eyes and with mouths blubbing open and closed like a room full of fish.

Lastly, as briefly mentioned in the previous chapter, an intervention produces the best results when it elicits immediate action. Know going into this intervention that you aren't looking for your son or daughter to say, "I'll go tomorrow," or "I'll go next week." As soon as your child agrees, put them in the car and take them directly to the facility or the airport. Get together the necessities in advance. Your son may get surly and ask to stop for cigarettes along the way. Your daughter may complain that you're sending her off without any toiletries or fresh underwear. In short, your kid will come up with any excuse to delay arrival at the unfamiliar destination. Pack up all the essentials and keep them hidden. When the whining starts, pull them out to use as mitigation tools and shut down excuses. This will avoid unnecessary stops on the way to rehab.

## Who Should Attend?

The idea of conducting an intervention may make you feel a little awkward. And honestly, interventions are awkward, and difficult. Thus, you may think it could alleviate some of the awkwardness to only include family members and friends who are very close to your child. This is *not* a good idea. Having only family members attend can make your son or daughter dismissive. I know if I had walked into my house and seen my parents and brother sitting in a circle expectantly, I probably would have said, "Go fuck yourselves," and gone up to my room without looking back.

You need at least one person there who isn't part of the family and who doesn't yet know your child personally. This could be someone from the medical team you've assembled, like an addiction specialist. It could be someone from the facility you plan to send them to. People from your local AA and NA groups are usually willing to help out if you ask. There are even licensed intervention professionals you can get in touch with, though their services aren't exactly cheap. N.A.D.A.I. (National Association of Drug and Alcohol Interventionists), for instance, may be able to refer you to a local intervention professional. Their website is www.nadai.us. You can also do a Google search and read advice straight from the pros online. Who knows? Maybe I'll show up in your living room one day.

Just like your medical and rehab team members, you need to screen your interventionist, too. Talk to others they've helped and check out any facilities they work at and have financial agreements with. Once you've selected someone, you need to take the time to talk with them and listen to their strategies. You should run scenarios by them, explain your strengths and weaknesses when dealing with your child, and explain why you've had trouble getting your kid help up to this point.

Having a professional stranger present is vital because it conveys the seriousness of the situation and will serve to grab your child's attention at the very least. Seeing someone who isn't in their inner circle will make your kid feel less in charge because the living room is now not their typical environment. Drugs have been controlling your household, and you and your child's lives. Having someone there who hasn't been effected by your child's use shifts the balance of power and boots your child out of their element. It's also harder to dismiss a stranger who is present in the home as a guest with a smart-aleck remark. Not impossible, by any means, but harder.

## Pre-Intervention Prep

Once you know who's coming, you need to establish a game plan with all of the players.

First off, you don't want everyone talking over each other. Decide who will speak first. In fact, it wouldn't hurt to establish the whole order of who speaks when for the whole intervention.

Have some stories prepared that will help your child see what their life has turned into. Remind her of the time she hocked the family computer behind your back. Remind him of the time he stole from you. Any crazy, dangerous, or illegal thing that put their wellbeing and lifestyle in jeopardy puts things in perspective all at once. The key is how you tell these stories. Yes, you want these stories to say, "Look what you've done to us and to your life," but you want to say it in the tone of a friend: half-joking and reminiscing, but enlightening. It's a way to say, "Come on now, man, can't you see you've hit rock bottom? Don't you want to give this change a shot?" Avoid the stereotypical image of Grandma crying through a story of what Johnny was like as a little boy and saying, "Why, Johnny, why?" Don't fill them with regret and nostalgia. Don't guilt trip. Guilt kills. It's not going to elicit the right response.

You need to rehearse the whole intervention, not just talk about it. Actually go through it. Make sure it has an opening, a middle, and a close. The dry run/mock session pays off. It raises the comfort level of everyone involved and emphasizes the gravity of the situation beforehand. The more preparation, the better.

Lastly, make sure everyone involved knows to keep the tone calm and comforting. No pointing, accusing, and yelling. The professional(s) you invite will already know this, but family members and friends may not.

## The Process

The addict is going to know damn well what's coming when he walks in the door. If you're leading him into the room, have him walk in in front of you, then stand in front of the exit in case he decides to run.

First, tell your child why you are all there and what got you all to this point. Explain that you don't want to have to see them high or hear their lies anymore—it hurts you. Tell them you don't want them to have to ask for money anymore, that you want them to be able to have a rewarding career and make their own way. Explain that you've spent way too many nights sitting up worried about them.

Then you need to let your child talk. I can assure you they will have something to say, even if it's just a dismissive scoff. The bullshit and excuses will flow freely, along with the empty promises and attempts to turn this around on you, but hear them out.

Then explain all of the prep work you've done. Tell them how the treatment will be paid for, making sure to emphasis that they won't be paying a dime for it; it's coming through the insurance you've paid for. Show them the facility, especially if it's a nice one in a vacation-like spot. If they are going somewhere like Florida, get a beach-themed shirt or a bathing suit, or just something cool they could use at the beach.

If you've been lucky enough to get insurance that pays for a real rehab facility and not just the few days of detox, explain how much nicer the process will be, how much easier on them it will go. Explain that they will get effective medicine that will get them through withdrawal without pain.

If they don't seem to be taking a liking to the facility you show them, don't worry. Have two or three backups that you discovered during your research for them to look at and choose from. Whatever center your child chooses, stick to the plan and the travel arrangements. Many treatment centers help get your child on a plane in less than 12 hours, if need be. Take advantage of this. Don't let your son or daughter dictate your actions. You did the research. You know the best facilities for them, and you've made the arrangements. Stick to them.

Let your loved one know that they will be among people who are like them, that this process isn't something radical that's never done. Millions of people do it every year, and you think it's worth giving it a shot. Ask them what they truly have to lose. They may interject with things like a boyfriend or a girlfriend or a job, but let them know that those things will be there when they get back.

Most importantly, let your child know that you've got it all figured out. It's all planned, and you've made sure it's the absolute best you can get. Let them know that you are in control of the whole process and that you've made sure it's going to be as painless as possible for them. Reinforce that they will be getting a proper medical detox, which includes plenty of medication. Promise them it will be painless and easy, that they will not even feel the withdrawal. Again, drug addicts will follow the next high, and if you have to dangle the detox meds in their face like an enticing carrot, so be it.

This is vital because what your addicted son or daughter fears the most is the unknown. Addiction is all about going back to the same thing, the same routine over and over. Change petrifies an addict. If your daughter knows that you've done your homework and that you can tell her what's going to happen without any surprises, she will feel more secure. If you can assure your son that he won't have to do any of the planning himself or shell out money that he doesn't have, the idea is going to be a lot more appealing to him.

The final step is to have someone very close to your child say, "You ready to wrap this up? Let's go hop in the car and get you over to the hospital for detox and then on a plane (or in a car or bus) to the treatment center."

## Prepare for the Refusal

No matter how much prepping and rehearsing you do, interventions do not always go smoothly. There will be tears and heightened emotions. There may be kicking and screaming.

Understand that the tears and the anger and the pleading on the part of the addict are just par for the course. You're going to hear a lot of tearful excuses, but stay strong. Just remember that no job or relationship or anything is more important than getting your baby clean. Without sobriety, those jobs and relationships are far more likely to fall apart anyway. Don't let them stand in the way. Explain all of this to your child. Let them know why you aren't buying it rather than just giving a tight-lipped no.

Your child may rattle off all of the things they are worried about when it comes to rehab, and you should listen. If you did the prep work from the previous chapter, you probably have the answers to assuage all or most of those worries. Remind them that they don't have to worry at all; you've got everything settled and planned to the last detail. The only thing they have to do is decide to take this huge step toward improving their life.

The key is to level with them. Listen and answer all of their questions and concerns to the best of your ability with a calm and reassuring demeanor. If things start going badly, don't get panicky and don't get loud or angry. Don't demand anything of them. Instead, request it.

Even in the face of their protests, keep things lighthearted. Any adverse reactions they have are stemming from nervousness and uncertainty, so keeping things upbeat will help to soothe them. Share some crazy stories of situations that the two of you had to deal with and got out of together. I'm sure you have plenty.

Your final words before asking them yes or no shouldn't be, "Do it now or else," but rather, "Hey, let's give this a try." In such an awkward setting like this, your son or daughter is going to feel vulnerable, so any commanding or harsh remarks will make them throw up a shield, which you most certainly don't want.

## Define Consequences

This may seem counterintuitive at first glance because I've just been talking about not demanding or being strict. Remember, though, that I was talking about tone and word choice. That's the key here. These consequences are also a last resort that won't be addressed unless absolutely necessary, meaning if your child is still saying no to treatment at the end of the intervention process.

Without consequences, the intervention can be seen as a joke to your child. If there is no threat of change at home, they will be more likely to reject the idea of making the big change in deciding to go to rehab. You need to let them know that things are going to change from this point on no matter what. It's up to them to decide if the change will be a positive or negative one.

These should be "if, then" type consequences, with the "if" always being saying no to treatment. You have to actually back them up, though. If they say no, don't let them stay at your house, don't let them borrow any more money. Don't pay their bills anymore. Saying no to treatment essentially means homelessness.

The urgency and immediacy of this should be the same as if they say yes. Remember, if they say yes, you get them on their way to treatment immediately. If they say no, you take them upstairs, pack their stuff, put them in a car, drop them off somewhere, and say goodbye.

If you want, an alternative to simply kicking them out on the street would be to drop them off at a hotel and pay for a single night. They will probably assume you've gone soft again and that you're going to keep taking care of them. They'll do whatever they want for a night, but the next day when someone comes knocking to collect another night's pay, the reality will set in. In this version of the plan, though, they've had some time to digest what was said the previous day before they are actually thrown out on the street. Some of the resentment and anger will have faded, they will have thought about the conversation, and only the next day after they've gone over it all do they see what it's truly going to mean to not get treatment from now on.

Of course, when you kick them out, let them know that it doesn't mean you don't love them, but stick to your guns. Let them know you can't and won't take it anymore. None of this is going to work unless you set hard boundaries and stick to them. If it comes down to kicking them out, don't torture yourself about it. Your child's addiction has already been torturing you. It's time to unburden yourself. At this point, you've done everything you can, and you've planted the seed. It's time to let go of all the guilt and get the poison out of your life if they won't get it out of theirs.

I will discuss boundaries, deadlines, and ultimatums more thoroughly later in the book.

## Don't Hesitate to Exaggerate

One of the best tactics you can keep in your arsenal is to hype up the treatment facility as much as possible. Now the idea of exaggerating the greatness of the clinic and the painlessness of the process may give you a guilty twinge in your gut, and I'm sorry to have to suggest it to you, but it's one of the most effective ways to reach the ultimate goal of getting your kid into treatment that very day.

Sitting in that intervention with all eyes on them is going to have your kid scared and confused. You need to tell them what they want to hear—that rehab isn't scary, it's actually extremely pleasant. It's not cold and dark; it's like a vacation.

Now, don't flat out lie. If the facility is absolutely nothing like you've described (aka if you've made it sound like they'll be sunbathing on the deck of a cruise ship in the tropics), when they arrive, your kid may very well look at you, say "Nope," and turn right back around. And then you will have destroyed their trust in the bargain. However, they have lied to you plenty, and a few fibs in the name of saving their lives isn't going to hurt. Get them to rehab! That is what matters most here.

What I'm saying is focus on the best and make rehab sound like wonderful place where they will enjoy themselves with likeminded peers and maybe even have some fun and make friends. The key is to ease all the worry.

## What If It Doesn't Work?

If your child refuses treatment after a formal intervention, first off, you have to stick by the consequences you laid out. Second, start working on an informal intervention. Your interventionist can help you here, too. He or she can coach you on how to approach your child in a more casual, less organized way. An informal intervention is essentially a serious of casual conversations that begin to guide the addict toward treatment. Ask those same probing questions you asked when you first found out for certain that your kid was using, like "Are drugs really so important to you that you're going to throw away ____?" The key is not telling the addict to do anything, but rather asking him questions and making suggestions that begin to make him think that rehab is his idea. Use verbiage like, "Man, it's freezing today. Wish I was on a beach in Florida. They have a lot of centers down there, too." If you've already done a formal intervention and talked about that rehab on the beach, this will be even more enticing because he already has the pictures from the brochure in his head.

If, God forbid, something worse happens in the time between the formal intervention and getting your child to agree to rehab, like an arrest or an overdose, use those opportunities to bring the option back up and ask questions like, "Honey, how do you think you got here?" and "Is this really how you thought your life would turn out?" If you feel like something you've said has struck a nerve and actually gotten your kid thinking, call your interventionist right then and there and hand the phone to your son or daughter. I have convinced many kids to go to rehab over the phone alone.

An informal intervention is often more effective than a formal intervention because it is a gradual process that tricks the addicts into coming to the idea by themselves, or so they think. However, it will take time to get a yes this way, so a formal intervention is always worth a shot first.

## Perfection vs. Possible

No matter which intervention technique you use, don't pressure your child with achieving a perfect outcome, and don't leave yourself open to disappointment by expecting absolute perfection. Don't go into the intervention telling your child that this will be the perfect way to make sure that they'll never touch drugs again. Your son or daughter is addicted to those drugs. Life without them doesn't sound like perfection right at this moment. Also, even if your kid is at the stage where he or she is truly starting to realize the suffering and destruction their use is causing (which is wonderful, but probably not actually the case at this point), the idea of quitting is still terribly daunting. If your daughter feels that you won't be satisfied unless she comes out of rehab and never touches drugs again, she may get discouraged. If your son feels pressure to completely throw off the burden of drugs all in one swoop before he even gets to the facility and starts making any progress, he may feel that it's an unattainable goal and that he shouldn't even try.

Instead, make it clear that all you want is for them to give it a shot. Ask them to please take a break and see how it goes. Say things like, "Let's just see what happens. You never know; you might like the way you feel afterward," or, "Look, if you hate it or it's that bad, we'll fly you home and you can act like it never happened, but don't you think it's worth a shot?" Pose loaded questions like these in a casual, sincere manner in order to steer them toward the decision you want for them. Make rehab sound good, then ask things like, "Don't you agree?" or "What do you think? Then they won't feel pressured. Instead, they feel like they are making the decision for themselves, on their terms, even though that's not the case. They need to feel as if they are the one choosing to go.

## Conclusion

Interventions don't always work, and you must be prepared for that possibility. Know that you can always try again, but that shouldn't keep you from putting your absolute best into this first one. Plan, rehearse, and try your hardest to make your child see why they need this so badly and that you're doing it all because you love them.

If your intervention is successful, allow yourself to feel that sense of pride, because you've just helped your child make their very first decision to try and get sober.

# PART 2:
# REHAB

## The New Parental Role

Once your child walks through the doors of a treatment facility, your role and mindset must shift. While your kid was actively using and making a mess of your home life, you had to take on an active role. You were the knight, charging onward in pursuit of real answers from your kid and solutions to their addiction.

This hands-on approach needs to subside a little bit now that your child is in treatment for the next several months. You must shift to a passive, supportive role. Now you're a watchman, observing other knights battle addiction from your tower farther from the battlefield. This can be a difficult shift. It's hard to let go after you've been the driving force behind your child's recovery thus far.

What you need to realize is that overbearing parental action can affect your child's recovery and your relationship with them adversely. You don't want to create codependency.

Effective treatment is about creating a portal from which your child can emerge and take on an independent life free of drugs and alcohol. You don't want them clinging to you for the rest of their lives. That's why your role at this stage needs to be a best friend or a concerned distant relative. Be there when they need you, be the voice of reason, be their vote of confidence. Let them know you'll always be in their corner, but don't hover around behind them in that corner micromanaging their whole life. You've helped them get into rehab. Now let them make their own decisions once there so they can feel empowered again, in control of their lives for the first time since they let drugs take the reins.

Remember how I talked about not letting grandma get too sappy and nostalgic at the intervention? The same thing applies to the rehab process. My mom used to say things like, "I'm so proud of the new person you are," and "Wow, my Adam is back." As much as I love her, that made me want to puke. Things like that are awkward, and they push unnecessary expectations and pressures onto your child which can endanger their recovery success. Being proud of their efforts and telling them so is great, but don't do it in the sappy-parent way. Remember, your relationship is more like a peer at this stage—hanging back, but around for support.

Don't start showering them with gushy praises as if they've achieved sobriety and can come back home and be "back to normal" after only a few days or weeks in detox and treatment. Getting detoxed and physically sober is only the first part of the process. The real healing that leads to a sober mindset takes a minimum of six months, at least in my experience. Keep that timeline in mind, and instead of gushing over them, keep letting them know you're still serious about this for the long haul while they are away.

The chapters in this section of the book are designed to help you explore and understand the step-by-step process of detox, treatment, and getting into aftercare. I hope that it will show you what it actually takes to get a solid footing in sobriety, so that you won't get overexcited and think you've "got your kid back" after the initial treatment is over. I also hope that having an idea of what your child is doing in the facility will give you some peace of mind.

Remember, be a friend and a parent, love them well, but make sure they know it's not all over once they walk back out those doors. Prepare yourself to hear that they're fixed—cured!—they don't need rehab anymore, and they want to come home.

You kid still has work to do after treatment. No coming home to lie on the couch. They have to work on themselves. Don't let them get complacent and say they are 100% cured. I'm eight years sober, and I still don't say that about myself—I won't, because I know where it can lead.

It's a delicate dance. Sure, you can call the facility on a regular basis to check on your child's progress, but let the professionals to their work and follow their advice. They will hold family therapy sessions while your child is going through treatment, and that is the time to discuss plans for the future and to make sure your child has been completely honest with their therapist.

The idea with these next chapters is to give you confidence that you know the basics of what is happening. That way, you won't feel a need to incessantly call the center. I can teach you what to look for during your visits to observe your child's progress. I'll teach you what to say in good times and bad. I'll teach you how to be an asset to your child that will help them change their lives for good.

# CHAPTER 8: THE KEY PLAYERS IN DRUG TREATMENT PROGRAMS

IF YOUR CHILD SAID YES to treatment at the end of your intervention, congratulations! The biggest step on your part is over now, and the light at the end of the tunnel has finally made its appearance, but that doesn't mean you should sit back and leave it all in your child's hands.

Staying actively aware of, if not being directly involved in your child's rehab treatment let's your son or daughter know you didn't just dump them off and "rid your hands of them," so to speak. It also lets them know they are going to have support when they come out, but doesn't go too far in making it seem like you're going to keep acting as their crutch.

One of the best ways to stay involved without hovering or inserting yourself too far into the whole process is to understand the key players. This gives you a good idea of what's going on inside the facility, and if you establish a relationship and keep in touch with the players in your child's care, it helps you keep tabs on your child's progress. Comprehending who each person is and knowing their role in the process will give you the leverage and ability to speak with the right person when you have questions. You'll know who to contact for updates that will give you peace of mind and a solid foundation for helping your kid adjust once treatment is over.

Full treatment involves physical and mental health, so

there will be a medical and psychological doctor involved, as well as directors, coordinators, and additional staff who keep things running smoothly.

Here is a list of professionals that you or your child will encounter at some point in the process. Make sure you know them.

## Player 1: The Admissions Coordinator

One of the first people you meet will be the admissions coordinator. This is the person who helps you get your child admitted into rehab and helps you get your insurance approval and benefit verifications. When you call the center, an admissions coordinator will ask questions about your child's prior drug use, previous mental/medical issues, prior treatment history, etc. This is called a pre-assessment, and it is how they qualify your child for treatment. Once your child is admitted, you will come into contact with a coordinator again when he or she walks you through all the necessary paperwork.

Admissions team coordinators are trained to understand the sensitivity of the situation, and they are often a great source of comfort from the first moment you decide to put your child in their center. You should save their name and number in your phone because they can help connect you to the people who will be taking up your child's care after admission.

## Player 2: The Medical Doctor

If you can, have your family doctor forward all of your child's records to the treatment facility's doctor, so that the treatment doctor will be fully up to date on your child's medical history—past medications and conditions. Sadly, the staff rarely asks for these things, believing they have sufficient knowledge. As a result, they often just give your child the common diagnosis based on a few minutes of interaction. Send the records over regardless of whether or not the staff asks. A more medically based program, such as the one my mother owns, Oceans Medical Centers, will see that there is communication between your regular physician and the treatment physician in charge of your child's care. In my opinion, this should be commonplace because your family doctor has well-documented records of any past mental health disorders or addiction issues that will allow the treatment physician to know the best course of action to take without having to make a quick, guess-based diagnosis.

The medical doctor watches over and improves your child's overall physical health during their stay. Your child will see this doctor upon intake and every thirty days thereafter at a minimum. The medical doctor will prescribe medications and order lab testing such as toxicology, blood work, HIV testing, STD testing, or anything they deem necessary. He or she will also assist in any necessary medical treatments.

## Player 3: The Psychiatrist

If your child has a dual diagnosis of mental health issues underlying their addiction, a psychiatrist will not only be involved but play a major role in the treatment. They help to manage the medications related to your child's overall brain health. They not only prescribe the medications, but also track how well they are taking hold in order to make the necessary adjustments over time.

Pro tip: if your child is on medications, bring the medicine bottles to the initial intake visit. Psychiatrists have to be wary of patients lying to get prescriptions, so bringing the bottles saves time by acting as concrete proof. Keeping in contact with the psychiatrist is important because you want to be able to pass those records on to other physicians later. In fact, you should always have a verified phone number or email for anyone who is prescribing medications for your child.

## Player 4: The Psychologist

A psychologist is not to be confused with a psychiatrist. The psychologist is the licensed therapist. They usually have an LCMS or some other fancy title tacked onto their name. A psychologist is vital, so make sure the treatment center has provided your son or daughter with a primary therapist with the proper qualifications and background in the area of substance abuse.

The psychologist is the meat and potatoes of one-on-one treatment, making them the key that unlocks the door to long-term solutions and sobriety. The psychologist will draw up a treatment plan specifically for your child and act as the lead in getting them through the program by sitting with them in hourly sessions each week to get at the core of your child's addiction motivations. Your child *must* feel comfortable with their therapist because they must be willing to offer up their innermost secrets and unwrap their darkest issues. If they can't share with the therapist, rehab becomes a waste of time. Let your son or daughter know that he or she can request a new therapist at any time.

At Oceans Medical Centers, we have a proprietary Oceans Therapist Matching Model™ that asks a series of questions and observations that help place patients with the staff therapist who fits them best, in order to achieve maximum results.

It took me a while to find the right therapist for me, but after going through several different ones, I found one with whom I have a lot in common. I still go to him today. He was in show business and did his fair share of cocaine during his quest to meet women. Though he's about fifty years older than me, I saw many similarities between myself and him. He's acts as a mentor and a life coach in addition to guiding and benefitting me with his clinical experience. Because we are so close, I get great, substantive advice during every session. That's why I recommend continuing therapy after rehab, whether at a private or government-run location—whatever you can afford. Think of it as going to see a chiropractor after a car accident or physical therapy after a major injury. Start by having your child see the therapist five days a week, and then taper it down to once a week, then every other week, then once a month until they are fully healthy. After a while, you or your child may wonder where the benefit of continuing to go is, as nothing new seems to be happening. Trust that while you may not notice that anything is the matter, the therapist might. They can hone in on aspects of your kid's life that should be addressed in order to avoid disaster down the road and improve their lifestyle overall. Several months can go by without major concerns, but when that one hard month rolls around, a regular therapy session can mean the difference between a relapse and continued sobriety. That's why I still go to my therapist once a month even after being eight years sober. It pays to always have someone in the loop to help you out.

Also, sticking to a productive schedule is one of the key's to staying sober. If your son makes seeing a therapist part of his schedule, it will not only keep him on track but also provide him with someone who can keep the right ideas at the forefront of his mind and in his life.

## Player 5: The Clinical Director

The clinical director is the chief therapist who oversees all programming for the entire treatment center. The clinical director creates different tracks for different kinds of treatment, whether it be mental health care, high level addiction care, or low level addiction care. Tracks are simply a subgrouping that makes sure your child follows a plan specially tailored to his or her needs. A track usually deals with the motivations behind your child's use. For instance, there is a mental health track, a trauma track, or an abusive track (for those with any sort of physical or mental abuse in their past), among others. Think of tracks as college minors. At the center, your child is majoring in addiction recovery, but they are minoring in correcting the underlying cause of their addiction. The clinical director is the one who determines the requirements for each of those "minors."

The clinical director also directs (surprise, surprise) the psychological and therapeutic models that the treatment center uses. If your child is having trouble connecting with a therapist and needs a new one, the clinical director is the one to call. This is also the person to call for updates or to discuss any serious issues regarding your child's care while they are in the program.

The program of any facility hinges upon the knowledge and experience of the clinical director. All of the lesson plans, groups, and activities included in the treatment and recovery process are designed by this one person, or are at least approved by them. The clinical director also reviews the case notes and treatment plans of every single patient in the center. He or she is also responsible for sending out the necessary information to your insurance company with *i*'s dotted and *t*'s crossed to make sure you receive your reimbursement or get requests for additional treatment days approved. This means that having the clinical director's info is undeniably important, as he or she is the team member you want to reach out to for big-picture answers as well as insurance matters.

## Player 6: Clinicians/Therapist

Clinician is a broad term that can apply to many different types of physicians and medical assistants, but in my experience, clinicians in rehab facilities are people trained under the psychologists/therapists. Usually, they're in the process of getting their license and are working at the center to put time toward their education. I have found them to be some of the most caring staff members, and they are usually always eager to help. A clinician makes phone calls for outreach, like setting up specialist or medical appointments, and helps run some groups and outings. They can also work as case managers who help patients with day to day issues like applying for food stamps, building a resume, finding a job, or getting a credit card. In some places, clinician is synonymous with therapist. They act as group therapy leaders or meet with patients one-on-one to talk through the struggles of recovery. Clinician is a broad term; they wear many hats.

The number of clinicians varies from center to center, with larger centers usually having more room for them on their staff.

## Player 7: Behavior Health Techs (BHT's)

BHT's or "techs" are the helping hands of the center. They supervise housing to watch out for the residents' safety and drive them to and from groups or outside meetings. Sometimes they may act as a kind of security, enforcing curfews, but mostly they are there to be a friend to your kid. Usually BHT's are people who have been through the rehab process themselves. They understand the situation your child is in, making them great workers and positive role models that your child can relate to on every level. They encourage clean living outside of the center, and though they aren't medical or therapeutic experts they can often provide help in a way other staff members can't.

## Player 8: Sobriety Coach

Not all facilities will offer a sobriety coach, but if your

child does get assigned to one, he or she will teach your child how to get and stay sober throughout your child's stay in the facility. It's coaching that will hopefully stick with them when they leave. Most coaches are other peers who have gone through the program, succeeded at staying sober, and earned a coaching certificate. They can share the hardships and pitfalls they faced and overcame, which can prepare your child for the challenges of long-term sobriety.

## Player 9: AA or NA Sponsor

Not to be confused with the in-house sobriety coach, an AA or NA sponsor is someone your son or daughter meets during the out-of-house AA or NA meetings. Pretty much every treatment center includes the twelve steps of Alcoholics Anonymous and Narcotics Anonymous. Usually, your child will be taken outside of the facility to attend these free meetings. If you or your child would like to donate to the program, you can, but you don't have to pay for the help your child receives there, and your kid can keep going to the meetings after rehab is over.

While at these meetings, your child will be encouraged to ask someone else in attendance to be their sponsor. The sponsor and your child go through the twelve steps together, keeping each other encouraged and motivated. They will also study the Big Book together, which is simply the handbook containing the practices and principles one should follow in order to live a sober life.

Getting a good sponsor makes all the difference in successfully getting through the steps. That's why I will be discussing the topic in detail in Chapter 12.

## Player 10: The Outreach/Discharge Coordinator

The outreach coordinator will become your main contact as your child nears the end of treatment. Just as change occurs inside the center, there will be changes in your child's life once they leave, as well. At least, there should be if they want to stay sober. Going back to old environments makes it much easier to start up old habits.

Thus, you will probably want to send your child to a sober living home or some similar kind of facility. Your child will also need help pulling the everyday details of their life back together. They may need a new social security card or rides to appointments (medical checkups, continued therapy, etc.). The outreach coordinator is the community liaison for the program and he or she will help your child do all of these things so that they can land on their feet right out of treatment.

## Player 11: Halfway House Owners and Managers

For the best chance of success, you want to transition your loved one from treatment to a lower level of care, such as a sober home or a halfway house. No need to be nervous. These places aren't slums. They are actually great if you select the right one. It's the same kind of process as picking a great rehab facility, really. Nothing you don't know how to do already.

What you are looking for in a halfway house is a zero tolerance policy. That means if your daughter slips up and uses again, they send her right back to rehab. Always talk to the owners and the house managers. They become the new eyes and ears watching over your child. They do what used to have you sitting up at the kitchen table all night worried sick, but they are trained and paid to do it.

They will collect rent and enforce the house curfews, on top of leading the sobriety program. They administer drug tests and breathalyzers both randomly and if they suspect anything. They report your child's behavior to both you and the treatment center.

## Player 12: The Sober Network

The sober network is comprised of whomever your child interacts with on a daily basis once sober. It could be the friends they made in rehab, their sponsor, a life coach, their old sober coach, etc. It's anyone they call or rely on in times they feel themselves struggling to stay sober and avoid the temptation of drugs.

You ought to be fully aware of who your child's network of support is, outside of yourself, of course. You don't want them talking to old friends unless those friends were never users or are users who have gone through treatment and are staying sober.

The network is the sphere of influence that your son surrounds himself with. They are the people your daughter calls in times of need to draw on their strength and encouragement. So the need to be good, reliable examples.

## Conclusion

I will refer to many of these people in the coming chapters, so hopefully this chapter will allow you to get your bearings and feel informed moving forward.

More importantly, staying connected with the people helping your child gives you peace of mind that they are in good hands. And if there are any problems, you will know about them. You will know where your child struggles most and prepare to help them through those areas when they come out of treatment.

You aren't being a hassle by staying in touch with these people (so long as you don't go overboard); you're making yourself an informed, prepared, and supportive parent.

# CHAPTER 9: THE DETAILS OF DETOX

TO TRULY UNDERSTAND WHAT YOUR child needs from you and to prepare for their reactions to detox, you need to put yourself in their heads for a minute.

To them, the past day probably feels like a week, flashing by in colors and sounds and glimpses of concerned faces and the landscape flying by as you drive them to the hospital or facility where they will undergo detox. They probably hardly remember saying yes at the intervention; things are moving too fast.

Once they walk into that setting and the doctor(s) start approaching them, it may all come crashing down on them, and the reality of it is terrifying. Huge change is happening faster than they can keep up. They don't want to get sober, to say goodbye to how the drugs make them feel ... momentarily, at least. They don't feel like they need to change. What will happen to them in there with all those doctors? What will they have to give up? The anxiety hits like a sumo wrestler belly slap in the face—sweaty and incredibly unpleasant.

What you need to make them realize is that this isn't for you, the parent. This isn't something you've forced on them. This is something they are doing for themselves. Drugs may give momentary pleasure, but because of those stories you've shared at the intervention, your child is getting a picture of what drugs have really done to them. They probably have known it for a while, deep down, but you've brought it to the light, and you need to keep it there. Remind them that detox is the first step to a better life where they are fully in control. Remind them that you've worked this all out and that they have nothing to be worried about. When detox is done correctly, it isn't painful at all. As you walk them through the doors, reassure them of all of this. Once they're in the hands of the doctors and caregivers, you can back off a bit, but stick around to let them get settled. Then, before you go, let them know that this is about them and it's in their hands. Ask them to give it a shot. If they can see that their life has to be a real mess for it all to come down to this—this alien environment where they need outside help just to get toxins out of their body—they will begin to see that the current road ahead (without change) is bound to lead to trouble. Remind them nothing can change for the better if they don't try and make a change.

As you tell your daughter goodbye and promise to bring her anything she might need, ask her to look around. Remind her that all of the people in this section of the hospital or in this in-patient facility are here for the same thing. Have your son take in his surroundings and remind him that he isn't alone. He will have like-minded company here. He isn't confined to a bed. He can interact with people who are in the same boat.

Leave your child in good spirits, alleviate some of their worries, and you can go home assured that they will be perfectly safe and comfortable.

When they come out, they will be completely drug free for the first time in what's probably been ages.

## What Does a Detox Really Do?

Detox is short for detoxification. It's the process by which toxins and abused substances are flushed from a body's system. To do so, there will first be an evaluation of which substances are being abused, how much is currently in the system, and the volume of use. These medical screenings can also reveal malnourishment, anemia, dehydration, and other illnesses that are a result of heavy drug use and which need to be addressed along with the substances. There will also be tests related to mental health in order to grasp the larger picture. Once the substances are identified, then the patient is stabilized, the drugs are flushed, and the patient's system is left entirely drug free.

Just know that a clean system doesn't mean a clean addict. You went through the insurance headache and did all this planning to send your child to treatment, not just detox. Long-term sobriety doesn't just magically spring from a cleaned out, sparkling, lemon-fresh system.

Medical detox also manages the unpleasant physical withdrawal symptoms, which brings me to my next point.

## Is Detox Necessary?

This question is likely to come out of your child's mouth at some point. Your response should be, "How do you feel after a few hours of not using?" That will probably shut them up pretty quick, because no matter what they are using or how serious of a substance it is, they've either experienced the uncomfortable effects of withdrawal or the anxiety-inducing need to find more.

On the other hand, you may be asking this question yourself. Why can't you just send them to the rehab center right away? Why this extra pit-stop? The simple answer is that traditional rehab centers always require patients to be medically cleared through a detox before they are allowed into the program.

## Detox Schools of Thought

In any detox, it is necessary to replenish vitamins and minerals in the body, especially calcium and magnesium. However, one form of detox does this more so than the other. There are two schools of thought when it comes to the detox process.

Passive Detox is just about getting your urine clean and your head out of a fog. This is the most typical form of detox, where legal prescription drugs and comfort meds are used to lessen the effects of illegal drug withdrawal.

However, using a toxin to combat a toxin isn't an effective long-term solution. Not to say that it's a bad thing; it will get your child clean for the most part and make sure they are mentally stable and clear-headed enough to handle rehab. However, another school of thought suggests it isn't going far enough.

The Active Detox theory is that once you're physically stable from toxins that show up on the 12-panel, there are still residual traces of the drugs metabolized in your fat belt. These residual drugs are hidden inside small molecules called metabolites. During high levels of stress or activity, those metabolites are released into your system.

While this isn't a universally accepted view, I feel it has some weight behind it. I remember that even after a year or two of being off opiates, I would still sometimes feel a mild high after strenuous activity like working out. Then I would have mild withdrawal symptoms at night—shaking, queasiness, etc.

A center which adheres to the Active Detox theory goes deeper that just going in, getting it out, and going home. With an Active Detox, the patient does exercise therapy, salt therapy, and sauna therapy to try and burn out the metabolites. Patients will also be put on a high fiber, vegetable, vitamin, and oil diet to try and get all that leftover residue out of the fat cells by replacing the fatty deposits with new clean ones.

If you have the option to send your child to an Active Detox center, do it. Even though the theory behind it isn't universally accepted as accurate, there's no harm in having your child go above and beyond with exercise and good diet.

## The Types of Detox

If you were to detox your child yourself by simply keeping them in the house and away from drugs, the symptoms would be very unpleasant and even dangerous. That's a cold turkey detox, and I'd never recommend it.

Another one I'd never recommend is the "detox" addicts try to give themselves. I used to detox from heroin by switching to cocaine. I'd take it easy on one substance and abuse another and call it detox. That definition is something of a stretch.

You definitely want a medical detox supervised by professionals. But hey, that's sort of a no brainer, right? The real question is what kind of medical detox to use. All do basically the same thing, but there are subtle differences in setting and method.

A local hospital unit is exactly what it sounds like, and we've covered it a few times already in this book, so I won't go into much detail. I will say, though, that this is the method I would suggest only for emergencies or if you have to get your kid into a detox program late at night for some reason.

There is also a private patient detox. This is a detox conducted at a small, private hospital/facility created especially for drug and alcohol detox. Your kid won't be shoved into a back wing. The whole building is designed for the comfort and security of patients undergoing a detox.

There is also outpatient detox, which is done from the comfort and privacy of your home. However, realize that with this version, you won't have the doctors there 24/7. You are swapping comfort and familiarity for accessibility.

Lastly, there is the option of sending your child to a detox program within a full spectrum treatment center. Some of the larger rehab centers have their own detox facility. The idea is that the people in that detox unit move on to the attached treatment facility. That's very convenient, but you may not want a large facility. You'll probably remember our discussion about how sometimes your child can get lost in the crowd at these big places. However, that doesn't mean you can't use their detox unit and then send them off to the treatment center of your choice afterward. Oceans sends the kids who come to their facility to other programs' detox units. Why? They know they are good ones, and their facility doesn't have the capacity to hold a full detox unit. So, Oceans sends them to a unit they know is nice, and then the patients come to Oceans after for treatment.

For the best results, you want to find someplace that focuses on a social detoxification setting. That simply means that your child isn't just lying in a hospital bed or even on their bed at home just getting pumped full of meds without interacting with other people—preferably others in the same situation. You want a program that has therapists around performing group sessions on a daily basis so your child has something productive and enlightening to do while getting clean.

One final tip: you want to avoid any facility that uses "rapid detox." This is passive medicinal detox in the extreme. Essentially, they lay the patients out on a bed, sedate them, and pump them full of a shitload of detox drugs. The centers that advocate this incredibly expensive treatment claim that when the patients wake up, they feel great and completely cured. Don't buy it. This is extremely dangerous, and some of these rapid detox methods are illegal thanks to some of the drugs used. This method is not the magic overnight cure-all it claims to be. In reality, it can be fatal, and the vast majority of experts do not recommend it.

## Preparation ... Or Lack Thereof

Now, as a parent (especially a mother), you may be thinking, "What do I need to bring?" "How long does she need to stay?" "How often should I go see him?"

Whoa, whoa, slow down. Let's start with the first one. What do you bring? *Just get there.* When you arrive, the staff will accommodate you and your child. They will have the necessities on-hand. The rest can be brought later. It's not a prison. You can send your kid pretty much anything you like. Some places do take cellphones away (you don't want your child calling up a dealer while they're supposed to be working to get clean), but you can bring clothes, books, snacks, even cigarettes and lighters if your child is a smoker. Of course, you could try bringing e-cigarettes or nicotine gum, but hey, one thing at a time, right? The point is, get them there as quickly as possible. I know I've said it over and over, but that's because it's so important, so no apologies here.

Now, if you're reading this chapter preemptively (kudos for planning ahead), and you want to go ahead and pack a bag of comfy clothes, reading materials, and snacks for your kid's detox stay, have at it. Just put it in the car before the intervention so there's no delay. And don't go overboard. No giant suitcases necessary. It's only for a couple of days.

That brings us to the second question: How long does your child have to stay for a detox?

If your child has had a relapse after being clean, only used for a short period, or only used low scale narcotics like marijuana or LSD, then they will probably only stay about three days or less.

If your child has been using harder drugs —like benzos, alcohol, and some opiates—at higher levels, or if they are somewhat mentally unstable, they will stay up to five days.

If your child is a hardened user who's been abusing hard drugs daily for longer than six months, is non-compliant, or even relapses while at the detox program (it happens), they will have to stay upward of seven days. This is because, in this case, your child will need more supervision and it may take longer to get their system stable.

So here we are at the last question. How many times should you visit? Remember what I said at the beginning of the section about backing off a little bit? It applies here. I'd say don't visit more than once unless your child really needs you to drop off something unexpectedly for some reason. Otherwise, it's only a couple of days. No need to show up every day at lunchtime and hover. You child needs to start communicating with others around them. They need to talk to the professionals and their peers, and if they can just look forward to you coming over every day for their little bit of social interaction and to tell the doctors what they've been too shy to say, they will be less likely to take matters into their own hands and take control of their healing process.

## The Day to Day of Detox

A number of things will start happening as soon as you and your child walk through the doors. Let me break it down for you a bit.

Prescreen: While in route or as soon as your child arrives, they will undergo a 15-20 minute interview that touches on who your child is, their history of drug use, and their mental and physical health. It gives the doctors a starting point from which to work in order to give your child personalized treatment and qualifies them for admission.

Admission: You will check your child in after the screening. There will be a bag search. They'll let you know what is allowed in and what isn't. For instance, some places don't allow strings in a hoodie or shoe laces. The rules are stricter depending on the level of care. It's a good idea to call ahead of time so your child doesn't have to waste time at check-in. It's always a good idea to bring some clothes. A staff member will take down all the necessary information and update the electronic medical records. Your child will then be given basic toiletries and a snack and shown to the bed. If you haven't said your goodbyes by this point, this is a good time to do it. After this, the medical staff takes over.

Before you leave, make sure you've signed all of the necessary forms needed to bypass privacy laws, if your child is over 18. If you don't, the staff will not be at liberty to update you on your child's progress.

Medical Analysis: The doctors come in and draw blood and test body functions, such as the liver and kidneys. They will then prescribe what are called "comfort meds" to alleviate withdrawal symptoms.

Treatment Plan: After the analysis, both the medical and behavioral health staff will create a personalized treatment plan that is followed to a tee throughout the whole stay. It determines how long your child will stay and what will be accomplished in that time.

After this, the exact events may vary because it is all based on the individual treatment plan. However, here is an overview of what generally happens on each day.

Day One: After the analysis is over and the treatment plan is in order, your child may be asked if they feel up to a non-mandatory group session. If they do not want to participate just yet, they are left alone to rest while the medications work to clear the funk out of their head and sober them up. A nurse will stop by regularly to check vitals and/or administer medication.

Day Two: By this point, your child is probably feeling much better. They've slept off the worst of the drugs, but now the reality is starker. They begin to fully realize where they are, and anxiety and restlessness can settle in. That's why the staff will try to keep them busy. The doctors and nurses will be in to check on them and talk to them. They will also be asked if they want to attend a group again. Hopefully, the staff can persuade them to do so in order to give them something beneficial to do. The groups will cover things like relapse prevention, triggers, treatment planning after detox, and the ins and outs of the whole sobriety process.

Day Three – Discharge: Remember, depending on your child's length and type of use, they can be out in as little as three days or as late seven. Still, from here on out, the routine won't change much. There will always be a schedule implemented based on the plan. Your child will wake up around 8 a.m. or earlier, eat breakfast, and then have a morning group session. Then they can take a break before going to a more specific/personalized small group session. Then they have lunch and usually go to a one-on-one therapy session. They will have free time before dinner and then head off to an AA or NA meeting before bed. You will also be called in at some point to do a family therapy consultation that covers the plan going forward.

Every center will have its own set of rules that must be followed. If you can, try to instill in your son or daughter how important it is to follow the rules in order to begin to feel better.

Also, if you are planning to visit outside of your scheduled family therapy session, know that those visits will have to be approved and scheduled ahead of time.

## Is It Really Painless?

Your child has probably experienced withdrawal pains before. Those memories are what's playing in their heads on the way to the detox facility. This is probably something you're a little anxious about, too. We're talking about your baby after all, and you may have even witnessed the discomfort of withdrawal before.

Let me set your mind at ease so that you can do the same for your son or daughter. As I touched on a moment ago, once admitted, your child will receive "comfort meds." Nearly every patient is given some sort of medication like Subutex. The exact medication varies based on which drugs your child is using. For instance, Suboxone and Methadone are used to relieve the symptoms of heroin and other opiate withdrawal. These medications are agonists that bind to the endorphin and opiate receptors in the brain to release "happy chemicals," ease cravings, and lessen the discomfort of withdrawal. These drugs are highly effective. Methadone was the very first recovery drug developed, and those who receive it are five times more likely not to relapse after a year. Suboxone can be even more effective. In fact, someone actually shooting heroin while Suboxone is in his system will hardly feel a high because this inhibitor is so powerful. Both these medications, though, can be addictive because they both can create a high if used in excess. Methadone has a higher addiction strength and must be administered by a doctor. Suboxone can be taken at home, but the dosage must be strictly regulated. The two medicines that make up Suboxone, naltrexone and buprenorphine, can be taken separately. Naltrexone by itself, however, has been linked to depression. Buprenorphine, on the other hand, is less addictive and has less side effects. These medicines work, but as with any medication, they must be used responsibly.

Anti-depressants are also common detox drugs used to combat both mental illness and drugs like cocaine, weed, and meth. No medicine has been created that can curb the cravings of those three drugs. Anti-depressants are the best method for fighting those cravings at the moment, but they are not 100% effective. Anti-anxiety medications like Ativan are also sometimes used to stabilize patients addicted to stimulants like cocaine.

Alcoholics are often given sedatives and anti-psychotics. Vivitrol (a brand name for naltrexone) is a common craving inhibitor that can prevent full blown relapse even if there is a slip up. There are a lot of inventive medications for alcoholics, too. For instance, Antabuse blocks the body's ability to metabolize alcohol, thus making the patient sick if they drink it. Not the kindest medication, but sometimes necessary. Baclofen, a muscle relaxant; topiramate, an anticonvulsant; and gabapentin, an anti-seizure medication are all used to combat and soothe the symptoms of alcohol withdrawal. Sadly, gabapentin (street name, "johnnies") is another one that is commonly abused. Addicts will mix it with Red Bull to get high.

The main thing you need to know is that these medicines make your child feel calm and relaxed. No jitters, no pains, no sickness. They will be given larger doses at first and then tapered off as the process continues. Sometimes the doctor will even prescribe them in small doses for a short time after the detox is complete.

These medications are delivered in a controlled environment in the correct dosages, and they make the detoxification process so much easier than quitting cold turkey. Rest assured that you and your child have nothing to be afraid of. The meds are tapered off gently so that as the symptoms begin to decrease, so do the medications, making the process as seamless as possible.

Ease your child's mind. Even if they don't express their anxieties about the pain, I can guarantee it's crossing their mind. Explain how it's going to work and emphasize the painlessness as much as possible. This is a fresh start, not a torture chamber. Worries about pain and discomfort shouldn't cloud the goal and block out the vision of a better life ahead.

## The Discharge Plan

At this point, you already know where you want your child to go after this detox, but you still probably have to refine some of the details. You need to know how you will get your child to the facility. Who will pick them up? Remember, no stopping (except maybe for a bite to eat from a drive-thru). The transition should be "Go, go, go." That's why you need a discharge plan. You will create one during that family therapy session I mentioned earlier. The program staff can schedule a drop off for you to save you some headache if you'd like.

You can hash out the practical details and voice where you want your child to go. If you put your child in a detox program attached to a larger rehab facility, they will probably try to get you to go to that facility, but don't be persuaded if that's not what you had in mind. It's your choice.

The therapy team will help you see where your kid's head is at about the whole process and act accordingly. If your child is acting reluctant, the therapist can help you re-voice the reasons your child should go. Both you and your child need to be open with the therapist during this time about all your feelings and concerns. Ask whatever question you feel like and as many as you feel like.

Just keep in mind that the therapist is the professional. They will be upfront with you about the reality of your child's mental state and behavior. Don't get defensive, even though it's easy to do so when hearing things you don't like.

## Some Final Tips

Here are a few productive/helpful things you can tell your child instead of "gushing" like we talked about in the intro to this section.

- Prepare for the worst, but don't expect it

- You can tough it out—it isn't so bad.
- Stay positive.
- Be honest and open rather than shy or timid—communication is key in therapy.
- Be vocal about how you feel.
- Stay out of your own head—things tend to seem far worse than they really are in there.
- Do what you are asked while in the program.
- You are here for yourself, no one else.
- Be proactive with your future sobriety.
- Remember how you feel now, and compare it to how you feel when you leave here.
- You are taking your life back, and this is the first step.

Now here's a few tips for you, the parent.

- While they are in detox, prepare for the next level of care.
- Get their personal things ready for their stay in rehab.
- Contact any relevant people—with your child's permission—to get things in order. For instance, you may need to call their school, their job, or personal friends to appraise them of the situation.
- Be available, but don't be overbearing.
- You can only do so much. Let the pros do what they do.
- Hope for the best and prepare for the worst.

## Too Good To Be True

Imagine you are your child again for a moment. You probably weren't all that eager to do this detox thing to begin with. Who wants to quit getting high every day with zero responsibility? You were probably terrified, and that made you a little resentful. But now, you've made it through the program, and it wasn't so bad. You feel much better. So much better! You can keep this up, right? That was no big deal. You knew your addiction wasn't that bad. In fact, you could probably control it better now, just have a little bit at a time. You just had to wipe the slate. Things got a little out of control, but now you can get back to where you were in the beginning, just having a little for fun. Because ... you're still thinking about that cocaine or heroin or whatever your fix is.

You're feeling pretty positive because you feel good. But you also miss your friends, and you're a little worried about what life is going to be like without using all the time. What will you even do? Are your parents going to want you to get a job now? Probably. That bites.

Your mom or dad is telling you that you have to go away for a month or two to some new place. You guess it won't be so bad, since this place wasn't, but it's for way longer this time. You don't really need it, do you? You can handle this. Your problem was never really as bad as Mom or Dad made it out to be—you always knew that. Maybe now that they see you this way, they'll get off your back and let you do what you want and come back home. Yeah, sure they will. You've just got to put on the happy face or the pouty face, whichever one works best, and things will be back to normal again.

As a parent, you have to prepare yourself for this type of thinking from your child. Prepare for the super happy bounce or the pouty face. Prepare for the, "I'm fine, Mom! I can come back home now," and, "I feel so much better, Dad. I think I'm cured." Detox is a great first step, but only 5% of people who go through detox alone actually stay sober. Detox makes getting sober feel easy because your kid isn't distinguishing between being clean and being truly sober. It can make him feel like there's an easy fix. He still wants to get high, make no mistake about it. A few days of sitting in a bed getting the drugs pumped out of him hasn't changed his addictive mentality. He wants the drugs, and now that he feels "together" again, he feels like he can have them, no problem. Also, the prospect of living a sober life is daunting. What will he do without them? What will you expect of him now? It seems easier to just fall back into old habits.

The only way for that low success percentage to increase is to go through all the recovery phases. That means rehab and then aftercare. You're in this for the long haul. Make sure your child knows it and explain to them why that's the right choice.

Right now, they're feeling great. You have to remind them of how it felt before. Do they really want to go back to that? To feeling out of control? To not accomplishing anything?

Be proud of them, praise them, but make it clear that this isn't anywhere near the end and those consequences from the intervention still apply.

## Conclusion

Make a plan to get them to the next step, and then when detox is complete, take some time to congratulate yourself and be happy. They've made it through the first phase!

Though it's still a while away, sobriety is on the horizon. Allow yourself to feel that triumph, and make sure your kid feels it, too. There's a great life awaiting them. Let them imagine it. Let it motivate them. Motivation and hope are going to carry them through to the life you know they can have. All *you* have to do is carry them from one phase to the next.

# INTERLUDE: THE VITAL IMPORTANCE OF REHAB

I'VE SAID IT ONCE, I'LL say it again; I really can't drill it home enough. *Detox alone is not enough to stay sober.* That's why you create that transition strategy with the detox center's therapist on how to get your child directly to an inpatient rehab. Now your child's body and brain have been cleared out and scrubbed clean of drugs and alcohol (at least for the most part), but they need guidance about how to make the right decisions to stay sober. Addiction is a mentality first and foremost, and it must be overcome with long-term therapy, coaching, and structuring.

As I've already mentioned, the relapse rates for those who come out of detox and seek no further care are astronomical. You must increase your child's chance of success by sending them to treatment program.

This is why I stressed finding a good, non-institutional rehab center. You have to combat the idea of hospital rooms and white lab coats in your child's head. In the right center, your loved one will basically live in a nice house in a nice setting (the beach, maybe) surrounded by peers. The people working there can show your child that if they apply themselves, they can affect radical positive change in their life.

Sending your child to rehab can not only turn their life around, but actually save it. If your child only does detox, that exponential chance of relapse becomes very, very dangerous. After their body has been cleaned of toxins, many addicts don't realize that they can't go back to using the same amounts they did previously.

Out of the huge number of people who relapse after detox alone, many die from accidental overdoses because they tried to use as much as they were using before getting cleaned up. Drug overdoses are the number one cause of injury-related deaths in the United States, killing an average of 44,000 people each year, and this is a huge contributing factor as to why.

Your child has probably heard all of this. I know I had. But I never believed it, because I didn't want to believe it. You may not want to believe it either, but it's very real. One of the kids I was housing in my sober living home experienced it firsthand. He and some of his friends had gone to detox and then gone straight into sober-living, choosing to skip rehab entirely. They all believed they didn't need it. They'd all been through the whole system once or twice (which isn't uncommon), and they thought it wasn't necessary. The second day after detoxing and trying to live basically on their own with only the help of a sober living house, they took "hotshots" together in a car: two girls and two boys. A hotshot is the term used for the first shot of heroin after a few days of detox and/or clean living, and it is the most lethal injection an addict can administer. The two girls in the back seat shot up first, then the boy in the passenger seat. By the time the boy in driver's seat was getting ready to shoot up, he looked around to find that all of his friends were dead. With freshly cleaned systems, the drugs had been too much. It happened that fast.

This is no joke. That is why convincing your loved one, and yourself, to take the next step is so vital. Some parents can't seem to let go or try desperately to hold onto their denial, so they postpone treatment. Sadly, sometimes by the time they come around, it's too little too late. It really is life and death. Dropping your child off at rehab can be painful as a parent. You may hear a little voice at the back of your head saying, "He needs to be home with me, not around *real* addicts." You have to shove these self lies aside and realize that denial is at the core of them. Your child is an addict, and in rehab he will be surrounded by peers, not some different breed of kid. The longer you postpone treatment, the harder it is for the center to help. You're only postponing the inevitable anyway, so do what you've got to do to shut those nagging thoughts up and just get your child to a center.

But you don't want them in just any rehab. You want a rehab that goes above and beyond teaching tricks and strategies for staying clean. It should get to the heart of why your child took up drugs in the first place. It should also help your child address the necessary life skills for living independently as well as sober. The staff should incorporate your child's medical history into their treatment plan. Lastly, and most importantly, it should be a judgement-free environment.

The last day I did cocaine, I was lying on a prison bench not caring about my charges or the damage I had done to myself and my loved ones. No, I was thinking about what my life would be like without cocaine, pills, weed, and alcohol. I thought I wouldn't be the same person. I wouldn't be as fun if I wasn't plastered. I'd been in the cycle so long, I couldn't imagine my life or myself without the drugs.

Now my days are full of things I actually love, not things that take over my mind. I don't have to constantly worry about when I'll get my next fix or how I'll pay for it. I can drive without worrying about getting pulled over and having to stash drugs and paraphernalia. I discovered that I have a talent for business, and because of that talent, I just bought my dream home: a five bedroom three car garage set up with a place to fish and kayak right in my own backyard! Getting sober didn't just improve my financial situation either; it made a positive mark on my social life too. I hang out with people who help me in my life and career instead of people who are detrimental to my peace of mind. I live in control, not chaos. *I* make my day go 'round, not heroin or cocaine. Rehab, prayer, and a lot of hard work got me here, and your child can get here too. My mom always told me, "You get back in life what you put into it."

Rehab is the place where they can begin to ask themselves who they really are without the drugs. The place where they can find out what really makes them laugh and what they really like to do, all free of the dictator-like influence of drugs and negative outside social influences.

In the next chapter, I'm going to make sure you're an expert on the ins and outs of rehab so that you don't have any doubts or worries. I want you to understand what your son or daughter is doing on a day-to-day basis so that you can better relate to him or her. For now, get them to rehab right out of detox. End of story.

# CHAPTER 10: EVERYTHING THERE IS TO KNOW ABOUT REHAB

Now that I've emphasized how important it is to get your child to rehab after detox, I feel I should add one more thing. Yes, I want to convey the urgency of the transition to you, but I don't want you to make that transition forced. You cannot force someone sober. To produce the best results, the abuser needs to want it, to be ready, and to start anticipating their new life. That's why I've talked so many times about conveying the benefits to your child and making it sound like an amazing experience.

Now I'd like to share with you everything I know about rehab so that you can feel confident that you know exactly what your child is experiencing day-to-day and put your mind at ease.

## What a Good Rehab Should and Shouldn't Do

<u>The Center Should</u>:

- Ease the hearts and minds of you, the parents.
- Do as they promise.
- Follow up and follow through.
- Do their homework.
- Get prior medical records from your child's long-time physician.
- Assess mental health in addition to substance abuse.

- Involve the family.
- Help you and your child plan for the future.
- Address life skills, so that your child has a leg up coming out and doesn't fall back into old habits.
- Have a history of success.
- Have great alumni who are still sober.
- Harbor a non-judgmental environment.
- Encourage independence.
- Exude professionalism.

The Center Shouldn't:

- Avoid medical concerns.
- Have greedy or shady motivations behind the creation and continuation of the program.
- Be more concerned with making money than helping patients.
- Have ties to politics that dictate how the program is run or how much funding it gets.
- Force or pressure you or your child in any way.

In short, a center should be focused on the residents' recovery, and the staff should genuinely care about what they do. The treatment must go deeper than changing the patients' actions. It must also focus on creating a change in their thinking.

## Addiction and the Addict Mindset

To better understand what rehab does, you must remember what it seeks to overcome.

Addiction is a sickness (though the definition of it as a disease is disputed by different groups of thought) that effects the addict's body and mind—making it more complex and much harder to reverse than a physical illness that can be cured with simple medicines. Some experts say there is no real cure for it, there are only ways to overcome it.

It's a malicious disease. It's progressive, meaning that once the addict turns back to it, the disease picks back up right where it left off. There is no gradual build. After the moment of relapse, the addict falls right back into the pit they were in before, and it's just as deep as when they first climbed out of it.

So if there's no real cure, what do you call people like myself who have been sober for years? Well, think of it as being in remission from cancer. There is always the chance that it will come back if I stray from my current path. That's why I continue to go to my therapist. That's why I don't let myself say that I'm cured, because it's a false notion that can lead to a dangerous slip up.

When your child first steps into rehab, their life is a rollercoaster. They have no real baseline for their life, nothing to root them to a chosen path. Their life is run by a mind-altering substance that literally affects their personality and how they approach the world. Now that they've done detox, that fog that allowed them to wander into crazy, unhealthy situations has lifted. Without direction, many people try to fill the void left by drugs with other habits. It can be a world of different things: sex, vaping, energy drinks, eating, exercise, etc. Some are good, and some are bad. However, even with the good ones, the former addict might develop obsessive behaviors. They might exercise until they literally can't stand. They need direction on how to fill that void with a healthy balance of good behaviors.

When your child exits detox, they are primed to start reversing the long-term effects of the addiction mindset. And that is what rehab seeks to help them do.

## Does It Work?

I'm not going to lie to you and say that rehab is the ultimate solution or that it cures the problem effectively each and every time. It isn't the ultimate solution, but it is the best one available right now.

There is no 100% guarantee. It's like any other medicine or "fix-it" product: results may vary. However, the percentages of success do rise as the addict actively and willingly completes each phase of the program. On average, 40-60% of all drug treatment patients relapse at some point.

Just know that the road to recovery isn't short and freshly paved. It's a dirt path through rugged terrain, and it never really ends. But the ground will begin to level out, and the traveler's muscles will grow stronger.

Don't set the bar too high and set yourself up to be let down. Understand the reality. Then, after your child has two to three years of clean living under their belt, you can start to relax a little. Sadly, though, the chance of relapse never goes away completely. After eight years, my mom is still prepared for the worst.

Know that everyone recovers differently, and sometimes what seems like recovery is something else entirely. There is a difference between abstaining and real recovery. Some people become what is known as a Dry Drunk. A Dry Drunk is abstaining from drugs and alcohol, but they are miserable doing it. They don't have the right mindset. They aren't living a sustainable, happy life. They're just going through the motions, forcing themselves not to use because they know it's what they're supposed to do.

These people will always eventually relapse. The Dry Drunk effect is most often seen in addicts who were forced into rehab.

Some people recover quicker than others. Some put up

more resistance than others. It all depends on what they must do to take the weight of the drug use and its consequences off their shoulders and find their path.

It also helps if they can find that one person who will make everything click for them. It could be a peer or a sober living coach or a therapist, but pretty much every successfully recovered addict has one person who said or did the right thing to spark the miracle, to make them "get it." This person is the one who helps your child dig up the root cause of their addiction.

Everyone finds that one person in their own time. There is no set timeline for when that burden is lifted. There's no specific point where you can say, "After this they won't use again." The timing will be different for everyone.

Usually, those who have been using the longest and the heaviest will take the longest to recover. If you walk into a dark wood and take a long hike, it's going to take you just as much or more time to find your way back out again. You can lose the trail along the way. Your journey may have made you tired, and you may need to take a break.

Make sure your child stays in treatment for as long as necessary. Sometimes addicts will cut and run as soon as they start doing good and feeling better. Whenever someone leaves suddenly this way, rehab staff call it an AMA, as in "John AMA'd last night." Running when treatment starts working seems counterintuitive, but fear is always irrational. That's what's at the core of pulling an AMA — fear. Sobriety, though it feels good to their bodies, can scare the living shit out of addicts because they realize that it means a huge change. Their life has revolved around drugs, and the prospect of life without them is confusing and terrifying. What will they do? How will they spend their time now? Rather than face these questions, they bolt. Rehab staff cannot force anyone to stay, but they do often try to make patients think they can in order to avoid this scenario. They will hold a patient's phone, money, and ID hostage if they sense an AMA coming.

The last thing you want is your child leaving too early. That just wastes all the effort you've put in and does your child no favors. Don't ever let your child convince you he's ready to leave. Talk to the doctors and the staff surrounding your child. They can tell you if they see a shift in your child's mindset and whether they believe he has adjusted enough and begun let go of the guilt and shame of past damages. It can be dangerous if patients are released too soon.

## Purpose of Treatment

Rehab will do a number of things for your loved one. First, they will uncover how they became an addict. Next, they will be taught what to do now—how to move forward and reverse whatever it is that got them into addiction in the first place. Then they will learn how to take control of their life outside of rehab. They will start to see the change in themselves, and hopefully be encouraged by it.

The first step of rehab is admitting you have a problem. That's why at group sessions everyone starts off their stories by introducing themselves like, "Hi, I'm Adam, and I'm an addict." It drills the idea home because they have to come to terms with it before the healing can begin.

Hopefully, your son or daughter will come to realize that resisting the process gets them nowhere. There may be parts they don't like. They may feel awkward at first. However, people will be experiencing positive change all around them. If they can observe that and take it to heart, they will begin to realize that they ought to make the best of the situation while there and at least try to participate to the fullest. This step is absolutely necessary for recovery, because only the addict can cure themselves.

## What You Can Do

You're not going to be around in rehab. Yes, you can visit, but you aren't going to be the active force behind your child's recovery anymore, the experts are. However, there are still plenty of things you can do for them.

Before your kid goes in, you can get them some new comfy clothes. My mom did that, and it meant the world to me.

While they're in the program, you can send them gift boxes full of things like razor blades, socks, underwear, shoes, a toothbrush, greeting cards, books, shaving cream, etc. The idea is to spoil them with necessities, not goodies. Get them the things they *need* to show that you are thinking about them and that you care.

You can also begin to actively prepare things for your child when they come out.

If your child has unpaid bills or loans, try to take care of them. You don't want your child walking out of rehab and falling into a large pile of debt.

Put money aside for them if you can, so that they have a starting point and a nice nest egg to live off of while they look for a job, even if it's only a couple hundred bucks.

Buy them clothes for interviews. Get them a cell phone.

Clear up the legal stuff. Your kid may have a pending possession trial or other legal matters as a consequence of their drug use. Get it all postponed, talk to the right people, and don't let your kid end up in even more legal trouble while they are away working to get better.

Get the medical side in order, too. Make sure your primary physician gets in touch with the center's medical staff so he or she will know what is going on with your child when they come out.

Prepare yourself for the family therapy sessions you'll

inevitably be called in for. Have the stories you want to tell prepared. Think through your feelings and come up with some concrete things you want to see your child do when they get out. If you know everything you want to say beforehand, you are less likely to end up kicking yourself an hour after the session is over saying, “Dang, I meant to say _____!”

Family involvement is very important, even at this stage. It just looks a little different than before. The best way to stay involved in your child’s recovery and show support is to show up. At this stage, that means participating in that family therapy session, even if it’s just via phone, and truly opening up. It can feel very awkward for some people. Your child will have talked to that therapist plenty of times before, but it may be your first time ever opening up to a professional like that. Don’t judge the process. Don’t fear it either. Follow the advice you’ve hopefully been hammering into your kid: it can’t hurt to try. Do it right and wholeheartedly.

## The Types of Rehab

1. Residential Treatment:

If you chose this type, your child will live at the center 24/7 for 30 days of medical and mental health treatment. Then they do the lower levels of care at the facility as well instead of out in the community, like with other programs. All-in-all they end up staying around 6 months.

Usually these programs are held in a large, remote building like a ranch that all of the patients live in together. They will only get to leave the residence on rare occasions because they will eat, sleep, do activities, and undergo therapy there. Even the AA and NA meetings are brought to them. Often such places require the residents to perform some sort of daily work duty.

This model isn’t normally used down here in Florida. We have smaller programs that get the patients in for 30-45 days and then begin to help them readjust to the real world instead of keeping them isolated.

2. Therapeutic Community:

This is more of a technique than a facility type, as some of the residential treatment centers are like this and some aren't. As you may have guessed by the name, a program like this works as an intimate community where the residents hold each other accountable for actions and behaviors. If one resident notices negative behavior from another, he or she can issue a "pull up," which is just a peer write up that is meant to help pull the other person to their feet and help them out by calling out negative actions. Honestly, though, nobody ever really gives out pull ups.

There are three phases that the residents must complete. For the first week to a month, residents have little freedom and are often paired with a "buddy" who is farther along in the program. Their days and activities are fully restricted with heavy structuring and lots of required group sessions. They will learn about what rehab can do for them, why people turn to addiction, and undergo an intro period where they are assessed by professionals.

In the second phase, more freedom within the center is granted. This is where the bulk of learning happens because the awkwardness is behind them. They will begin to share more in groups and be more comfortable with their peers. There is lots of therapy in this phase (groups and one-on-one) to try and root out the resident's reasons for using.

The last phase usually requires that they get a job in the community. They then go to the job during the day and their only requirement is to come back to eat, do some therapy, and sleep there at night. They will also be expected to take on more of a leadership role in the program and learn how helping others can help themselves. They will feel more comfortable with sobriety. As a result, this is when things begin to shift toward aftercare, relapse prevention, and creating a game plan with support teams.

3. Partial Hospitalization Program

PHPs are a hybrid of inpatient and outpatient facilities with a community that is still peer driven. PHPs offer residents far more liberty than the Residential Treatment centers do.

In this model, the residents live in a nice house or development with a roommate. They will eat and sleep at this residence and then go to the treatment center during the day. It's much more like living at home, but there is still 24/7 staff supervision.

Usually a program like this lasts between 30 and 45 days, depending on the individual. Up to fourteen of those days are designated for stabilization.

Your child will be required to put in 23 clinical hours per week minimum, but there are a lot of group activity options for downtime, like going to the gym, the beach, a mini golf course, etc. They will be allowed to leave the development with a staff member to go to the grocery store or shopping for things they may need around the house. They also get to leave to go to outside AA and NA meetings in the community and attend recovery events.

These kinds of programs are very comfortable and relaxed and take place in upscale settings, which is why they are very popular in Florida and California where the recovery community is abundant. No rent is required for this room and board (or at any rehab facility, for that matter). It's all included in the price of admission, which is hopefully covered by your insurance.

## Rules of Rehab

All rehab centers usually have the same basic rules that

your child must follow if he or she is to stay there. In all honesty, the list of typical rules reads like a long list of "Thou Shalt Nots" or the rant of a scolding mother waggling her finger at a toddler, but such structure and discipline is necessary at this stage. All of the rules are in place for good reason.

The list goes a little something like this:

NO phones

NO holding prescription medications

NO money, at least in the first phase

NO video games

NO sex

NO drugs (duh!)

NO leaving the property

NO missing curfew

NO isolation

NO sleeping until noon

NO dirty rooms

NO messy beds

NO being rude

NO aggression or violence

NO self-harm

NO contraband / prohibited items

NO porn

These rules are the most common gripes patients have with their centers, and your child is unlikely to be an exception. You're probably going to hear a lot of whining about these things during your phone calls. Now, your child could have a totally legitimate complaint, but you need to know how to pick those out and ignore the bull. If your child's complaint has anything to do with the typical rehab rules, let her know you think they are for the best. Don't simper or pout along with her if she says, "Mom, they have me scrubbing the bathrooms like a servant," or, "Dad, they force us to go to meetings. I told them I didn't want to go today, and they took my phone. It's like a prison!" Yes, you need to hear your child out, and yes, sometimes the center's rules are a little overly strict, but it's all for a reason, and you need to let your child know that. Drugs equal chaos. Rehab provides extreme structure to counteract that and make sure your child stays firmly on the path to recovery.

A warning sign for legitimate complaints is if the center goes radio silent when you try to check in and ask about progress while, at the same time, your child is continuously complaining about mistreatment. That's a major red flag, and it may be time to get back in touch with that second or third rehab option that you prepared for the intervention.

Those backup options also come in handy if your child breaks a center's zero tolerance drug rule. With most centers, there is no playing games if your child is caught with drugs or found high. They can't risk having that around the other patients, and they will not hesitate to kick your child out *that day*. When that call comes in, you need to be ready with that backup center because the last thing you want is your child getting dumped off at a hotel on a Saturday afternoon and having to wait for you until Monday. Hotels and a disgruntled addict are a terrible combo.

That's why Oceans Medical does its best to make sure that the patient who slipped up is not chucked out the door with nowhere to go. Sometimes, the high person can become belligerent, causing serious trouble and drawing the attention of the other patients who really don't need to be in the presence of drugs or anyone on drugs. However, in this case, a good center ought to have referral programs to a detox center or another rehab to help you out with the transfer. Not all do this, though, so you need to be prepared yourself.

## Day In, Day Out

While there may be slight variations, the rehab process is pretty much the same everywhere, and thus most centers follow the same basic schedule.

To give you an idea of what your child's daily activities will be like, here's a sample schedule split into weekday and weekend activities.

Monday-Friday:

7 a.m. — Wakeup call

7:30 a.m. — Breakfast

8 a.m. — Morning Meeting

9 a.m. — Phase Group or Medical Break

10:30 a.m. — Didactic group

Noon — Lunch

1 p.m. — Specialty groups

2 p.m. — Small group OR individual therapy

BREAK

3 p.m. — Process group OR one-on-one

4 p.m. — Closing group

5 p.m. — Back to housing

5:30 p.m. — Clean up

6 p.m. — Dinner

7 p.m. — Downtime / group fun time

8:30 p.m. — AA, NA meeting

9:30 p.m. — Nightly wrap up

FREE TIME

11 p.m. Bed

Weekend:

9 a.m. — On Sundays go to church

10 a.m. — Breakfast

11a.m. — Morning meeting

FREE TIME

1 p.m. — Group activities. (These often include beach sports, mini golf, horse-back riding, movies, bowling, and go-karts depending on the area. Some facilities are stricter than others about this. Some require that patients go through certain phases and accomplish certain things before they are given this freedom. Just make sure the center you choose has group activities in some form. I think it's vital that residents get to have a little fun.)

6 p.m. — Dinner

7 p.m. — GI (General Inspection), deep cleaning

8 p.m. — AA, NA meeting

FREE TIME

1 a.m. — lights out

## Group Therapy

You probably noticed that a lot of therapy sessions go on during rehab, all with different names and processes. However, all of them adhere to certain predetermined qualities which I will explain to give you a better idea of how they work and what they seek to do.

Factors All Sessions Share

All group sessions are moderated and run by a trained therapist or professional, obviously. Usually, the participants sit in a circle and are encouraged by prompts from the therapist to discuss their experience with drug use, what they are currently feeling about rehab and recovery, problems they've faced, etc.

The participants are expected to encourage one another as well, but they are told that their focus should be on advancing themselves through the steps before trying to help others advance. The professionals are there for everyone; your child is there for his or herself.

All group therapy only works if the participants actually participate, not in just talking about themselves but listening to others. The participants must actively contribute at some point. It's normal for them to be shy and uncertain at first, but for healing to happen they must overcome that, and the therapist is there to encourage active behavior. When participants do contribute, it's only effective it they are honest and sincere about their answers and stories.

When your child listens to the stories of others, they will begin to realize that they aren't alone in the difficulties they've faced, and that can encourage them to participate, too, without feeling silly.

Group Etiquette

When participating in a group session, certain behaviors will be expected of your child to keep the process ordered and effective. Keep these in mind for your family session later on.

Usually, participants are asked to raise a hand to request to speak or share, as it keeps things from getting chaotic and overly noisy.

Jokes should be kept to a minimum, so as not to undermine someone's suffering or accidentally offend. People who are sharing often feel vulnerable. Sometimes jokes can cheer them up, which is why they aren't discouraged altogether, but sometimes they can be perceived as insulting in such a vulnerable state.

It is understood that everyone arrives on time and people don't leave early. Having people milling in and out can be disruptive. Not to mention it's pretty rude to walk out while someone is in the middle of spilling their darkest, long-harbored secrets.

Reasons Behind Group Sessions

In addition to allowing participants to learn from each other and take encouragement from the fact that they aren't alone, group sessions work to create bonds between the patients. It's hard to share your deepest secrets with people and not feel some sort of comradery toward them.

Sometimes it's easier to talk to a peer than a professional. While a good professional comes off as personable and non-judgmental, they are still an authority figure and can be unintentionally intimidating. In a group session, your child can look to others like them as they share, and feel more comfortable with their admissions.

Group sessions can also improve your child's social skills for when they come out of rehab. If they begin to struggle with temptation once they're back to their daily lives, they need to open up to someone about it and ask for help. If they've done so in group therapy, they will be less nervous about doing it outside of therapy.

Perhaps most importantly, it keeps your child from feeling isolated. If left alone in a clinical setting with only doctors to talk to, your child has far too much time to dwell on things, which can lead to depression and shame. Your child needs to think positive in order to recover.

Lastly, your child will get to witness the progress and recovery of others. Watching friends succeed encourages your child, letting them know it's possible. It also pushes them to do the same.

## Different Types of Group Sessions

Now that we've covered the general attributes of group therapy, let's dive deeper into the different types and the purposes they serve.

1. Process Group

This type of group discusses your child's experience in the program itself and in the recovery process. It's designed to encourage patients to openly share and discuss what they've been learning in other groups and activities, and ask questions if something needs clarifying.

There is a subcategory of this type called an Interpersonal Process Group which helps the patients resolve social issues. For some people, their inability to relate to others is what pushed them toward addictive substances in the first place. This type of group helps them overcome those issues and better relate to their peers so they can reap the full benefits of the other group sessions.

2. Didactic Group

This group is based around the participants' feelings and finding meaning in their actions, both past and present. In these sessions, they will seek a moral compass to steer them along. They may participate in prayer lead by whomever is in charge, depending on the type of group. This sort of session has a classroom-type feel.

3. Support Group

AA and NA meetings fall into this category. Depending on the program your child is in, they will either be held at the facility or outside in the community. Either way, your child will reap the benefits of this social networking group. It educates addicts about how to achieve sobriety with the help of experts on the subject who have gone through the same things. The sponsor system of AA and NA allows addicts to support each other through the twelve steps.

Really, there is a support group for just about anything you can think of. Bible studies and men's/women's groups are some big ones, but you can also find LGBT groups, trauma groups, etc. There are also groups like Al-Anon, which is a kind of family AA group meant for parents like you and others who have addicted children. Al-Anon is about teaching family members how to deal with an alcoholic loved one.

4. Trauma/Specialty Group

These are the specialty groups that deal with the different tracks I discussed in Chapter 8. There are trauma groups for those who have a history of domestic abuse, sexual abuse, eating disorders, anger management, PTSD, suicidal tendencies, or mental health issues to make sure all of your child's obstacles are addressed and overcome. The specialty groups pair your child with peers in the same boat and are led by a specialist on the given subject.

5. Small Groups

Most of the other groups I've discussed are very large with a lot of people participating at once. That's why programs also offer sessions that break up these large groups into small groups. These sessions provide a more intimate environment where everyone can be heard in a shorter amount of time. Usually, people who are in the same phase of the program are paired together here to add an extra connection and sense of comradery.

What is said in a small group stays there, and when done correctly, the same people will always be in the small group together throughout the process. That way, the participants grow comfortable enough with each other to share deeper thoughts and feelings. It forms a team that knows each other very well and seeks to help each other along.

6. Mental Health Groups

These groups focus on dealing with different types of

mental health issues and maintaining a healthy mindset. While substance abuse groups focus entirely on drug use, these groups help participants learn how to identify and be aware of their behaviors. They teach participants how to combat specific issues that arise regularly as a result of mental health problems. Some are designed for people with substance abuse problems in addition to a mental illness, while others only deal with mental health issues. For instance, at Oceans, we can admit you solely on mental health. If a client is sober but still doesn't feel 100% due to obstacles pertaining to mental health, we can admit him or her into the program to provide the proper support.

## One-on-One Therapy

After all of this discussion about groups, let's not forget that your child will be required to speak one-on-one with a therapist for an hour at least once a week.

These are the sessions you see in movies and on TV, though there isn't always a lounging couch for your kid to lay back on and stare up at the ceiling.

The main person in charge of your child's treatment (the primary therapist) runs these sessions. Thus, they are up to speed on your child's history and progress. They are excellent listeners—better than people in group sessions—because they are trained in it. They give open and honest feedback.

If your child finds the right therapist with whom they really connect, this is where they will open up the most because this professional therapist knows how to help your child dig deeper into the causes of their drug abuse.

The therapist is who your child should turn to if they are truly struggling. A peer can be sympathetic, but a therapist knows how to actually help and move things forward for the better.

These sessions aren't meant to be an hour-long vent or

a place for your child to whine about how unfair it is for them to be there. These sessions are where the ghosts are forced from the closet. They are about getting your child's mind past the hang ups and difficulties and steering them toward change. These sessions will teach them to take responsibility for their actions rather than moaning about life's unfairness.

## What's Being Discussed?

While each group has its own special area, there are a few general things that all the different types of therapy will teach your child.

They will learn to communicate better and understand the ins and outs of rehab and sober living. They will admit to their addictions. They will learn their triggers and other ways to prevent relapse. They will make amends with you and anyone else they've hurt. They will become more self-aware and learn to assess themselves and their behavior. They will learn more about why they crave substances, the science behind addiction, and its effects on the brain. This sort of education can have a profound effect because most addicts don't understand or don't want to admit that they are sick. When they learn that their struggles are due to a rewiring of their brain, it becomes a tangible problem that puts their hardships in perspective. They now know why they can't seem to quit on their own. Identifying the problem is just the first step, though; they are also taught how they can combat it. They will learn how to stop addictive and negative thoughts that drive them to reach for drugs. They will learn meditation techniques to keep themselves on task, in the present, and out of their own head whenever a craving should strike. Lastly, they will be taught how to schedule their day around non-triggering activities and how to build proper life skills to help them adjust to independent life after rehab.

Essentially, they are learning to let go of whatever is holding them back and forging a tangible plan for staying sober for the long run.

## The Medical Side

While in rehab, your son or daughter will be required to see a program medical doctor once a week. This isn't just a check up to make sure they haven't gotten hold of drugs somehow either.

Many hard drug users develops additional health issues such as horrendously bad teeth (Google "meth mouth" if you don't believe me), kidney damage, and liver damage.

It's also quite common for serious drug addicts to catch STD's like Hepatitis C or even HIV due to a lack of self-restraint or lack of consideration about consequences. Your child will not only be tested for these diseases, but also educated on the dangers of them by a medical professional on staff.

On a lighter note, your son or daughter will also be educated on the importance of good nutrition and tips on how to craft meals and live a lifestyle that promotes good health. They will also pair that nutritional education with a workout routine to give their body the boost of strength and endorphins it needs to make a speedy recovery.

Traditional rehab centers do not use heavy-duty medications like detox meds during treatment. Sometimes lighter medications are administered. For instance, if a patient is struggling with bipolar disorder, they may be given Seroquel. Medications have been proven to aid addiction recovery, especially in the detox stage, but they must be prescribed sparingly, adjusted regularly, and heavily monitored. If your child suffers from a mental health disorder, medication can be lifesaving, and the rehab doctor will absolutely provide them. Giving medication for mental disorders is a more common practice than administering strong drugs for addiction treatment. The only time strong detox drugs like Suboxone (for opiate addiction) are administered during rehab is if the patient has struggled to complete rehab multiple times or continues to relapse after completing multiple programs. If your child is in this position, you may need to spend some extra time seeking out a program that specializes in or accepts this.

## Are They Feeding My Baby Right?

Don't worry, Momma Bear, your kid's not going to starve. There are three square meals a day listed in that schedule I gave you, remember? The center will also provide some snacks.

Some programs provide a weekly budget for residents to purchase extra food items on the Walmart trip every weekend. They get to go pick out those Doritos or Flamin' Hot Cheetos they love so much, don't worry.

You can also bring them snacks when you come to visit, so long as they're fully sealed and not overly messy.

## Home Sickness

It's going to happen. Your child will start to feel overwhelmed by the whole process, and they will long for their old life and "normalcy." They will use their limited phone call privileges to call you up and beg you to come get them out.

You have to stay strong and resist the pleas. Remember, they are better off where they are; you brought them there for a reason. Go back over those reasons with yourself or your spouse if you have to; think back to all the problems you were having.

When they call with tears in their voice, tell them that

home will still be there when they get out. Remind them why they are there. Assure them nothing has changed at home; they aren't missing out. Quell the homesickness as best you can because it is an unneeded distraction.

Leaving your child in rehab isn't abandonment, it's an act of love. Don't worry, there are plenty of ways you can see and talk to your child every now and then while they are in rehab.

## Special Passes

The program your child is in may allow them to request overnight, day, or weekend passes to get out and go home or stay with someone outside rehab for an approved amount of time.

All passes must be signed and approved by your child's main therapist.

An overnight pass is usually granted if you child needs to get to an out-of-town court date or wants to spend the night with you if you've come to see them out of state.

A day pass is usually granted for a short family visit, a medical or dentist appointment, or if your child needs to deal with some sort of legal issue close by.

A weekend pass is usually only given out at long-term centers and only once your child has reached the final phase of treatment. Its main purpose is to help them get used to reintegrating into society, but it's also a way for them to come visit you in your home state.

## Visitation

Just like the detox center, visits at the rehab facility must be scheduled. Usually, you can't even make an appointment until a certain amount of time has passed, like two weeks or so. In most places, your visits will be supervised, simply as procedure so that no contraband is snuck in. In fact, they may search your bag.

It may sound like a bit of a pain in the butt, but hey, it's worth it to go see your kid, right?

You can spend a Saturday or Sunday morning with them, just talking. Ask them what they've been doing, what parts they've been enjoying, and what they've learned.

Ask them if they've set goals for life after rehab. If not, go over the options. Set clear, obtainable goals that don't overreach. Ideally, your child should have daily, short term, and long term goals laid out that they are actively pursuing. The therapist will have probably already been working with them on this.

Ask if they've made any new friends. In short, talk about and inquire after the good and keep the attitude positive. Encourage them, let them know you're proud, but remember, don't gush or you may induce a gag reflex.

## Final Tips

When your child is off at rehab, maybe out of state and far away from you, you can start to get antsy, feeling like you need to do something like you did in the first stage of this process. I'd like to leave you with a few tips on your mentality and what you can do at this stage.

- Be there but don't be overbearing: make the most out of a visit or two.
- Trust the process.
- Start preparing for the next phase (I'll tell you how to do that in the next chapter).
- Assess your role in the addiction process and adjust your actions accordingly.
- Get counseling for yourself. You have things you need

to deal with as a result of all of this, too. Don't be afraid to open up to a professional.

- If you expect your kid to honestly assess their faults, you should be willing to do the same.
- Get strong.
- Be open to change.
- Don't be critical.
- Don't make it harder than it is.
- Learn all that you can. Hey, that's why you're reading this book, right?

## Conclusion

Rehab is a full-time study of addiction for your child. It is where they will begin to rewire themselves, clear the funk, and learn how to prevent relapse. They will make new friends and form their own support group. They will begin to see the potential of what life can be like without drugs. They will begin to see that though they may be a different person when off drugs, the change is a positive one, and they most certainly aren't going to lose those characteristics that truly make them who they are at heart. I have been through this process; it's hard but worth it. Remember, though, that it's still early in the big picture.

The next and final phase is where they will start taking action to become an active, fully functioning member of society again.

# PART 3: AFTERCARE

## The New, New Parental Role

We've come to the end of the second phase of recovery. The rehab program is about to release your child, and I'm sure both you and your kid are practically skipping with joy about that. Hopefully your child has some new confidence and a real desire to live sober and keep feeling the way they do right now: in control, healthy, and motivated. I know that sounds like a chorus of angels to your ears, and that's why I really hate to tell you that the work is far from done. But deep down you probably suspected that, right? I mean, you've still got a nice chunk of book left to read at this point.

For the last few months, professionals have watched your child 24/7, making sure temptation stays out of reach and that they keep their eyes on the course ahead. Going back out into the community to live entirely independently again is a whole different challenge. That's why I recommended finding a rehab program that allows integration back into the community as part of the third and/or final phase of treatment. If your child got to go to a facility like that, they are a step ahead, but they still aren't home free.

Once again, your role is going to shift. First, you were a battering ram, knocking down every obstacle in your way to wake your child up and arrange serious help for them. Next, you were a concerned watchman, communicating with everyone involved in your child's care and observing them from afar. You provided encouragement and gifts to keep your child happy and motivated throughout treatment, without hovering.

Now, you're eventually going to slowly pull back more and let your child start to live their own life. However, for a brief moment, you may need to swoop in again. When they first graduate from the program, it's okay to help them get on their feet. In fact, I highly encourage it if they haven't been allowed to get a job during their time at treatment. You don't want them to come out hopeful and encouraged only to have to face homelessness while they search for a job.

If you need to help them with the first weeks' rent at the sober living house or get them some new clothes for interviews, do it. However, don't give in to every little request they may have. Support them with necessities, not luxuries. They need to prove to you that they can continue to move toward a positive, productive sober life on their own recognizance.

There are only two things your kid can do coming out of rehab: make the right choices or the wrong ones. It's really as simple as that. What you're rooting and praying for is that rehab was successful in instilling a desire to make a change. This will motivate your loved one to go to a reputable, zero tolerance sober house rather than a flop house (a joke of a halfway house where addicts basically just hang out and slip back into addiction). When you're working with the rehab program's coordinator and therapist before discharge, make sure you provide your child a few different high quality homes to choose from.

After I graduated from rehab, my folks gave me just enough to pay my bills while searching for a job. They made it clear they wouldn't stand for any lying or conniving. If I hadn't done the right thing and actively looked for a job, I would have been on my own. You need to adopt this attitude. It shows you mean business even though you are lending a helping hand.

At a sober living house I managed, I knew a few parents who paid for a week or two of rent and asked that I not tell their kid. They wanted me to help their child stay active. By not letting on that the rent was already covered, they sought to keep their kid actively hunting for a job instead of letting him or her just lounge on the couch thinking, "I'm covered for a few weeks."

Spoiling your child with constant help makes you an enabler. A lot of young kids do drugs because they simply have too much downtime on their hands and they've never had pressing responsibilities. They need to grow up and learn the life skills necessary to live independently. So, give just enough support to keep them from falling on their face in the beginning, but after that, begin to draw back.

That doesn't mean withdraw emotionally. You can still be there for them if they need to talk. Let them know that you're there to listen and give advice. Just don't hand them everything they want, they need to earn it. Let them solve life issues for themselves, and understand that any extra money instantly shoves temptation in their face. Even if it's only $5 or $10, if they don't have to spend it on bills and groceries, they may spend it on drugs.

I highly recommend having your child continue outpatient treatment. That way, they have professionals to turn to as they make the transition, but they are out in the community making a new life for themselves at the same time.

I recommend a security blanket like this because a lot of times for the first month and a half or so they are riding on the high of rehab, but afterwards, the red lights and sirens go off. At first, they may obsess over the sobriety process (such personality traits are common in addicts), but the "high," so to speak, will begin to wear off. For the next two to three months, you should be on high alert. Try to see them and talk to them casually more often during this time to observe their behavior for any red flags. This is when relapse begins to sneak up behind them with a chloroform rag.

They may begin to express frustration with "getting nowhere." They may slack off and lose their job. They may come to you upset that a boyfriend or girlfriend has cut it off with them. They will use these things as an excuse to justify relapse. Nip that in the bud as soon as it comes up.

Get them in a good sober living home and continue an outpatient program through the rehab center. Know where they are, and communicate with the house manager who runs the sober living home. He or she can also alert you to any danger signs so that the both of you can step in with encouragement when it's needed most.

In the coming chapters, I'll discuss all you need to know about sober living houses, avoiding relapse, and everything else about life after rehab. For now, start adjusting to your new role. While you need to step back in the area of responsibility and let your son or daughter take care of his or herself, your mental and emotional support role will become more active. Your kid has access to a phone now. (Be leery.) They may be able to come see you or at least call you whenever they want. They can also get on social media and reconnect with the wrong people.

They may call you with grievances some days and with great news others. Be loving and enthusiastic no matter what type of call it is, and try to let them do most of the talking. Advise them to think through every decision. Praise them when they're up, and encourage them when they're down. Keep financial help to a minimum and put your efforts into rebuilding your relationship with them instead.

# CHAPTER 11: HOME AWAY FROM HOME: SOBER LIVING HOUSING

THE FIRST STEP OF AFTERCARE is settling your child in a good halfway house. As a former owner and current interventionist/consultant at a sober living home, I want you to understand just how vital this next step is for a recovering addict. It's the key transitional piece of puzzle, and if you skip it, your child's chances of long-term sobriety plummet exponentially.

Not all sober living homes are created equal, and the concept itself can be confusing. In this chapter, I'll walk you through what a sober living home is, it's purpose, and tips on selecting the best one.

## Graduation Day

When your son or daughter has successfully completed all the phases of rehab, it's cause for celebration. There will be a small graduation ceremony that you can attend to show your support and pride with ruckus cheers and hoots that will make your kid blush on the outside but smile on the inside. They will receive a completion certificate which represents their achievement and their readiness to begin taking on the world through clear, sober lenses.

Some people feel more prepared than others. Some attack sober living with passion and enthusiasm while others feel as though they're finally being released from prison. The latter type are in danger of becoming what's known as spin cycle clients.

## Don't Turn on the Spin Cycle

Spin cycle clients are chronic relapsers who become professionals at going to rehab and working the system. As soon as they get out of a program, they go back to using. They will party until they have exhausted all resources or until their parents stage another intervention, and then check themselves back into a program to appease their parents and make it seem like they're actually putting in an effort to change. Some will even go so far as to check in just to get a shower and do the laundry, get some detox medication when they are out of drugs, or simply regroup before heading back out to do the same old things. They know their insurance cards work, and they quickly become rehab professionals. They'll say it just isn't working even though they're trying really hard ("I've been four times, but it just hasn't clicked! I just need someplace better."). There is always some sort of excuse. The blame game is always in play.

Don't fall for this. This type of behavior suggests they aren't taking the programs seriously and they aren't really interested in living sober; they're just trying to keep you off their back so they can continue to live the addict lifestyle.

Relapse happens, so don't automatically assume that this is your child's attitude if they slip up. There is a real difference between someone who gets a job, displays a real desire to stay clean, but slips from grace in a moment of temptation, and someone who starts getting high as soon as they walk out of the rehab center doors.

Every time they go back in it's on your dime, so don't be suckered by this spin cycle behavior. The best way to avoid it is to stick by those boundaries and consequences you created for the intervention.

However, if your child relapses after putting in a solid effort, don't get angry with them and don't be discouraged. Many programs offer a second chance for their alumni. Talk to the rehab center's alumni coordinator. This person coordinates the game plan for release and checks in on rehab graduates every now and then. Ask the alumni coordinator if they offer to take a relapsed patient back for free. For instance, at Oceans Medical Centers, if a patient completes the year program and then relapses within a year after, we take that person back in for free. If there is no alumni program, centers often have a stabilization program, which is two weeks of inpatient care to get them back on track. After a slip up, just sitting at home in outpatient to get sober isn't really safe (especially with drugs like heroin). Your child should go into a structured program in order to recover in a safe, monitored environment. Many centers also offer a warrantee option, so if someone relapses shortly after leaving the program, they bring them back in free of charge. If your child gives a serious effort and slides backward once or twice, that's okay and there are options for you that will save you headaches and money.

## The Game Plan

When your child graduates from rehab, a plan should already be in place about where they will go after the ceremony. That plan is created with your child's primary therapist at your family sessions, along with the program's discharge coordinator, who arranges the sober home details.

You will need to know:

- Which sober living home will they stay at?
- Who will pay the rent there? You or your child? If you are going to pay until your child gets on their feet, make it clear exactly how long you are willing to pay. One week? Two weeks? A month?

- How will they get to the sober living home?
- Are you going to buy them a bike or a car to help them get around and get a job?
- What supplies will they need?
- Do they need new interview clothes?
- How will they pay for food until they get a job? Can you get them on food stamps?
- Who's going to pay for a phone and a service plan? They ought to pay for the service eventually, but how long will you pay for it at first?

## What Is a Sober Living Home?

Sober home, halfway house, or transitional living—no matter what you call it, it's the halfway point between addiction and recovery. A sober home is an independent housing community where recovering addicts live together and work to put their lives back on track. Your child will have a roommate or two with whom they can begin to learn life skills, start a career path, and work on staying sober.

Make sure you choose a house that's all male or all female. The couples houses that allow both sexes in one development are just asking for trouble.

These houses may or may not be owned by a rehab center, but they often have strong ties with a particular rehab facility. In fact some places will only take residents from a certain facility. Your child's rehab coordinator will push you to go to the house affiliated with them. This isn't necessarily a bad thing. If it's a good rehab program, one can assume that they will be paired with a housing component that best continues their practices and has a good reputation. Also, a strong connection between the rehab center and the sober home means the staff at both places will better communicate about your child's progress. I just want you to understand that you don't *have* to send your kid to the housing community they suggest. NARR (National Alliance for Recovery Residences) sets the national standard for sober homes. If you're in doubt about the facility your child's rehab staff is pushing you toward, NARR is a great resource to check with first.

Your child will enter a sober home straight out of a highly structured, highly supervised rehab facility. A sober home tries to mimic some of the structure and security while granting your child the freedom to begin putting their life back together. As a result, their day will not be meticulously planned down to the last activity anymore, but they will have a curfew and a set of house rules.

Curfew is usually around 11 p.m. on weekdays and 1 a.m. on weekends. The rules usually include clean up duties and always require that the residents get jobs so that they can pay the rent. Usually, the rule on guests is always the same: anyone who doesn't live in the house shouldn't be in the house. I highly suggest that you choose a facility that strictly implements this rule. This doesn't mean your child's friends can't come pick them up or even hang out on the front porch, but it's not a good idea at this point to let friends and significant others in the house. The house is a private area where temptation can lure your child behind closed doors. Also, if one of the residents lets in someone unsavory and that person robs the place or destroys property or whatnot, it effects that resident's roommates too, which isn't fair.

Pretty much all sober homes have a zero tolerance policy. If one you are interested in doesn't, run the other way because you are most likely being enticed by a flop house where structure goes out the window and drugs inevitably find their way into every room in the place.

A zero tolerance facility will conduct random drug tests and inspections on a weekly basis, and if drug use or paraphernalia is discovered, the offending person is sent packing back to rehab immediately.

While at the home, your child is also encouraged to receive outpatient care from their rehab facility. They will continue therapy and AA/NA meetings, and follow an individualized treatment program that will teach them how to reintegrate back into the community. This outpatient treatment is gradually tapered off to help make the transition from rehab to independence as smooth as humanly possible.

The person who oversees all the mechanics of the sober home is called the house manager. They are often a former addict with many years of sobriety. This allows them to better connect with the residents and act as a reminder that sobriety is possible. The house manager usually lives on the property with the residents. He or she collects rent and enforces the rules.

The facility is usually owned by someone other than the house manager. The owner is a business man or woman who doesn't live there and usually just drops by every now and then, but he or she is often highly experienced in the recovery process and readily available. Recently, new recovery residency certification courses were created for owners to further their knowledge on the whole rehabilitation process. You want a facility that also has regular employees who come in the morning and leave at night. These employees are a lot like the Behavioral Health Technicians (BHT's) at a rehab center (see Chapter 8). They will help out with transportation when needed, handle the day to day of the facility's business, and keep a friendly but watchful eye on the residents. Try to avoid houses that are solely run by a house manager; they are easily bribed and often relapse themselves. Having extra staff around keeps the house manager accountable and makes sure he or she isn't overworked or overstressed.

## The Continuation of Care

If the high dive from strictly disciplined structure to total freedom is made too quickly, your child will belly flop. That's why sober homes partner with rehab facilities for outpatient care.

So what is outpatient care?

Well, there are two types: Intensive Outpatient (IOP) and Outpatient (OP). Your child will start off with IOP five days a week for two weeks, move down to three days a week for a subsequent 30+ days, and then move to OP which only requires a minimum of three hours a week. OP should last for about six or more months before everything is tapered off and your child is considered entirely independent.

Both IOP and OP are a continuation of therapy that specifically addresses staying sober while transitioning into independence. Check your benefits and see how many days of IOP and OP your insurance will cover. Usually the policy lists a set amount of days that are fully covered, as with rehab.

The IOP curriculum will teach your child to incorporate strategies and tricks to stay sober as new temptations and stressors emerge. These group lessons are almost identical to the group therapy sessions back in rehab, but the material covered veers toward the practical. The topics will focus on things like time management, goal setting, fellowship, school, and work. Participation is highly encouraged, just like in the group therapy sessions. A therapist leads the group, and as such, participants will also be asked to share their thoughts on things like relapse and personal insecurities.

The curriculum also requires weekly one-on-one therapy sessions and daily NA and AA meeting attendance. During this time your child will be developing a working relationship with their sponsor and the group at the home.

IOP will also begin to address the damage done to your child's life before rehab. They will work through any legal ramifications, family rifts, financial issues, or health issues. They will see a medical doctor once a month to help with medication management or any medical issues they are still working through.

Once your child moves on to OP care, some facilities allow patients the option to continue care remotely through telephone or Skype rather than on site. Either way, they will still be required to attend individualized therapy and continue the 12-step program, sponsorship, and fellowship of AA and NA meetings.

Throughout the week, the staff will do a check-in with each resident. They will ask your child how they are doing, how their job search is going, and generally make sure your child stays on track and has everything they need.

OP also requires family sessions, so expect to be called in for those. By now you should be a natural.

## Selecting a Qualified Sober Home / Halfway House

Deciding ahead of time where your child will stay after rehab is extremely important. Don't let them come home and live on your couch eating pizza in a bathrobe all day. In order to have the greatest chance at success, they need to immediately go into a sober living home where a professional can keep them on track without babysitting them all day long.

You will need to research and vet each home like you did with the detox and rehab centers. Find a few that look promising and call them up.

Questions to Ask:

- Where are you located?

Try to find a housing complex close to your child's rehab center. They have to go to a facility for IOP and OP, and if they are close to their old rehab, they will be able to continue outpatient care in a familiar setting with familiar staff.

- Do you require meetings?

If they don't require AA and NA meetings, throw up a red flag; you may be dealing with a flop house.

- What do you charge for rent?

The average rental rate is $100-$200. However, the really swanky places can run upwards of $300 or even $600 weekly.

- How much is it to move in?

Most places charge a move-in fee in the form of a deposit (around $500 bucks or so). Sometimes the fee is just the first month's rent upfront. As you can imagine, sober living homes have a lot of residents flake out on rent, so they do this to ensure some sort of payment to keep the place running. Usually the deposit is refunded after your child has been there for six months.

- How much supervision does the facility have?

Some sort of staff should always be on duty to make sure rules are followed and dangerous situations are avoided.

- Are there live-in managers or is there only outside staff?

If there is a house manager, he or she ought to live at the facility, but additional outside staffing is always a good sign.

- Are your properties single family homes or apartments?

Sometimes a house is a little cheaper simply because up to six people are sharing the rent, but really it doesn't make a difference. Some complexes offer upscale apartments that run higher than most houses. Essentially, it comes down to your son or daughter's preference.

- How many beds are in each property?

This will give you an idea of how many roommates your child will have.

- How many houses do you have?

Having an idea of how large the program is gives you an idea of how many residents the staff has to oversee. So, a good follow up question might be, "How many staff members are on duty at one time?"

- Are you currently full?

Even if they will have a bed open when your child is ready to move in, just take into consideration how busy this complex must be if they are completely full at the moment. It's also wise to factor in how many beds they have. If they only have a dozen beds that are all filled, that's much more manageable than fifty full beds.

- Do you conduct mandatory drug tests?

Stick that red flag in the ground if they say no. You could be dealing with a flop house. All zero tolerance houses conduct drug tests.

- When is rent due? Monthly or weekly?

Both have their benefits. If it's monthly, your child has some breathing room to come up with the money, but if it's weekly they are less likely to blow the money on things they shouldn't before they have to hand it over. If the home charges by the week, try to cut a deal that allows your kid a small discount if they pay the full month upfront instead.

- Are you affiliated with a rehab center?

Now, I've already discussed the pros and cons of this, but make sure you always ask, because some houses only admit patients from a certain rehab center. The complex may sound like a real gem, but if your kid didn't go to that specific affiliated rehab, you don't want to waste any more time on this sober home because your child won't be allowed in.

- Will my child have to go to IOP?

Some places only require regular OP, but if your

insurance covers IOP, I say why not go for it? IOP provides more structure during the most critical transitional period. Try to get your child in it if you can. But at no time should your child be forced into anything. Sometimes when your insurance runs out or your IOP days are no longer approved, the sober home will kick your kid out. You need to ask if participation in an IOP program is a *requirement* for living at the residence to make sure this won't be an issue.

- Can I come for a tour to see the properties?

The place may look great on the brochure and sound awesome on the phone, but as with buying a house, you should always do a walkthrough to make sure the reality matches the expectation.

- Could I get a copy of the house rules?

Always a good thing to have for reference. If there aren't any predetermined rules in place, it's another sign of a flop house.

- Do you help residents out if they don't have transportation?

Eventually, your child should at least get a bike or a bus pass, but it's an extra bonus if the property provides free transport in the beginning.

- Is there a grace period on rent to allow my child to get a job?

Some places do offer "scholarships" for the first week's rent. You can also ask about secretly paying for the first week or two yourself, as discussed at the opening of Part 3.

- On average, how many months of sobriety do your current clients have?

This is more important than you might think. If one house has six beds and five of the people in those beds (including your son or daughter) only have 30 days or less of sobriety under their belts, they are more likely to talk about drugs and other temptations. However, if your child gets in a house where most of the other residents have been sober for a few months, those more experienced residents will steer the conversation to the fun things they do without drugs and the things they've achieved while sober.

- What are your rules on house guests?

Remember, anyone who doesn't live in the house shouldn't be allowed in the house.

- How do you handle relapse? Do you have a zero tolerance policy?

No zero tolerance policy, no dice. You want your child sent straight back to rehab if they have even the slightest slip up. You should be notified immediately, as well.

- How long have you been in business?

Longevity doesn't always prove success, but it's often a pretty good indicator.

- Can I talk to a resident or get any sort of reference?

If they don't have any references, walk. If they do, actually take the time to call the person. An actual resident can offer insight that the customer service representative may leave out.

## The Daily Grind

On your child's first day, there will be lots of paperwork like releases allowing the sober home staff to speak with you and the treatment center, a signed acknowledgement of the rules, medical privacy agreements, a rental commitment, and a medical waiver. After that, though, the sober home will become a place to socialize.

Your child will mingle with their housemates and hopefully form bonds that last for years to come. Though they are granted more freedom, they are also given more responsibility. In rehab, they were basically shuttled from one place to the next. In the sober home, they will have to carry out required tasks on their own time. They will have cleaning duties both in their own house and around the property at large. Mostly it's just typical chores: keep your part of the room clean, take out the trash, sweep up your messes. They will also be required to do weekly deep cleans. So moms, next time your child tries to pull the "I don't know how to dust the baseboards," or "Why do I have to clean out the oven; it's just going to get dirty again?" you can call their bluff.

If they want to maintain this newfound freedom, they'll have to get a job to keep up the rent. Otherwise, they'll be sent back to rehab or put out on the street with nowhere to go, because you're not going to let them crash at your place. *Right*?

I know firsthand that many kids come into sober homes with absolutely no handle on any basic life skills. Why would they know how to do the laundry or make a doctor's appointment or even work the air conditioner? They got hooked on drugs at a young age, and all responsibility and awareness went out the window.

A sober home will force those life skills upon them. Of course the staff will be there to step in and answer questions, but your child will actually begin to learn the difference between dish soap and laundry detergent. These are little things, but they are the necessities that keep life running smoothly. It's best that they learn them in a controlled environment rather than out on their own.

Just to give you a clue about how oblivious most kids are (though you mothers probably have a pretty good idea). While working as a consultant at a sober home down in Florida, I started chatting to a kid doing his laundry. He told me he was having to do the wash in a rush because he didn't have any clean socks for work. I had a sneaking suspicion and opened the up the lid. There, swirling around in a huge vat of soapy water, was a single pair of socks. A whole load of laundry for one pair of socks. These sorts of things are what slip through the cracks while you're trying your hardest just to keep them alive and get them help for their addictions. A sober living home is where they start to make up for lost time and learn to take care of themselves.

Working, cleaning, living, and chasing after long-term sobriety with a group of peers will not only teach your child valuable life skills but also provide them with a sense of achievement and comradery. If they stick to the rules and actually apply themselves, they can take back control of their lives. That control feels good, and once they get a taste of it, they won't want to give it up.

# CHAPTER 12: HOMECOMING

THE DECISION TO ALLOW YOUR child to move back in with you is going to arise at some point in the process. Maybe your son went to rehab in a different state, and now that he's out, he wants to come home and stay with you for a bit before transitioning to a sober home. Maybe your daughter has been in the sober home for a good while and she's ready to strike out on her own, but she wants to stay with you until she finds the right apartment or home. You will get these sorts of calls often. An independent life is not easy, and young recovering addicts struggling to get a handle on life don't want the responsibility. Many times they choose to run from it by heading back home.

No matter the case, your child has been away for up to nine months, maybe more. Things have changed, and the home situation needs to change, too. New preparations should be made. No matter how many months it's been, some sober time doesn't mean an addict is cured, and coming back home could potentially be a move in the wrong direction.

If your kid comes back to live with you, it means returning to old stomping grounds, old friends, and old habits. Whenever I go back to the Philly area to see my parents, I don't like to stay for more than a few days, maybe just over the weekend. Otherwise, even now, I know that staying too long can potentially lead to traversing the same haunts, meeting up with the same old people, and doing the same old things. It has in the past. The calls to go out and the party WILL come. It happens every time I go back, not just the first few times. You tell yourself it will be different and that you will act differently, but in reality, the temptation to relive it all can convince you that the old life was better than it really was. It's too great a risk and should be avoided altogether. There is too much history in an addict's former home or hometown: old friends, old lovers, and all sorts of all-too-familiar things that the addict may not be ready to deal with yet.

Even just being in your home may bring the temptation to get high back into your child's head. It's an old environment, and it holds old memories and familiar places to hide drugs. It's easy to remember old arguments. It's easy to remember the things they did to you, the way they behaved. Those unpleasant memories may bring drugs back to the forefront of their mind.

If you're considering letting your kid come back and stay with you for a while, you need to take steps to weigh the pros and cons and to make absolutely sure it's the right move before committing.

## Test the Waters

Before you settle on anything regarding your child's possible return home, invite him or her to come back and stay for a week or two. It can't just be an over-the-weekend, go out to dinner, have some fun, and then go back sort of visit. It isn't a vacation.

You need to observe your son on a normal day and see what he does, what habits he leans toward, and what choices he makes in everyday situations. Observe who he calls and who he meets up with. See if he goes to AA meetings of his own volition. Is he asking around about jobs? Has he looked up a local therapist? Maybe he needs a slight nudge. Suggest those things once, and then see if he acts on them. You shouldn't have to repeat yourself over and over. He must be making a conscious, trackable effort to establish a life in your hometown. Otherwise, he isn't really serious about living there on his own; he's just wanting to piggyback off of you.

This is also a testing period for you. It may not create the healthiest dynamic to have your kid back in the house again. When your daughter is staying over for the week, do you find yourself questioning all her actions? Do you feel a little paranoid? Are you hovering? Do you find yourself hashing out old issues and old arguments in your head? If so, it would probably be better just to help her find a sober home, or if she's already been to one, help her find her own place.

Also question your motives for wanting to allow your kid back home. Is it simply because you miss him? If so, pull back. If inviting him back home is going to pull him away from a steady job and a recovery network he built during his stay at an out-of-state sober home, you shouldn't jeopardize that positive situation just because you miss him.

My mom misses me like crazy, but she knows and accepts that the Adam who lives here in Florida is better than the Adam who might exist if I moved back to Philly.

## Create a Contractual Agreement

There are a number of things you need to address before allowing your child back into your home. If you don't address rules and lay down the law about how you expect your child to behave while under your roof, your son or daughter may easily fall back into his or her old ways and ruin everything in just a few weeks' or even a few days' time.

I suggest writing up an actual contract that lays everything out. Make it clear that if any of the big clauses are violated, your child will have to find a new place to live, immediately.

I think it wise to follow the structure of a sober home as

closely as possible. That means, of course, a zero tolerance for drug use or drinking. If that clause is broken, it's straight back to treatment.

Make the rules stricter for the first 90 days. Set a curfew of 11 p.m. for weeknights and 1 a.m. on weekends. Require that your kid attends one AA/NA meeting per day and that he finds a sponsor within a set amount of days—roughly five should be enough time. Make sure he cleans his room and does a set list of chores. (If I were you, I would turn that room inside out before he comes back. Kids hide drugs in the craziest places. Flip everything over, go through all the clothes pockets, etc.)

Require that he work full time or attend school full time. If he's working, make him pay rent at a rate similar to a sober home: about $100 a week. If you feel bad about charging rent, let your kid know you're putting that money toward a new car for him or a down payment on a small house, but make sure you charge him something. His money ought to be going somewhere positive, and he must have the discipline to handle it wisely. You may want to see if you can get a hold of your kid's first month's paycheck at her new job and keep it for the whole month or hand it over in installments so that she won't be tempted to go grab some drugs from an old local dealer she knows or blow it all on childish things like video games and expensive shoes.

Just like a sober home, administer drug tests randomly about three times per week. You may be able to do a long-distance testing program with the rehab center, but if not, pay to mail in a test to a lab once a week and then use the instant, at-home test for the other two times. That way at least one test will be checked for a large number of drug panels.

Have your kid attend an outpatient group where she can talk to a therapist and handle the new changes, at least until she finds a job or gets enrolled in school. Check and see if her rehab facility has an online program where she can Skype with an outpatient therapist. Lay down the law about no friends over at your house and no sleeping at a friend's. She must return home by curfew every night. She must attend all scheduled doctor's appointments and take all her medications as prescribed. If she wants something special, other than basic necessities, she has to earn it in some way.

You may want to make a no smoking in the house rule or one that requires that your kid head to church every Sunday. Whatever concerns you have, lay them out in a rule and then stick to the contract.

After 90 days, you can start giving your child some small liberties like a later curfew, allowing a friend to come over every now and then, or letting him stay at his girlfriend's place for one night. Gradually ease back until you've restored independence and you feel confident in giving your child his or her freedom.

Trust that your kid will probably say yes to all of your requirements *at first*. Kids in this situation almost always want to come home because they've been fending for themselves for a while now, doing their own laundry and grocery shopping, and they decide they want to get back on easy street and come home to have Mom and Dad do everything again. When they realize Mom and/or Dad aren't going to play that way again, their agreeable attitude starts to slip. Be aware of this and monitor them closely so that they don't slip back into their old ways. If they do, hold fast to your new rules and make sure there are consequences.

If your kid whines about the contract, tough shit. If he wants to live there with you, he follows it. End of story. If he breaks the rules, there must be consequences. You can lay out varying levels of punishment. If your daughter doesn't show up to a doctor's appointment or is an hour late on curfew, her curfew is cut back or her phone is taken away for a week. However, for really serious things like her drug test comes back positive or she disappears for three days, the consequences must reflect the action. Serious offenses result in returning to treatment or getting sent directly to a sober home.

Ninety days with some strict rules is not too much to ask. Make it clear that the restrictions will ease up after that period. If your child plans to keep doing the right thing and get his or her life back in order, the contract shouldn't be an issue. Your child must earn back your trust and the life he or she wants. By laying out these rules, you're letting your kid know you're never again going to just sit back on pins and needles while he wreaks havoc.

## Get an MD Involved

Maybe your local family doctor is the one you briefed on your child's situation for the intervention. If so, great. If not, do so. It's imperative that you have a doctor on hand who knows what's going on and what stage of recovery your child is at. Set up an appointment as soon as your child moves back home, refill any needed medications, and monitor a medication management program.

## Find a Therapist

You probably already know a psychologist from the intervention process, but now that your child has been through rehab and hopefully discovered what issues are at the core of the use, he may need to see a specialist.

Unsure if you need to find a specialist? Get in touch with the therapist in charge of your child's care at the rehab center and ask. Your child may need a therapist who specializes in trauma, eating disorders, mental health disorders, etc. Make sure your child clicks with them because this is someone they should be seeing regularly for several months.

## Put on the Big Kid Pants

You don't need to be scheduling your kid's life; you have your own schedule to deal with. Once you've called up the doctor and found that specialist, it's time to step back and let your kid manage her own day to day life. She ought to set up her own appointments, and you shouldn't have to remind her and prod her to go. She should find her own NA meetings to attend and get up for work on time on her own. The holding your kid's hand days are over.

## Continual Care

It's never a bad idea to keep your child in some sort of professional program. See if you can find an aftercare program that just requires a quick session or two a week. Oceans Medical Centers offers an online aftercare program that allows our clients to keep in touch after they go home. Get in touch with the aftercare or alumni coordinator of your kid's center and ask if they provide something like that.

## Observe Their Attitude

Remember that over-the-top excitement and trying to convince you they're totally cured is one way addicts overcompensate. They aren't totally cured, and if they're covering up their real feelings, they may actually be dealing with severe doubts and temptations, but are trying to cover it up. You want to see sincerity as well as happiness. You want to see that your kid is working through his problems by acknowledging them, not acting like rehab was a magic cure-all that's made him never want to touch a needle again for as long as he lives.

You also need to watch out for a lack of motivation. This can manifest in negative talk, such as, "I'll never be able to ____," or "What's the point of ____?" Sleeping all day is bad news. Questioning the need for AA meetings spells trouble.

All of these are signs of backsliding. Relapse comes next. Be on the alert, and catch it before it happens.

## Meetings, Meetings, Meetings

In order to see better results and stay grounded in sobriety, it is essential for addicts to keep up with the same meetings they participated in during rehab. AA strongly encourages members to take part in the 90-in-90 challenge, in which addicts attend 90 meetings in 90 days upon release from rehab. Those 90 meetings can be arranged in whatever is most convenient—one a day for 90 days, two a day every other day, etc. The key is regularity. After the 90 days, it can be tapered off to 60 then to 30, but meetings need to remain a constant source of support and guidance in your child's life because they hold her accountable for her recovery.

## Keep Things Interesting

Addicts need motion and excitement—something to do to keep their minds off getting high or heading out to old haunts. Have some projects lined up, like things that need to get done around the house. Maybe the deck needs a new coat of paint. Maybe you need some landscaping done. Ask your child to help you.

Have outings and monthly fun activities planned so that your child has something to look forward to if she sticks to her schedule, goes to work and meetings, and sticks to your contract. These can be anything your kid likes to do: canoeing, going to see a baseball game, seeing a concert, etc.

Life needs to be cool and fun, or else getting high and saying goodbye to responsibilities looks like the better option. These activities can become something fun you do together. You need to repair your relationship; it's undoubtedly been damaged by the strain brought on by drugs. Just making the effort to arrange something fun every month rewards your child for positive behavior and occasionally lets you reconnect in the best way possible—sharing fun experiences. You don't need to go with them every time; in fact, avoid doing so. This isn't about smothering them, it's about getting them out into the world to have good, clean fun. They need to be going out with sober peers. Arrange to pay for a dinner out for your son and his sponsor. Tailor the rewards to what your child likes to do. If your son's into video games, one month's reward could be a gift card to GameStop. The goal here is to make your son or daughter realize that a sober life can be just as fun as and ten times more rewarding than a life fueled by drugs.

## Discuss Dating

In Chapter 17, I'm going to deal with the hazards of dating in detail, but for now just know that this is something that can make or break your child's success with sobriety. If the right partner turns up, he or she can provide your child with renewed motivation. However, the wrong relationship can lead to disaster. In a new relationship, people act irrationally, and sometimes they cling to the other person in an unhealthy, symbiotic way. So though it may sound invasive and not all that fun, keep an eye on the people your child dates, and voice your opinions about the significant other calmly and in confidence.

## Making Amends

Drugs are cruel. They care for no one. They only take. So there's a good chance that there are plenty of people in your hometown who were hurt by your child while he was under the influence of drugs. Make sure your child works to itemize the damage and make amends when possible. Maybe there are some family members or close friends your child stole from. Make sure your kid gets on the phone with those people and lets them know he's coming home and would like to make it up to them. When he gets in town, apologies should be made where needed.

Your child could have done something serious that might illicit retribution, and you need to know about that. Sit down with your child and ask. Did she have to give out the names of some not-so-nice people in a court case? Did he work over a drug dealer for cash and supplies? You need to know these things.

Does he have some warrants out on him that he never told you about? You need to settle these things or at least have a course of action before he comes back into the state.

When dealing with any of these issues, you want to minimize uncomfortable or high stress situations as best as possible. If Aunt Janie is a bit of a loose cannon and she might verbally attack your child when she tries to make her apology, maybe that apology can be left unsaid for a while. Too much stress on your child at this point in recovery is something you want to avoid, but on the other hand, do your best to get all the cards on the table pretty quickly. As soon as you get all the ghosts out of the closet, there is no reason to hide.

## Get a Job

This could potentially be a huge hurdle. I've met many kids who really, really don't want to work, and they fight it hard. It could be that your child got the notion of coming back home because he was sick of having to pay his own way at the sober home, and he thought to himself that maybe Mom and Dad would let him skate by on freebies again.

That's why you need to have a conversation about what you expect well before your child comes home. I've known parents who actually made their kid get a job position lined up before they allowed the kid back into their home. I think it's a good idea. You could have your kid go out and try to find something during that week-long trial period.

Getting a job is vital for reasons beyond integrating your kid back into society and giving him or her responsibility. Think about it. The last thing you want is to have your kid sitting at home alone all day when everyone else is out at school or work. That's a recipe for complete and utter disaster.

## Finding Purpose

In order for your child to maintain a desire to stay sober, his sober life needs to somehow be cooler and more engaging than his life on drugs. Your kid needs a purpose, an underlying desire that gives him the drive to get things done. Your kid needs to feel he or she belongs somewhere, that there is something in his or her life to look forward to, something to accomplish. Perhaps your son wants to be a firefighter. Encourage him to take the exam. Being a firefighter is cooler than being a drug addict. Maybe your daughter wants to be an internet mogul someday. Getting a job as an app designer is cooler than being a drug addict.

I love what I do. It's rewarding, and it's a whole lot more fun than my old life. My job keeps me busy and productive; I don't even have time to consider using again.

Help your child work out what he wants to do in life and then help and encourage him to push forward to achieve it.

Maybe you want to even evaluate your own life. Are you doing something that gives you a purpose, something that fulfills your inner desires? If you aren't, start looking for it. It's never too late. You and your child can reach for your desires together. Once you begin to fulfill that desire, the hard work doesn't seem so hard because you're doing what you love.

## Drill Home the Habits

Good things come from good habits. Your child has begun to dump old destructive habits as a result of treatment. Now it's time to pick up new ones. Your child has probably already picked up some new habits at the treatment center and the sober home, but those habits must be continued as your kid makes the transition of coming home.

If you see your child practicing a good habit, praise it, and keep an eye out to make sure your kid sticks with it. Help them foster new good habits like reading self-help or motivational books. Encourage positive hobbies that lead to personal betterment. Athletics better the body. Reading and learning better the mind. Religion, meditation, and therapy better the soul.

Help your kid drop bad habits like smoking or even cursing (I struggle with that last one, personally). Buy your son his first set of patches and gum. Make your daughter put money in a swear jar. At the same time, reward your child for good behavior. Show up at her sporting events. Give him a treat of some sort for good grades. Feeling your support and praise for the good things he or she does will encourage your son or daughter to continue those habits.

## The Importance of Sleep

This is a big one for me due to my bipolar disorder. It's a good idea for everyone to maintain a healthy sleeping schedule. It keeps the days running smoothly and helps prevent burnout that can lead to dangerous downtime.

Your child needs a full eight hours of sleep at decent times. No going to bed at 3 a.m. and waking up at 11 a.m. A curfew can help you regulate this. They ought to head to bed when curfew hits. You can encourage this further by creating a rule like no TV on downstairs after midnight.

Don't just implement the rule, explain why it's there. That way it doesn't turn into a "because I said so" situation. Good sleep keeps the body energized and the mind on track.

Make a rule that your kid has to make his bed every morning before work or before heading out on the weekends. That keeps him getting up at a decent hour to get stuff done before he has to leave.

## People, Places, Things

During their rehab program, your child will learn that people, places, and things can trigger feelings that may push an addict toward bad behavior or relapse. Your child has to think about and discover those triggers and avoid them. Any people or places from days of heavy use is a definite trigger because those things evoke memories, and in those memories your child was high.

Keep an eye out on who your child is hanging out with and where your child goes. Don't let your kid convince you it's okay for them to go hang out with that old friend who's still strung out just to reminisce about old times. Reminiscence in itself is dangerous, not to mention the influence of someone who is still using.

## Stay Open

When your kid comes home, it's time to implement the 2.0 version of yourself to match the changes your son or daughter has made in his or her life. You're now armed with all the education needed to move forward and create a new way of life for everyone.

You must keep an open mind. Having your kid back in your house may trigger old emotions of stress and anger that must be pushed away. You can't be judgmental and bring up old crap. This is about moving on.

Don't be too harsh. Don't take personal jabs at your kid or put too much pressure on her. There is a fine balance between being harsh and being tough. You need the rules, but the rules must be reasonable requirements that will actually help your child. You can't just employ rules left and right with no real purpose in mind.

The biggest thing you can do for your child at this stage is be supportive. You need to set aside time to give specially to your child and talk things out, even if the conversations get uncomfortable.

This whole arrangement of coming home is going to be strange at first, and difficult. To get through it, you have to stay flexible and be receptive to what your kid needs to do and think about what part you play in those things.

## Be Sensitive to Their Temptations

Just because your kid has been sober for a while doesn't mean he's not an addict anymore. Your child will face enough temptation without you unwittingly presenting it to him.

If you like drinking wine or beer while laid back on the couch after a long day at work, I hate to break it to you, but if your kid is coming to live with you, you can't do that anymore. At least not when she's in the house. You getting tipsy every night is not a good thing for someone in recovery to see. Seeing alcohol on the counter or in the fridge can also be a trigger.

The best plan is to get all of that stuff out of the house, but if you can't part with it, lock it up. Your pills, too. You could even keep your medications at work, far out of your kid's reach. You have to make sure there is not anything in the house to compromise your child's sobriety. Just opening a medicine cabinet and seeing some pain pills on the shelf can set off a battle in an addict's head. You don't want your son or daughter to have to fight that battle in your own home. Home should be a place to relax and get away from the outside world, a sanctuary where they can rest and feel safe.

## Don't Get Stagnant

If life gets stale, the temptation of drugs grows significantly larger. You must push your child to be active, both physically and mentally.

If your daughter is waiting for classes to start, give her a book on something she enjoys, introduce her to a new game she can puzzle over, or drop her off at the library. The point is to keep her mind active just like it would be in classes. If your son hasn't got a job yet, make sure he's going out and actively looking for one for the majority of his day. He needs to be working even when he's not working.

Yes, everyone deserves a break at some point, but for former addicts any sort of break is a break in their routine, which can open up negative situations and allow negative thoughts to creep in. If something in their life is making them a degree off today, in a few more days, they could be five or ten degrees off. That is a recipe for relapse. Former addicts must stay busy throughout the day and stick to a schedule. When breaks happen, they need to be planned in advance, and they should be a one-day event.

## Conclusion

I've laid out the details of what can go wrong when your child moves back in, and some ways you can steer things away from disaster, but there is one thing that encompasses all of that stuff and makes it a lot easier.

Life with a recovering addict living in your home will be so much easier if you are open about your feelings and if you initiate conversations with your child. Vocalize any concerns you have and then work together to create ways to overcome them.

Maybe you ought to make a contract for yourself. Vow to talk. Vow to stick by your rules. Vow to support and not judge. Let your child see that contract as well as the one you made for him.

Make time for your kid. As this chapter has made abundantly clear, you must pay attention to your child's actions and moods. That shouldn't be done like a stalker, lurking around in dark corners and peering out at your child from a distance. The best way to know what your kid is doing and who she's doing it with is to reestablish trust by being there and asking her face-to-face in casual daily conversation.

Strive with all your might to do things right this time around. Apply what you've learned, stick to your own contract, and then no matter how things end up—whether your child relapses or goes on to live completely drug free until the day he dies—you know that you did everything you could. You spoke to him when you observed both good and bad behaviors. You offered proper, well thought out advice. You got him into the programs that got him clean, and you continued to help him progress through recovery with the ultimate goal of allowing him to live a fruitful, independent life.

# CHAPTER 13: AA/NA SUPPORT GROUPS

ONE DAY AT A TIME. You will hear this said frequently among recovering addicts. That's because it's a staple at AA and NA meetings. It embodies the realities of a recovering addict's life. The only way to keep pushing forward toward an independent, successful, and fulfilling drug-free life without getting bogged down by all the major adjustments is to take it one day at a time. If you ever sense your child is becoming overwhelmed, you can instill great comfort simply by reminding them of another AA favorite: "Just for today."

You may have already picked up on the prominence of AA and NA meetings during the recovery process. There is a reason rehab centers and sober living homes mostly all require attendance at these community support group meetings. The main reason is that they provide a structured environment where addicts can make recordable progress toward recovery with the support of like-minded peers. Yes, your child will get group therapy in rehab, but AA and NA meetings are more tightly woven into the community itself. They are also free, and your son or daughter can attend them for as long as he or she needs without having to worry about what insurance covers. Make it a habit to ask your child if he or she might want to try and hit a meeting, especially when you catch him or her lying around the house in the middle of the day.

Since these groups play such an integral role in the life of an addict, familiarizing yourself with Alcoholics Anonymous and what it requires will help you better chart your child's progress and get a better understanding of what is required for long-term sober success.

## The History of Alcoholics Anonymous

Alcoholics Anonymous was founded in 1935 by stockbroker Bill Wilson and Dr. Bob Smith. Both men struggled with alcoholism and found that sobriety was easier to achieve when surrounded by others in similar situations. Bill Wilson achieved sobriety first, with the help of a clergyman, Dr. Samuel Shoemaker. Wilson found that meeting with other alcoholics still seeking sobriety gave him a worthwhile purpose that pushed him to stay sober himself. When Dr. Bob Smith met Wilson, he found that talking to someone who not only understood the struggles of alcoholism firsthand but had also overcome them gave him hope that he could do the same. Under Wilson's guidance, Smith achieved sobriety, making the pair AA's first sponsor success story. They wanted to repeat this relationship-building in order to help others like them, and Alcoholics Anonymous was born. Wilson wrote the group's textbook—otherwise known as the Big Book, in 1939—which outlined the now famous Twelve Steps of Alcoholics Anonymous. The Twelve Steps are the core of the program.

The program has anonymous in the name, so a common practice is for members to just go by their first name and last initials. However, as addiction is becoming more widely recognized as a disease, this anonymous trend is changing. Addicts should not feel shame for their problems, especially among other addicts. Many are coming to believe there is no need to hide identities anymore.

Another staple is the Serenity Prayer, which reads, "God, grant me the serenity to accept the things I cannot change, courage to change the things I can, and wisdom to know the difference." Meetings close with this prayer, and faith is an underlying theme within the Big Book's core values and ideals. One of their common slogans is, "Let go and let God." Some other popular ones are, "Fake it till you make it," and the KISS anagram, which stands for "Keep it simple, stupid."

Another cornerstone is the bestowing of sobriety chips to members as a representation of the days they have remained sober. The chips are medallions or coins roughly the size of a poker chip, and different colors represent different lengths of sobriety. At NA, they often hand out keychains rather than chips, but the idea is the same. On their first day at AA, members receive the 24 hour white sobriety chip. The white represents cleansing. The coins are a symbolic representation of an accomplishment. Is a piece of metal going to keep your child sober? No. But it will remind them of what they've already achieved and acknowledge that the effort made to get there is worth rewarding. It can act as a motivational tool to get to the next step. After the 24-hour mark, chips are handed out at 30 days, 60 days, 90 days, 6 months, 9 months, and then every year of sobriety. Every chip is presented with a sort of mini ceremony where the person's name and clean time is announced to the group, and everyone applauds the achievement. Personally, I think this practice can be a double-edged sword. On one hand, the addict looks at that chip when he feels a craving and says, "I've got six months; I'm not going to screw this up," and it helps him stay on the right path. However, if a slip-up does occur, counting those days can hit hard. The addict thinks, "I had four months, and I just threw it all away." He beats himself up, and that shame may keep him from attending meetings. Attendance is key, as studies have shown that AA's success rate is largely if not solely due to the fact that it requires addicts to just show up and interact with others. That interaction is the best motivation. If your child slips, and you pick up on that guilt, the best thing you can do is drive him or her to that next meeting yourself.

## Extreme Accessibility

One of the great things about support groups is that they are so readily available and easy to attend. You are now familiar with how many hoops you have to jump through to get your child into detox, rehab, and a sober home. No heavy lifting is required with AA and NA meetings. True, they aren't as structured or professional as a group or one-on-one therapy session in rehab, but they are entirely free and take place pretty much all day long. This means your child can find a meeting whenever they are feeling the lure of drugs. Instead of seeking out a dealer, they can seek out a meeting instead, and they will be able to find one easily. AA and NA groups are a global phenomenon. They take place in church halls, club houses, and all sorts of public places.

When I was a kid, the odd group of people standing outside the church by my favorite convenience store always caught my attention. They were always smoking outside on Friday night, and they didn't look like my idea of "church people." I could never solve the mystery of who they were or what they were doing there, sending clouds of smoke into the night air on the church steps. Little did I know that 15 years later, I would be one of them.

## The Downside

Let's go ahead and get the shortcomings out of the way. The reason you can't just send your child to AA and NA meetings instead of rehab is because they are a casual, non-mandatory thing (unless you're in a rehab program that requires them for a certain period). The medical help and rigorous structure are not present. However, some people mistakenly believe that these support groups are a quick fix. Parents pressure their kids to go there, or addicts attend of their own volition just to get loved ones off their back.

As a result, your child may come across people at these

meetings who are making no real effort to change. In fact, they will show up high, and this can act as a trigger for your child. That's why it's great to have your kid in a program that sends them to these meetings with peers in the same rehab or sober home. If your child goes with someone they know who is actively making an effort, they will be more insulated and less likely to wander toward those sky high attendees and ask for help getting a fix.

## Getting In and Staying In

It is recommended that during early recovery, an addict becomes an AA or NA member and attends 90 meetings in 90 days. If your child is on probation or has any sort of legal trouble, they may be also be required to get a sheet signed by the group chair of every meeting. The group chair brings the meetings into session and keeps things on course. After the meeting is over, they will sign their name, the date, and the meeting location on the sheet as proof that your child attended the full session.

There are many different meeting types that apply to both AA and NA groups. When looking up meetings, you will come across these abbreviations:

- O = Open Speaker. This means the public is welcome. It's a sort of introductory meeting where people can see if they want to join the program.
- C = Closed. This means members only.
- OD = Open Discussion. This means that the discussion is for anyone suffering from any addiction.
- CD = Closed Discussion. This means that the topic of discussion is only for alcoholics (AA) or only for those addicted to narcotics (NA) specifically.
- CS = Closed Speaker. Usually, this means one person comes in as a guest speaker and talks the whole time.

- SD = Speaker Discussion. This means all of the members share their stories.
- BB = Big Book Discussion. The Big Book is the guidebook for the whole program.
- 12 = 12 Step Meeting. At this meeting, attendees will specifically work on progressing through the 12 steps.
- T = 12 Tradition Meeting. Like the 12 Steps, the 12 Traditions are simply another category in the Big Book. This meeting will deal with progressing through them.
- M = Men only.
- W = Women only.
- Beginner's Meeting = For people just starting out as a member. These take place about an hour and a half before the regular meetings.
- YP = Young People.
- NS = No Smoking at this meeting.
- G = Gay, Lesbian, Bisexual, and Transgender.
- # = Must Sign to Enter.
- H = This symbol is usually found at the end of the listed address, and it means that the meeting is accessible for people with disabilities.

Your child will have attended the beginner meetings back in rehab. By the time they are in aftercare, they will be full-fledged members hopefully making their way through the 12 steps. They can attend whichever meetings they want, so long as they attend regularly.

In places like South Florida and California, where recovery is abundant and , and other major cities, AA and NA programs will have their own club houses that have separate rooms for all of the different types of meetings. If there aren't any club houses near your child, that's fine, it just means that everything isn't all in one place.

There are many different types of groups that deal with many subcategories. For instance, there is CA, which is cocaine anonymous. However, the two biggest are AA and NA. AA is actually the largest of the two, and its guidebook, the Big Book or Blue Book, is the one that all of the other programs' individualized books are based off. (Each program will also provide a workbook that helps participants chart their way through the steps.)

That's why anyone can attend an AA meeting, even if drinking is not their particular problem. The principles for recovery and staying sober are the same. In fact, you may want to advise your child to go to an AA meeting or two even if they struggle with narcotics because the AA crowd is usually more mature and has more experience. Many of the people there will be a great influence, and one may even end up being a great sponsor to your child.

Another piece of advice you want to make sure your child hears is to pick a regular meeting time that isn't a strain on their new schedule. An addict needs structure to stay on track, so it is highly recommended that they attend a meeting in the same time slot to make it part of their routine. Jumping from meeting to meeting can lead to relapse because your child can easily fall into the habit of saying "Oh, I'll just attend the later one today," but then they forget or just don't go. Attending support groups should become a habit. Same time every day of the week. That regular meeting slot becomes your child's "Home Group," which forms greater comradery and accountability than sporadic meetings ever could.

## Sponsors

A sponsor is an essential part of the program. The idea is simple, but has a huge impact. Two members who click over a shared interest or a hardship or anything make a commitment to help each other through the 12 steps. When members feel themselves slipping backward or if something triggers the urge to use, they are taught to call their sponsor immediately. Sometimes the group sessions themselves can be a trigger because they require everyone to face the causes of their addictions and talk about upsetting things. If turning to a sponsor becomes an automatic response, though, it acts as a shield against relapse. Instead of responding to a trigger, they make a phone call to their sponsor.

Going into the program, your child must understand that a sponsor should be someone with a significantly larger amount of clean time than him. A sponsor is a beacon of leadership who helps you work through the steps he or she has already completed. If your child is 30 days clean and he buddies up with a guy in the exact same boat, it's great that he's found a likeminded friend, but that friend won't make a good sponsor. That new friend can't give your son solid advice on how to complete a step if he hasn't done it himself. A sponsor is both friend and guide who will work with your child both in an out of meetings to do step work and study the Big Book. Ideally, a sponsor has similar interests to your child, but experience is the real key. AA and NA are about giving back to others, and sponsorship is the main way that goal is achieved.

During my time in AA, I chose the guy with 25 years of sobriety behind him and the nicest car in the parking lot (Hi, Ralph!). Turned out to be a good choice. He was very supportive, and a phone call from him was just about the best thing I could ask for when feeling down.

## The Full Scope

There are two main group types in AA/NA: Home Groups and Commitments. Your child's Home Group is the one they are never to miss. It's with the same people at the same time with the same group chair. This group is your child's main source of networking, socializing, support, and volunteering. Commitments are the outside speaker meetings, where someone in the fellowship volunteers to speak at a treatment center or rehab. These occur daily, just like the Home Groups, but it isn't essential for everyone in the program to attend them all the time. The main idea behind these types of meetings is "giving back what was so freely given to you."

The program encourages volunteering in many small ways. I'm not talking about bake sales or rallies or picking trash off the side of the road. But someone has to set up the chairs and make the coffee. Someone has to plan outside conventions and fun outings with the fellowship. Someone will need to bring food to those events. Everyone there has suffered with addiction on some level. The meetings themselves are free, but the program has to stay afloat somehow. There's always a donation basket passed around. People usually only give a dollar or two, but hey, these are people who have just gotten back into the job force. There's no judgement about the size of donations. There's no "mommy figure" who takes care of everything, so small acts of generosity and helpfulness have to be taken up by everyone.

In helping each other out, working together to set up meetings, and sharing their experiences, the people in a home group begin to form a strong bond. The fellowship encourages this even more by setting up special outings like group softball games. These activities usually require the groups to work together, strengthening their friendship so that they automatically turn to their fellow group members in times of need. But there's a delicate balance to be had. Support groups aren't just for clowning around and making buddies. The core of the group discussions and steps is tailored to keep your child focused on their recovery and continued sobriety.

## Other Options

AA and NA aren't going to click with everyone, and that's okay. If your child is refusing to go to AA or shows no enthusiasm for the program after attending a number of meetings, ask why. If your son or daughter simply hates the program and isn't connecting with it or the people, know that there are alternatives. Here are some options to consider.

*Rational Recovery*: This program, based on a book of the same name, concedes that things like alcoholism are diseases but does not adhere to the idea that addiction itself is a disease. Instead, this program centers around the idea that addiction is a separate disorder (not a byproduct) from diseases like alcoholism, and that this disorder can be abandoned with the correct application of will. Its core method is called the Addictive Voice Recognition Technique, which seeks to help addicts make those willful, deliberate steps toward shaking their addictive habits.

*SMART Recovery* (self-management and recovering training): this program is developed to work whether you adhere to the idea of addiction as a disease or not. It focuses on helping addicts recognize environmental and emotional factors that contribute to their addictive behaviors and counteract them with productive new strategies. The program also includes motivational interviews to empower members to not see themselves as a victim of disease but as strong individuals able to take back control and balance their lives.

*My Way Out*: This program is based in medicine. It seeks to use a mixture or medications, natural supplements, hypnotherapy, and exercise to fully detox the body of adverse substances and combat the destructive behaviors of addiction.

These are just a few options available to you. If AA and NA aren't working out, try as many of these alternative groups as necessary. The most important thing is to help your child find a group that speaks to their personal needs and preferences so that they have an adequate support system of peers and leaders around them for their continued sobriety journey.

## Church

Most AA and NA programs work on the assumption that there is a higher power, whatever yours may be, and they try to impart that on members. Personally, mine is Christianity and God. I was raised Catholic, and I sometimes still go to mass, but I have since turned more to Protestant churches. The modern Christian churches, especially, have great bands and a casual feel that I find inviting. Many of them house AA and NA meetings or have some form of support for recovering addicts. Today, you don't get so much of the Bible beating, especially if you pick the right congregation. Churches have come a long way in that regard since I was young, and I think it's worth looking into. It might be a good idea to encourage your child to attend a service and give the atmosphere a chance. Churches nowadays really help a lot of addicts.

If your child does have a sense of a higher power but doesn't like the more formal feel of a regular church service, suggest they attend a bible study or other church group. These will provide spiritual support that uplift moods and bolster hope.

I got into men's Bible study because, while on supervised release, I became friends with a man who had done 25 years in jail for manslaughter who recommended his group. He was older, and he really took me under his wing. He said it was really helping him out, and he asked me to tag along and see what I thought. This particular group was made up entirely of men who had suffered from some sort of addiction, but we didn't talk about drugs. We read a Bible verse and discussed it for an hour. We talked about what it means to be a man, what it means to grow up, what it takes to do the right thing, and how God touches our lives in ways that mold us for the better

Almost everyone there had been sober far longer than I had, and they held me accountable. In a lot of ways, it was like an NA group, but the key difference was that we didn't dwell on drug use and drug related problems.

A Bible study group, especially one like I was lucky enough to find made up of fellow former addicts, works as a support system that deals with life and living it to the fullest. AA and NA are crucial, but once your child gets a significant amount of clean time under their belt, they are going to need to move on from those general groups and find something that's an expansion of the idea without the constant drug-related topics. It's always best, too, if your kid can find a group that is gender specific. The genders tend to clam up more around each other. The conversation is more open and the level of comfort is higher when members are amongst the same gender.

A Bible study group is a great support system to seek out during recovery because its positive effects can extend beyond aftercare. Once your child has gone through all the recovery steps, they can grow complacent and lazy, and little by little they can be corrupted again—if not by the same addiction, then by a new one. A Bible study group is a great way to keep them on a pure life track by keeping moral values at the forefront.

## Non-Profits for Parents

You and your family have not come out of this unscathed. You probably need some sort of recovery support too. You need someone to turn to when you're feeling low—someone who understands. Don't be afraid to seek out help. There are free support groups for you as well.

I already touched on Al-Anon. That's one of the biggest support groups for families of addicts. Just like AA, it focuses primarily on alcohol abuse, but the basic principles are the same and they welcome others.

There is also a non-profit called The Addict's Mom which focuses specifically on mothers of narcotics addicts. They have meetings and forums where they implement their motto, "Share without Shame."

Another reputable one is Recovery Advocates of America. They cover the whole scope of recovery and work with addicts and their families on many levels.

You can find local chapters of the larger support groups or local meetings by non-profits in your area online. Just know that there are many groups out there for your child with others who have been in her shoes and are now committed to helping. Whether your child's underlying issue is mental health, addiction, medical, or grief related, there are groups for everything. Your child can find people to help her and commune with her, and it works.

## Conclusion

Support groups are an integral part of the rehab and recovery process because they show results. They give your child ties to the community and provide a peer-based support system that becomes like a second family.

As a result, the meetings should become something they look forward to. They should be a pleasant commitment and not a chore. If your son or daughter starts talking about not needing to go, that's when you need to encourage him or her to go. It is when addicts become complacent and think they no longer need meetings that relapse occurs.

If your child can find and commit to a home group and stay accountable to the people and rules of that group, they will have established a strong foundation that will hopefully keep them rooted in a sober life for years and years to come.

I am a success story of these groups. I saw the miracles that can be worked in those environments firsthand. Trust the process and be open to change, and change will happen.

# CHAPTER 14:
# ADDRESSING MENTAL HEALTH

MENTAL HEALTH ISSUES ARE INCREDIBLY common amongst addicts. This is because nine out of ten addicts start using around age 13. When used during these early formative years, drugs slow down development. As a result, teens are more prone to make bad decisions. This postponed mental development can also bring out an underlying mental issue faster. Mental illnesses, just like the addiction gene, can lie dormant in the form of a switch in the brain. If that switch exists, drugs will flip it on as soon as they walk through the door. During early stages of life, the body doesn't have all the necessary natural coping mechanisms, and things can quickly spiral out of control. That is why it is so vital to make mental health care just as much a priority as regular rehab (or even more so). Rehab, in all honesty, can seem like a shot in the dark. It doesn't have the greatest success rate. Mental health treatment, on the other hand, has a significantly larger percentage of success. This is why Oceans actively strays from the structure of bubblegum addiction programs and puts a heavy focus on mental health treatment.

The term mental health or mental health disorder can make many shy away. Only in recent years have physicians and society at large truly come to view it as an ailment on the same level as ordinary medical problems like strep throat or arthritis. The taboo surrounding mental health disorders sprang from the medical community's initial inability to truly identify the cause of such conditions and the public's inability to comprehend the complexities of such conditions.

The brain is a beautiful but extraordinarily complex thing that we are yet to fully understand, and the smallest nuances in a brain's makeup can create idiosyncrasies in behavior. The idea that "something is wrong with my brain" is scary, but it's really a misunderstanding. Mental health can be healed just like a regular medical condition, and a person affected by a mental health disorder doesn't have a deformed brain—their brain just functions differently than others. While physical health deals with the function of the body, mental health deals with the psychological and emotional well-being of a person.

Recently, new schools of thought are arising that propose that everyone should undergo an annual psychological health examination, just like a yearly physical. Politicians and doctors and public figures are beginning to work toward erasing the social stigma surrounding mental illness and ensuring that it is always taken seriously and addressed in the proper manner.

At one time, mental illness was not considered an insurable condition by any insurance company. In the past, mental health has been seen as a ruse—a way for parents to shrug off a child's inappropriate behavior or for people to try and excuse themselves from consequences. That's been proven false time and time again. Still, people have tried to hush up the mental illness of a family member for fear of embarrassment or to protect the affected loved one from the judgement of others. Thankfully, though, times are changing.

There are classifications for mental illnesses, ranging from very minor to extremely severe, and now insurance companies cover all of them. The facts are coming out into the open and professionals are learning more and more about how to help those in need.

While mental health conditions can be handled by a primary care physician, a true psychiatrist is the best guide for assisting in coping with mental illness symptoms.

Mental illness is not something to be afraid of. Please let your child know that. If they are diagnosed with a mental health disorder, let them know you don't think they're a freak. They aren't. Hiding the condition and trying to ignore it only allows it to grow into a true beast that can take over a person completely. Help is now readily available, and it does produce results. Why keep it caged and foaming at the mouth when you can let it out and tame it through skilled care?

## My Bipolar Disorder Diagnosis

When I was young, I was an extreme motor mouth. I'd talk so fast I was unintelligible. I'd get so excited my eyes would bug out of my head. I was labeled (often with a tone of slight amusement) a hypermaniac. The term ADD was slung around a lot, too, but never with any real seriousness. I always performed well in school; my hyper attitude never affected my grades. So, nobody ever even thought to question my mental state. However, as I got older, my mania became destructive.

I would excel at anything I tried ... for a short while. I would be hyper focused and extra enthusiastic about whatever project I had in mind for myself next. But then I would suddenly burn out, and I'd mess up the opportunities I'd set up for myself. My life became a pattern of doing exceptionally good, then crashing and burning. During the crashes—and honestly, even during the mania—I felt that something wasn't right. I wasn't in control. I turned to drugs during the crashes to try and reach that mania high again. First it was pot, but that wasn't quite right; it didn't give me that overly energetic buzz. That's when cocaine came in.

Essentially, I was self-medicating, trying to balance myself out. That's no excuse for picking up drugs. There's always another solution; it was my choice to seek out drugs as the answer. But the up and down rollercoaster of my mental state was what made me look for a solution in the first place. It's just that I, like many others before and after me, pursued the wrong solution.

When I was on a mental high, working on a huge project that I just knew would work out great, I didn't do drugs. I didn't feel I needed them then. But once that big project was over or if it fell through, I would have way too much downtime on my hands, and that's when I would relapse.

After I got casted onto the TV show *Big Brother* and actually won the damn thing, it fueled my mania even further. While I was on the show, I was completely clean. After I won, I was shuttled around the country to parties and TV appearances with a half million dollars in my pockets. Those parties had drugs galore. I was riding the aftermath of a big project. I slipped back into the life.

That's when I got arrested for selling pills. I didn't care I'd been arrested; I was simply devastated by the thought that I couldn't do coke. I had nothing but downtime while sitting in jail, and I wanted to feel the high more than anything. Instead, I got into a rehab program for six months and then did outpatient rehabilitation while living at my parents' house to start getting my life back in order.

I was clean, but something still wasn't right. Something still felt off, but I knew it couldn't be drugs. I did some research and began to suspect that I might be bipolar. So when I found out about a medical study on bipolar disorder being conducted at the University of Pennsylvania, I applied to see if I would qualify to participate. The main doctor met with me and said I wasn't eligible, but not because I wasn't bipolar. I just didn't fit the exact parameters of this specific study. The doctor told me he believed I was in fact bipolar, and he looked me in the eye and said, "You're not going to suffer anymore; I'm going to get you better."

I was put into psychotherapy and a mental health outpatient program. Sure enough, I was diagnosed with Bipolar Mania One and put on the proper medications to stabilize my mood and behavior. I was taught to get plenty of exercise during the day to expend all that extra energy and to make sure I actually slept right at night to keep myself healthy. Now my ups aren't crazy high and my downs aren't nearly as long. I feel like me again, and healing my mental state opened my eyes to a life I never imagined could exist for me.

Rehab got me off drugs, but that mental health treatment program saved my life.

## First Layer of the Onion

As I've discussed before in this book, the rehab center may admit your child under a dual diagnosis if they have already been diagnosed with a mental illness. However, there is a huge difference between a dual diagnosis and an actual mental health treatment program. Most rehabs can only admit clients for addiction, but they treat secondary conditions like mental health on the side during specialized group sessions. However, some of these rehabs don't even have a true psychiatric team, and that leads to piss poor treatment. Some programs can admit clients solely for mental health as well as for substance abuse, like Oceans Medical Centers. Those are the programs you want because it means that they are fully staffed in both areas. Either way, someone suffering from a mental health condition also needs to go into a mental health treatment facility *after* drug rehab, in my opinion.

There are two reasons for this. One, it takes time—somewhere in the range of two months of close observation—

to accurately diagnose a mental illness. If your child's first evaluation is in rehab, there may not be time to both diagnose and fully address the issue before release. Two, sometimes things like ADD and depression will subside after the drug abuse stops because the drugs are actually causing those conditions. After your child completes rehab and has been clean for 6 months (whether actually inside rehab or after it), get them a new examination and diagnosis. Once they are sober, there may still be an untreated mental illness affecting their ability to move forward and live a true recovered, healthy lifestyle.

More often than not, drugs are just the first layer of the onion and a mental health condition may be a driving force behind your child's drug use. However, it's only when the drugs are taken away that the underlying problem can be seen clearly.

I cannot stress enough the importance of preparing to address your child's underlying mental health. Prepare for it even if you don't think that your child actually has a mental illness. You never know, and if you aren't aware of the possibility, your child can suffer. Some rehab facilities without a real mental health program will keep a patient who is suffering from mental illness in the program for substance abuse without truly addressing the motivation behind it. The client knows something isn't right, and the facility just tells them that they need some more substance abuse help because they want to keep the money coming in, even though the client doesn't need that particular kind of help anymore. Other times, the insurance money runs out while the client is still scrambling to figure out what's wrong, and then they are removed from the rehab facility and put into a loop of housing programs that don't address mental health, leaving the client to fend for his or herself.

Always prepare to get your child into some sort of outpatient program that teaches them how to cope with mental illness as well as the substance abuse component. You never know if they might need it.

## Common Types of Mental Illness

Bipolar I:

Symptoms – severe mood swings, hypermania followed or preceded by a period of low mood/sadness, fully manic with heightened excitement, heightened irritability, decreasing appetite, rash/impulsive decisions, distractibility

Common Medications – Olanzapine, Quetiapine, Risperidone, Ariprazole, Ziprasidone, Clozapine, Trazodone

Bipolar II:

Symptoms – severe depression followed or preceded by mania, difficulty sleeping, loss of energy, inability to concentrate, poor mood, suicidal thoughts

Common Medications – Olanzapine, Quetiapine, Risperidone, Ariprazole, Ziprasidone, Clozapine, Trazodone

Attention Deficit Disorder (ADD):

Symptoms – Inattentive, inability to concentrate, highly energetic and impulsive

Common Medications – Ritalin, Adderall, Dexedrine

Depression:

Symptoms – difficulty sleeping, loss of energy, inability to concentrate, poor mood, suicidal thoughts

Common Medications – Trazodone, Sertraline, Fluoxetine, Citalopram, Escitalopram, Paroxetine, Fluvoxamine

Anxiety Disorders:

Symptoms – inability to relax, constant concern, sweaty palms, nervousness/fear, palpitations, upset stomach

Common Medications – Prozac, Luvox, Zoloft, Paxil, Celexa, Lexapro

Obsessive Compulsive Disorder (OCD):

Symptoms – obsessive, ritualized, or excessive behaviors that the sufferer is aware of but cannot stop

Common Medications – clomipramine, Prozac, Zoloft, Paxil

Post-Traumatic Stress Disorder (PTSD):

Symptoms – persistent frightening memories of a traumatic experience, episodes of extreme fear, emotional numbness

Common Medications – Prozac, Zoloft, Paxil, Prazosin, Clonidine

Eating Disorders:

Symptoms – some sufferers may refuse to eat or throw up what they eat to lose weight rapidly, while others may gorge themselves when not actually hungry

Schizophrenia:

Symptoms – hallucinations (auditory, visual, tactile, or olfactory), paranoia, odd delusions/ideas

Common Medications – Haldol, Clozapine, Geodon, Seroquel, Risperdal, Zyprexa, Abilify

Impulse Disorders:

Symptoms – there are various unique impulse disorders (trichotillomania, kleptomania, intermittent explosive disorder), and the symptoms range from pulling out hair to impulsive theft to bursts of rage, but all display an inability to control an irrational impulsive behavior

Common Medications – Prozac, Luvox, Zoloft, Effexor

<u>Tic Disorders/Tourette's:</u>

Symptoms – sudden, erratic, uncontrollable movements of a body part like the eye, hands, face, etc. that is not stimulated by a substance or other medical disorder

Common Medication – Prolixin, Haldol, Risperdal, Zyprexa

## Plan to Address It

If you suspect a mental illness may be the hidden motivator your child is trying to uncover in therapy, there needs to be a course of action in place. If they get enrolled into a rehab with a dual diagnoses, great, but they will need more than that at some point.

Check your insurance policy and make sure it offers benefits for mental health treatment as well as substance abuse treatment. If not, switch policies if you can. Thankfully, many insurance companies provide unlimited outpatient benefits for mental health care these days. Just know your policy.

After your child has been clean for six months and a solid diagnosis has been made, they need to get the proper medications and care. You will need to readmit them into a specialized outpatient program for mental health care alone. This isn't like rehab all over again. They won't be stuck in a facility. It's another form of aftercare that allows your child to continue living the new life they're building for themselves while getting specialized treatment for their mental health needs at the same time.

If there isn't a nearby mental health outpatient program near you, you can piece together your own program if you must. Find a psychiatrist for medication management and have you child visit them a minimum of once per month. Next, find a psychologist for therapy, starting at once a week and tapering down to once a month.

## Common Types of Treatment

Emotional Brain Training (EBT):

This therapy, originally called Solution Training, was created by Laurel Mellin, M.A., R.D. in the 70s. It was originally created to help cure obesity in children, but it has since been found to work for a number of disorders such as binge eating, anxiety, depression, excessive drinking, and certain personality disorders. The core idea is that excessive levels of stress rewire the brain, causing it to seek out excessive amounts of something (whether it be food, alcohol, exercise, etc.) as a form of relief. EBT seeks to rewire the brain to steer away from stress pathways and instead seek out joy. Harkening back to Paul MacLean's Triune Brain Theory, the training revolves around the idea that these stress circuits dwell in the emotional part of the brain, not the logical part, so you can't "think yourself out of it." That is why the training focuses on teaching emotional skills that teach patients how to push stress aside — gradually weakening those circuits altogether — and bring joy to the forefront of the mind.

Cognitive Behavioral Therapy (CBT):

This well-known therapy is a mix of psychotherapy (focusing on how a person's way of thinking was shaped in childhood) and behavioral therapy (focusing on how problems arise based on the relationship between a person's behavior and thoughts). It was created by a psychiatrist named Aaron Beck in the 60s when he realized that his patients often had internal dialogues with themselves that sprang up as a result of unpleasant emotions, such as worrying why he, the therapist, wasn't talking much, worrying that he was annoyed with them, etc. The core of CBT is identifying the negative emotional thoughts that are at the root of the patient's suffering, finding their core, and then working to provide the patient with actionable steps to break old patterns.

The idea is that real problems only arise from negative thoughts when we actually give into them and believe them. For instance, patients suffering from depression wallow in the thought that today will be no different from yesterday, that the sorrow and misery will only continue, that they can't go to work, that they are a failure. By believing that today won't get better, they convince themselves that there is no point in looking for something enjoyable to do today. In one week sessions of 50 minutes per piece over the course of five to ten months, CBT works to teach patients to recognize that they are in fact believing these automatic negative thoughts without any proof. Once the patient can recognize when they are doing this, CBT provides them with steps to combat these negative thoughts. The steps will vary depending on the disorder the patient suffers from and will be further individualized for every patient's needs. The sessions themselves have a structure; it isn't lying on a couch and venting about whatever comes to mind. The therapist first works with the patient to identify the main problems the patient wishes to overcome. Then, together, therapist and patient create goals for the therapy. Maybe a depressed patient wants to be able to not dread heading off to work each morning. Maybe an OCD patient wants to find relief from a certain destructive compulsion by the end of the therapy. Once the goals are identified, the therapist starts outlining a certain topic or step to cover each week, and then the patient is given homework. Homework will vary based on the patient and his or her disorder. An example might be asking a patient with extreme anxiety to keep a diary of everything that triggered her that week. That helps both her and the therapist narrow down her specific stressors. One of the key things that sets CBT apart is that by working *with* the therapist to outline goals and doing homework on their own, patients do not become overly dependent on the therapist. The relationship is personable but still somewhat business-like, and the patient works independently during the week in between sessions. This prevents the patient from feeling like she can't continue progress without the help of the therapist and lets her take back control of her own life.

Interpersonal Therapy:

This therapy focuses on helping patients improve their relationships by helping them better express their emotions. This therapy works well with mood-related disorders like depression and bipolar disorder. However, the therapy used for bipolar patients is a slight variation called "interpersonal and social rhythm therapy." The difference is that this variation helps patients develop fixed, healthy routines to balance their lives, channel their mania into productive avenues, and have a path to follow all the way through recovery.

Family Therapy:

We have already touched on this type a little bit. You, of course, will need to participate in this therapy should it be deemed a good fit for your child. These sessions help patients learn how to handle conflicts, resolve issues, and communicate with family members in a healthier, more productive way. This is a highly recommended therapy for bipolar patients and those with eating disorders.

Psychodynamic Therapy:

This therapy is more of the traditional "talk-it-out" style. Through personal conversations that become gradually more probing as the patient becomes comfortable, this therapy seeks to uncover the unconscious motivations behind the patient's largest problems. Oftentimes, buried emotions or experiences cause people to create patterns of denial or faulty rationalizations that help them cope with pain or stress. This therapy seeks to bring those unconscious barriers to the surface and tear them down to eradicate the problem at the heart of the issues, whatever they may be.

## Medication Management

A vital part of your child's mental health outpatient care will be finding the meds that work best for them. There are countless medications available to stabilize the symptoms of every mental health condition, but they all have their own list of potential side effects, and what works for some people may not work for your child.

Once the right combination and balance is found, the medications mediate the symptoms that can act as your child's biggest trigger and will also help them progress through therapy smoothly.

Once a good balance is found, your son or daughter needs to stick to that prescription unless there is some major change. That can happen. After a while, one medication won't work as well anymore or new symptoms may arise. These are serious medications that can cause odd side effects like weight gain, lethargy, and fogginess. That's why it's so important that your child is in constant contact with the medical team and remains honest about how they are feeling and the effects of the medications. They ought to feel like themselves. They ought to feel comfortable. If they don't, they have to speak up to the doctor about it or it's all just a waste of time.

It took me four years to figure out the perfect medication combination. I went through six different ones; sometimes the doses were too high, other times the medication just wasn't working for me. When I at last found that ideal combination, I stuck to it religiously for about three or four years, while also consistently going to weekly therapy and monthly medication management sessions. After that, I began tapering myself off the harder medications. Then I began tapering down the dosage of all of my medications. As of today, I'm taking almost nothing. Still, I keep the stronger medicines in my cabinet just in case.

I'm comfortable not taking the harder medicines now, but I stuck with them for a long time because I recognized the good they were doing. Those meds saved my life. They allowed my brain the chance to stabilize while healing. I decided to slowly taper off them because I didn't want to use more medications than necessary. That's why I advocate for being vocal about how the meds make you feel.

Some people with very serious disorders like schizophrenia must always stay on their meds. Even if it isn't something as serious as schizophrenia, it's fine for your child to stay on the medication for their whole life if they want, so long as they are truly using it to feel balanced and not as a substitute for the illegal drugs they were taking before. When used correctly, mental health medications are like a daily vitamin, not a legal way to get high. Some addicts seek out legal medications to try and imitate the feelings of heavy drugs like cocaine and heroin. However, a professional will probably be able to figure out if that's the case and will make sure your child steers clear of the potentially dangerous/ addictive drugs like Ativan and "Johnnies".

When I was diagnosed bipolar and started testing out different medications, my dad didn't get it. He would say, "You can't take drugs to get off drugs." While I'm sure just about everyone can see where he was coming from, there is a serious difference.

Cocaine was my way of self-medicating to get through the lows of my disorder. It didn't help my symptoms, it amped them up. Cocaine took the wheel of my life, spun it as hard as it could, and then let go, sending me into a crazy tailspin that not even a Tom Cruise character could get out of unscathed.

The bipolar medications my psychiatrist gave me were carefully selected by a professional, monitored, and tweaked accordingly. They steadied the wheel and gently tapped the breaks until everything righted itself and I could progress through life at a steady cruising speed. I also learned productive ways to lessen the effects of my bipolar disorder naturally. I learned to begin shutting down and relaxing after 5 p.m. so that I get into bed at a decent time. I'm aware of my symptoms when they begin to show themselves so that I can address and restrain them. I know what sort of environments cause stress and present triggers so that I can avoid them. I can feel an episode coming on thanks to the knowledge I have gained through therapy. When that happens, I grab those stronger meds out of my cabinet and take them until I feel balanced again. I stick to a healthy diet and exercise routine to balance myself and expend extra energy in a productive way. Spirituality and meditation also help me stay in the sweet spot between the highs and lows of bipolar disorder by providing comfort and creating a calm environment. Lastly, I still go to therapy once a month to this day. The bad times are few and far between for me now, and sometimes going every month and not having much to discuss can be boring, but when the bad spells do come, that one much-needed session is worth all the other visits.

## It's a Cause, Not an Excuse

My parents had very different reactions when I was diagnosed. My dad wanted to deny it all. He didn't like the idea of me being labeled as mentally ill. He didn't see me that way. Back when I was flying through school on manic highs and doing well, he would brag about me. He didn't want those achievements to be marred by the mental illness label. He would always brag about how in control and happy I was and refused to say there was anything wrong with me. As long as my mania was allowing me to break down walls and succeed at impressive tasks, there couldn't possibly be anything wrong. What he didn't understand was that I was suffering; mania can make you feel just about as out of control as drugs can. He's still very much anti-medication, so it's something we don't talk about much. To him, my mania has always just been "good spirits."

My mom, on the other hand, was overjoyed. It was the cure-all excuse she'd been looking for. I wasn't a junky for no reason; all of my past actions were justified under the umbrella of my disorder. I couldn't help myself, right? Well, no. I didn't have to do cocaine. My bipolar disorder didn't put a gun to my head and make me do a line.

A mental illness is not an excuse for poor judgement and criminal behavior. Was it one of the causes that drove me to drug use and made it more appealing? Yes, absolutely. It was my root cause, but there is a difference between a cause and an excuse. I made the decision to pick up drugs of my own free will.

If your child is diagnosed with a mental health disorder, don't let that be the cure-all that lets them off the hook. What they did was their choice, and it still has consequences. What you can do, however, is help them get the care they need to get that condition under control so that the temptations it presents are squashed out.

## Conclusion

If you take away nothing else from this book, I hope you understand the importance of properly addressing your child's mental health. If your child as a disorder that is leading them back to drugs over and over, it won't matter how many times they go through drug rehab if that disorder is not addressed. Your son or daughter must then minor in drug recovery and major in mental health treatment.

# PART 4: LONG-TERM CONTINUATION OF CARE

WHY DID YOU PICK UP this book? Did you suspect your child was using drugs? Had your child been arrested for drug use? Had your child just relapsed for the first, fifth, or tenth time?

No matter the reason, the process for reversing things remains the same. Even if your child has relapsed multiple times and you're beginning to wonder if rehab is really the answer, the process is still the same. You just need to make adjustments to how you approach it, and I hope this book has helped you with that so far.

We've covered the intensive, hands-on process from intervention to aftercare, but we still aren't finished. We must still cover some of the after-effects of drugs that can leave a mark on your child's life even after they've successfully completed all the professional steps.

Maybe your son was brought up on serious charges like distribution or armed robbery. Maybe your daughter's dating life is getting her into trouble and presenting temptation on a whole new level because she can't seem to drop the addicted boyfriend she met before going into rehab. Maybe you are still struggling with self-blame and doubt of your parental abilities, which makes it harder for you to remain a rock that steadies your child in times of temptation. Things like this are all side effects of drug use that can linger even after recovery is achieved.

After all the professional recovery steps are completed,

your role changes once more. First, you had a highly active, hands-on role. Next, you stepped back a little and provided passive support. Now, it's about actively working on yourself in order to help your loved one. Your role is an educated, self-assessed one. You're already working on the education part by reading this book and educating yourself on addiction and the recovery process. Now it's time to step back and assess yourself and your parental approaches and make the little necessary adjustments that will make you the best possible parent you can be for a child wrestling with addiction. To do this, you must know what they need and how to give it to them in the most productive and healthy way, and that's what I'm here for. I've been where your child is, but I've also redirected my life and gained experience helping kids get out of the same tight spot I was in. My specialty is next steps. I'm always looking for the next thing I should do. When I was sitting in jail, reevaluating my life, I decided to take that time to quit smoking cigarettes. I couldn't do much sitting in jail, but I could take that one step toward personal betterment before I was even released. It's this attitude that makes me great at long-term care, honing in on what struggling kids need and discovering what they should do next.

Your role now is to treat your child like an equal. The bond you have with your child is a relationship, and relationships only work out positively if both members look at themselves honestly and figure out the changes they need to make. If your child is out of rehab, they have done this already in their countless group therapy sessions. Now it's your turn. It doesn't matter if you read this book before your kid went into rehab or if you've been reading it as you go along through the process; take the time now to make this evaluation. If you need to, you can do it again down the line after your child actually comes out of rehab and aftercare. But please know it's a two-way street. You can't expect your child to change and then do nothing to change yourself and your attitudes in the whole situation.

In the coming chapters, I'm going to not only help you get over the humps that remain after aftercare, but also help you assess your own role/behaviors and put strategies in place to make sure that you never again reach the same lows you experienced before reading this book.

My family and friends never gave 100% on the self-evaluation part, and I think it made my transition back into regular life a little harder. For instance, some of them thought that rehab was some miracle cure that fixed me for good and eradicated all my struggles. As a result, they would often refer to the "old Adam" and remind me of things I'd done in the past that they were "so glad" I was over, without thinking about how that would affect me. Others took the opposite approach and kept throwing old sins in my face and assuring me that I was going to mess up again—it was inevitable. That sort of thing is extremely harmful to a recovering addict's psyche. I had to bolster myself up even more to get where I am today as a result.

Still, with all that said, many of my relationships within my family were made stronger by the process, and hopefully yours will be too. So, for the next few chapters, put any guilt, ignorance, or doubts about your ability to make the right choices for your child aside, and listen to some advice from someone who's experienced these after-effects firsthand. That's all my words about parenting and handling the next steps are, though—educated advice. So use what works for you, and if you don't agree with something, that's fine too.

The finer points of your role in this long-term recovery continuation stage will vary depending on your child and their own personal struggles, but it all comes down to them making the right choices or the wrong ones. If they do the right things, you won't have to step in or worry. If, because nobody is perfect, they slip up and do the wrong thing, you'll need to act quickly and efficiently. A wrong decision can slip in between many right ones. It's unfair, but true.

So I am here to prepare you specifically for those wrong decisions that lead to relapse during long-term continuation of recovery, a.k.a when your child is living on his or her own or coming home to live with you. Recovery is never over for an addict. Temptation is always present, though it weakens significantly with time. That's why it's so important for you to have a firm relationship with your child in which you are a parent, an educated source of advice, and a strong foundation to lean on.

If you haven't yet done some of the things I'm going to mention in the next few chapters, please don't jump to the conclusion that you've failed as a parent or acted as a cause for your child's problem. Addiction isn't something anyone knows how to deal with at first; you're not alone. I've crafted the following chapters around what I've spent years studying and seeing firsthand in order to help you assist your child with a continued prosperous and drug-free life for decades to come.

# CHAPTER 15:
# CRIME AND ITS CONSEQUENCES

ONCE YOUR CHILD HAS SUCCESSFULLY completed aftercare, they will have all of the necessary tools to continue that hard-earned sobriety for the rest of their life. However, that doesn't mean that they still won't slip up. It's terribly frustrating, but it happens. That's just the nature of addiction.

Some of you may be reading this book step-by-step and only moving onto the next chapter after each phase is completed. If that's the case, your child is now out of aftercare and firmly planted on the road to recovery. But early recovery is extremely fragile, and one slip causes a fast-moving backslide of regression. When an addict returns to drugs, just once, the addiction picks up right back where it started.

Others of you may be reading this book entirely pre-emptively, trying to come up with a full strategy before you put any of these steps in play. That's fine, too, and will make sure your plan is rock solid. However, if that's the case, your child is still wallowing in addiction.

Either way, it's time to return to the nitty gritty. The seedy side of addiction is a topic that can't be avoided, whether your child has relapsed or hasn't even begun to make progress and is still in active addiction.

I feel it's necessary to clue you in on the ugly side. I'm sure you've seen some of it, but as a former addict, I know there are probably some things you are unaware of—perhaps blissfully so. However, if you want to be 100% prepared to help your child triumph over their addictions, you need to know the uglier, crazier truths.

Addicts are often intelligent and highly resourceful. They become master manipulators, and they run cons on the smallest things. There's always a story or a strategy, even if the goal is just $5 and a pack of cigarettes. Pretty much all their money is shoveled into the drug mill, so they constantly need to manipulate more money out of others, like you.

They probably call you with crazy stories about why they need money this time. If they're calling you at all hours, they're probably doing the same to other family members, friends, and just about anybody they know. You'll be able to pick up on this conning because all of a sudden it will seem like your child's life has suddenly become an unmanageable set of unlucky circumstances. One day your son's car breaks down. The next day, his dog ("He has a dog?") needs to go to the vet because it swallowed a bunch of pennies. A few days later his car runs out of gas, and he just realized that he left his wallet at home. The next week, he calls you in the middle of the night to say some girl he met stole his I.D. and wallet in a hotel room, and he has no money to get home. The words Western Union are always a warning sign. Call his bluff.

If you've been conned before, don't beat yourself up. It's pretty inevitable because most people aren't familiar with the ins and outs of addiction until they have to be, and by that time the conning has already started. Just remember that you are being conned by the drugs, not your child. Yes, your child makes the decision to use drugs in the first place, but it's the drugs and the desperation they fuel that have them calling you day and night asking for money.

Even the best cons fall through and get discovered, though, and the addict has to go to new lengths for their daily fix. Many times, the new solution involves illegal activities.

That's why in this chapter I want to cover how to recognize illegal behavior so you can try to prevent it and what to do if your child ends up facing legal ramifications. To do that, you need to understand exactly why your child turns to illegal activities and exactly what they're getting into.

## How Did/Do They Support Their Habit?

You must always ask yourself this question, and the answer may surprise you. An addict can quickly become destitute, so many people get it in their head that drugs are high price items. Now, some of the higher grade drugs are expensive, but that's probably not what your child is hooked on. They only need about $20 bucks to get enough dope to kill them, should they use it all at once. (*Check the appendix for a full list of the street value of common drugs.)*

The misconception that your child needs to be raking in hundreds of dollars to buy one supply of drugs leads many parents to mistakenly assume that giving their child $5 will only help them buy necessities like toothpaste and food instead of drugs.

The reason addicts end up homeless is that they keep needing to buy more and more. The drugs themselves are cheap, but keeping up the habit is not. Teen addicts, especially, develop an obsessive "I need more, and I need it NOW!" mentality. Once a strong habit is formed where they need large amounts to get high and they need to get high more often, it becomes a $50 to $100 a day habit, easy.

After you and grandma and everyone else get wise to the games and the money is no longer coming, odds are your child will set their sights on illegal activities if they don't get in treatment.

When your child is high and out of their mind, there is no right or wrong, legal or illegal. There is only the constant thought of, "I need drugs now."

You definitely don't want to give your child any money because then you are fueling the habit, but you don't want them to become desperate enough to turn to crime. The answer? Nip things in the bud and get them into detox and rehab as quickly as possible.

## Legal Issues and Illegal Behaviors

Addiction can move quickly, and you may not have caught on to the true depth of the problem fast enough. Addiction is a progressive disease, and if your child is on hard drugs like crack, meth, or heroin, casual use turns into abuse at an incredible speed. Addiction is a disease that affects the mind in just about every possible way, and no matter how good of a person your child truly is deep down, the drugs smudge the line of morality until it is indistinguishable. (I know this firsthand.)

Your child will turn to crime to support their habit. Drugs are the number one cause of crime, so it's not so much a question of "if" as it is "when and how."

There are many different ways addicts fund their habit. One of the first options addicts turn to is petty theft. They will steal anything they can sell on the streets, at a pawn shop, online, or even to their dealer. They'll nab tools from Home Depot, DVDs from Walmart, you name it. I've even known addicts to sell their food stamps for half price to get some extra drug money.

Other times they will run a sort of con on the store where they will steal expensive but mundane things like razorblades that they can return to the store for a refund or a store credit in the shape of a gift card that they can turn around and sell. Keep this in mind when you take your child to the store. Many parents try to avoid giving money by just buying their child the necessities they need. It's a good idea, but if you buy your child anything remotely valuable—even razor blades—they may bring them back to the store later to get cash or a gift card they can sell. Some things you can do to prevent this are destroying the receipt or making your kid open the product right away. These simple measures will make the return process harder.

If they've managed to hold down a job, they may end up stealing from their employer, swiping cash out of the register during their shift or writing themselves fake checks. They will start stealing from you, right out of your wallet laying on the kitchen counter. My mom was always good for $20 out of her wallet.

Some common signs that your child's habit is getting serious are missing items and money around your house. You may even find sales slips from pawn shops. If you're missing an expensive heirloom, go check your nearest pawn shop.

Those same pawn shops that help your child turn a profit are also a common way addicts get caught. Pawn shop owners keep records of everything sold to them and who sold it. The shops are one of the first places cops check for stolen goods once the owner of the missing item files a report. Cops will also do online searches on eBay and Craigslist for missing goods. Once they find the item, they can trace the sale back to the seller.

It's hard to steal more than a few items at once, so some addicts look for a bigger payout. That means resorting to robbery. It does happen; I've actually known a few guys who stuck up drug dealers, pharmacies, and banks. Such drastic action springs from the complete desperation that can affect anyone hooked on drugs. Many addicts refer to these stick ups for drug money as "come ups" or "licks." So keep your ears open for that sort of lingo.

Another slightly more sophisticated form of stealing is prescription fraud. Some addicts will steal prescription medications from other people and either use or sell them. Others steal prescription pads from their psychiatrists or other doctors and write themselves "scripts." Some simply change the amount of pills, the milligram dosage, or the number of refills on the prescription slips they are given.

Sadly, many addicts (mostly females) turn to prostitution. Sometimes they sleep with their drug dealer for free drugs and a place to stay. Check online for local Backpage or Craigslist prostitution ads to make sure your daughter is not selling herself there. You can also google her phone number, which will pull up any ads she has running. I've known parents who actually found such ads. It is rarer for males to resort to this tactic, but it isn't unheard of. Some entirely straight males resort to homosexual prostitution to obtain the drugs they crave.

One of the most popular ways to get some extra cash is dealing drugs. It allows an addict to get high and make money at the same time. Many addicts are drawn to this method because the more drugs you buy at once, the lower the price gets. They will pool their money for a while, collecting those $5 handouts until they have enough to buy their first stash, and then they have all the drugs they need to satisfy their own habit and still sell to others for a profit.

This is the method I chose, and honestly, it becomes more addictive than the drugs. Starting as early as high school, I got high for free for over a decade. I was a pill pusher, and I obtained my supply by "doctor shopping." Back in '08 and '09, right after I won *Big Brother*, Florida was a hub for opiate pill trade, with stuff like oxycodone getting handed out like candy by doctors more concerned with money than their patients' wellbeing. These doctors' offices were dubbed "pill mills." I would go to a doctor in my county on Monday and then head off to another doctor in the next county on Tuesday and get a generous prescription from each doctor. When I say generous, I'm talking like 250 pills of oxy a month. That's about ten times what someone would need if taking it properly. I would then sell the pills to other addicts for ridiculously high rates. Prescription writing is monitored more closely now, but back then, doctors were helping me fuel my drug habit and the habits of the people I sold to. Eventually, I was arrested on charges of distribution.

Another method dealers use is forming connections that allow them to skip the middle man and go directly to the main source of the drug supply. This main source will have the raw form of the drug that hasn't yet been mixed with cheap, sometimes dangerously cut ingredients to increase the volume and lower the purity. The dealer can buy the uncut stuff wholesale, do the cutting themselves, and then sell the larger volume of drugs for a profit. However, a dealer who does this will get slapped with an automatic manufacturing charge if they get caught with the raw stuff. I was a professional at rerocking cocaine at the age of 20.

This method is pretty much as dangerous as robbery. If you're a known drug dealer, you're going to make enemies. There's also a very high likelihood that someone will overdose when such large quantities of drugs are in play, whether the dealer himself overdoses or someone dies of an overdose on the dealer's watch. There's also a high likelihood that someone will rat out the dealer, and if the dealer is your child, you can expect some nice legal expenses.

If you suspect your child may be dealing, look for the essential items of the drug dealer tool box: a backpack, baggies, a scale, large wads of money, a cell phone, and rubber bands. If their brand new cellphone is constantly ringing and they always seem to have money but don't have a job, it's a safe bet they're dealing.

## Handling an Arrest

Eventually, an arrest will happen. Hopefully, you can

catch things before it gets to that point, but a lot of people aren't that lucky. The main thing is to stay calm when it happens. Rushed, frightened decisions can mess things up even worse.

Arrest isn't all bad. Many times it can scare your child into realizing they need help. If it's a first offense, you can breathe a little easier, as the courts are usually more lenient with the sentencing. However, the more convictions your child gets, the harsher the sentences will become.

If your child is arrested for a first time offense, push as hard as you can to fight a felony conviction and get things dropped to a misdemeanor. A felony charge on a kid's record is just about impossible to scrub clean, and it can dictate their future for the rest of their life. It definitely gives them an excuse as to why they can't get a job, and they will use it to their advantage. Every time you push them to take responsibility and earn a living, they will hit you with the "I can't get a job; I'm a felon" line. This just isn't true. However, that felony can limit the types of jobs your child is eligible for, so for everyone's sake, it's best to avoid it if you can.

Sadly, some parents become very familiar with the whole arrest process before their child gets clean. But if your child has recently been arrested for the first time, here's a few tips about things that often get overlooked.

First, if a car was impounded during the arrest, get it back ASAP. Many parents, understandably, hardly think about the car when they see their child in handcuffs, but those daily impound charges can get expensive fast.

Second, your child will get a free call, and you will most likely be the recipient of that tearful exchange. Those calls are usually made collect, so you need to make sure that you can accept collect calls on your phone. Also, you ought to make sure that your child actually knows your number. Now that cell phones allow kids to save their parents' numbers in their contacts, they don't even bother to memorize them.

Third, make sure your child knows to keep their mouth shut until a lawyer arrives. If you can't afford to get them a lawyer, they will still get a public defender, so there is no reason for them to talk to the cops on their own. If your child is involved in something serious like armed robbery or a drug ring, the cops will try to bait your child into giving someone up or participating a sting for a lesser charge. If your child watches crime dramas a lot, they will already have an idea of this, but make sure they know that such "deals" are often ruses and they need to avoid falling for it.

Some of the most common charges brought against addicts are DUI (driving under the influence), possession, possession with the attempt to distribute, conspiracy to distribute, theft, robbery, and prostitution. Simple possession charges rarely receive actual jail time, but the more serious stuff like armed robbery is a whole different beast.

## How Do I Get a Lawyer?

First, start by asking your friends and family if they know a good lawyer. It's nice to know that someone you trust has used that lawyer and found them helpful. The best option is to hire a private local lawyer who is familiar with the local courts and judges. A public attorney is cheaper and may be a better option for your budget, but just remember you get the quality you pay for. Also, whether public or private, local is always the key. If you can't afford a lawyer, your child will still be represented by a court-appointed public defender.

No matter what sort of lawyer your child ends up with, they need to be completely honest with him or her. Everything they say is protected by client-lawyer privilege, and letting the lawyer know all the ins and outs of the situation will help them best form a solid case.

It's paying a lawyer that makes most people cringe. The money out of pocket is going to be drastically different if the lawyer is working on a misdemeanor case or a federal case. When I had to pay my lawyer for a simple drug possession charge, it was only about $1,000. However, when I paid my federal lawyer for my felony conviction, it cost a whopping $50,000.

When negotiating the price of a lawyer's services, always get a flat rate. You don't want the lawyer tacking on extra costs as the process goes forward, and never pay by the hour.

Even if your child hasn't been arrested, it would be a good idea to have a lawyer in mind. Start searching and call a few candidates. You want to make sure you actually like the person, for one thing. You can also ask them about what they charge for different types of cases. When you make those calls, you may get asked if you want to put down a retainer. A retainer is a deposit-like fee that sort of holds your place with that firm to ensure that the lawyer you want will represent your child at all times no matter what. I don't recommend a retainer. Just have a good criminal lawyer in mind, and after that consultation, part ways amicably and say something like, "It was nice talking to you. Hope I never have to call."

## How Does Bail Work?

Bail is a sum you pay to allow your child to get out of a jail cell while they await trial. It's a deposit that you will get back if you child appears in court when they are supposed to and sees the case through.

To find a good bail bondsman, you will need to go through a selection process similar to finding a lawyer. Try to find a nice one that you feel comfortable with. As a nonrefundable payment, the bondsman receives 10% of the bail amount set by the judge, which you will not receive back. This can get confusing, so let me break down the difference for you. Without a bondsman, if bail is $1,000, you can put it all up and get your kid out right then. If all goes well, and your child appears back in court, you get the $1,000 back, but it's out of your pocket until then. With a bondsman, you can pay just $100 to get your kid out, but you never see that $100 again. Additionally, if your child skips out on bail, you are still responsible for the full $1,000, minus the $100 you already paid.

Your lawyer can actually help you appeal the bail amount a week or so after it's first set, and you may end up getting the bail amount lowered, making it more affordable to get your child out of jail.

## What to Do Before the Next Court Date

Once you post your child's bail, a court date is immediately set. So what do you do between now and then? Get your child straight into rehab. Any kind—inpatient, outpatient, simple detox, I don't care. Just make sure you take some step toward getting your child help. Once your child is in a program, give the court liaison or the probation officer assigned to their case the phone number and the info of the center and the length of stay. Chances are the judge is going to assign some form of rehab later anyway, so being proactive and taking that step without being asked looks real good at sentencing time.

## Appearing in Court

The idea of sitting in a courtroom can be nerve wracking, but your child won't be alone. You can be in the courtroom for support, and the lawyer will be there as well. Impressions are critical. Make sure your child dresses appropriately and speaks respectfully to the judge, addressing him or her with "Yes, Your Honor," and "No, Your Honor." Your child can address the court and ask for leniency and help, but it will only work if your son or daughter speaks openly and respectfully. A judge must see remorse. Your child needs to tell the court that they understand the severity and foolishness of their mistakes and that they would greatly appreciate the help needed for them to get better.

These words need to be backed up, so make sure your child understands the consequences of a making a bad impression, and make sure they stay on their best, angelic behavior from the day they are arrested to the day they appear in court. The judge will hear about their behavior, and if they've caused problems during the process or gotten in trouble again, it won't reflect well. Actions speak louder than words. Your child should go to rehab, get help, volunteer, get a sponsor, and document it all.

You can also provide letters of character and recommendations for leniency from the court. You can get these from a medical professional (whether it be a family doctor or a psychiatrist/psychologist who has met with your child a time or two since the arrest) or from other respectable people who know your child. You can even write one yourself, and definitely get one from the rehab center.

Once your child is released on bail, they will appear at their first hearing where they plead guilty or not guilty. Everyone always pleads not guilty at this stage. Then your lawyer will review the charges and look for holes in the prosecution's case.

What most often results is a plea deal. This is an agreement between the prosecutor and your lawyer about the penalty. Usually it's a more lenient penalty than the prosecutor would have pursued in open court.

After the plea is made, the next appearance is at sentencing. This is where the judge officially lays down the penalty and sets it in stone. Your child can either get a dismissal, be sentenced to rehab, receive probation, or serve jail time. No matter what sort of sentence your child gets, there will be a fine you must pay to cover court costs and possible restitution.

The ideal sentence is rehab, that's why it's beneficial to go earlier. Your child can then essentially say, "I already did what I had to, so please let me go." You're already a pro at that option by now. It's also the most productive solution. Try to push for it in your character letter asking for leniency or continuing treatment if your kid's already in a program.

Often, if your child is found guilty on a first offense, they will be sentenced to a term of state monitored probation. Right after court, your child will need to check in at the probation office and speak to their newly assigned probation officer. The probation officer enforces the guidelines set by the court. Those guidelines always include regular drug testing. In fact, your child will likely be tested when they report to the officer that first day and any time they check in after that. Your child will receive a schedule of when they need to report to their probation officer, and it is critical that they actually appear on those days. Travel restrictions will be put in place; they won't be allowed to leave the state or some other designated area. Your child must have a job or be in school, or else probation is revoked and some other form of punishment (a.k.a. jail time, usually) will be put in place. Lastly, the officer will regularly check on your child's residence to make sure the living conditions are drug free and safe.

There is a new form of probation that is steadily growing popular, though still not an option in every court system. It's called drug court. It's most often a six month period in which your child must report to the court house multiple times a week for drug screening and attend drug related groups. This option requires stricter discipline, which can be a good or bad thing depending on your child. They have to show up at a designated place more often, but if they can do it, it's a shorter period than most probations and offers a tight structure to help them stay clean.

Your child may also be sentenced to house arrest, which is an interim between probation and jail. Instead of a probation officer checking in on them every now and then to make sure they stay where they're supposed to and stay clean, your child will have an ankle bracelet that alerts authorities if they leave the house for anything other than an approved, scheduled appointment. This sort of penalty is usually assigned to more serious cases, repeat offenders, or those who failed at regular probation. You don't want your child in this situation. Yes, it's better than jail time, but it's not productive. Your child can't get a job or go to school or start turning their life around just sitting at home.

If your child's crimes are very serious and your child has offended multiple times, they will probably be given a stint in prison. I myself did federal time. It's not pleasant, by any means, but it is what it is. Sometimes, a prison's closed, disciplined environment is best for kids who just need to get under control. It forces them to get clean and stay clean; not in a way that will teach them how to stay sober for the long-term, but it's still something. It clears up their brain and allows them to think about the current state of their life. However, the jail system takes a toll on the family both emotionally and financially. Parents worry about their kids in jail, and if they want their child to be able to make phone calls, eat anything besides prison food, or have any sort of small luxury, they must pay for it (and not at Walmart prices).

If your child ends up doing jail time, do your best to stay positive. Remember that at least they're getting sober in there, and hopefully realizing they need to turn their life around. Visit a lot to keep their spirits high and keep yourself assured that they're doing okay. Every prison will handle money for prisoners a little differently, but keep money on the prison "books" so that your child can make phone calls and buy necessities from the commissary.

If your child is currently in jail, it's the perfect time for you to start making a treatment plan for them. They can't go anywhere and get in anymore trouble (hopefully). You can take the time necessary to create a solid, structured plan for an intervention, detox, rehab, and after care. When they come out, many addicts get wild because they're overwhelmed by the newly restored freedom. Have the plan ready to reel them in before things get crazy all over again.

After a jail sentence is served, it's usually followed with probation, but you can arrange to do the probation and still get your child through rehab. In fact, that effort looks really good to the parole officer and the courts in general.

## Conclusion

The recidivism rate is very high amongst felons. Please keep that at the front of your mind. No matter how contrite your child acts in jail, be wary when he or she gets out. By staying vigilant, you can help avoid further trouble.

I'm not saying your child *will* end up in jail. I truly hope they don't, but I think you need to be aware of the high possibility that they will. Crime stems from addiction because a drug habit requires money—lots of it. And someone without a job or any stability in their life isn't going to be able to get that money by legal means. I want you to be prepared for the worst so that if it doesn't happened you can feel relieved and thankful, and if it does happen you can be prepared to handle it well.

I didn't write this book just to talk about getting over addiction. I wrote it to give insight into the overall world of addiction and deal with the consequences that stem from it, such as criminal behavior and legal ramifications. Those things affect parents as much as their children, and I want to make sure you're ready and confident if the time should come that you have to look the ugliest parts of addiction in the eyes.

# CHAPTER 16:
# YOUR LIFE, YOUR LAWS

YOUR CHILD ISN'T GOING TO want to go to treatment or get better. Not at first. There's no desire to get better if you believe nothing's wrong with you, as most addicts do. That's why I told you to set consequences for your child's continued drug use at the intervention. Those consequences have to be stark enough to snap your child back into reality. Not allowing them back into the house, not providing them transportation, not providing them with food and handouts forces reality to sink in a little bit. That's why, while outlining all the steps of recovery, I have continuously reminded you to stick by those consequences when your child begins to get surly about moving from detox to rehab to aftercare.

Setting boundaries with your child and actually sticking to them is how you cease being an unwitting enabler and take back control of your life. In order to steer your child's life down the correct path, you first have to be the boss of your own life again.

Many parents find setting strict boundaries incredibly hard. Many begin to blame themselves for their child's addiction, thinking, "I must have done something wrong," or "I could have done more to prevent this." Sometimes it's not just blaming; they are in a rut, afraid of change. They have fallen into a routine, and making a change becomes difficult. If you're feeling this way, remember what we discussed in the very first chapter about finding strength in the realization that you are powerless against drugs.

You had no control over the appearance of drugs in your child's life, and alone, you are powerless to stop the effects of addiction. Your child's addiction doesn't reflect on you, and once you realize that, you can let go of that weight and begin seeking professionals who have been trained to deal with these issues.

Other parents find it impossible to set boundaries because their child's suffering hurts them, and they can't help but try and bandage up the wounds over and over again to try and relieve some of the pain. If you're feeling this way, remember the old adage, "No pain, no gain." Yes, it hurts to see your child struggling, but your child needs stitches, not Band-Aids. You have to dish out some harsh realities and feel that pain for a while in order to truly make a difference in your child's progress. Think of it like building up muscle at the gym. The first few times you work out hard, you're very sore the next day. If you only go once or twice and then give up, you never make any real progress and the pain was for nothing. If you actually stick to a regimen, that initial pain will dissipate and begin to produce positive results.

Kicking your child out if they don't make an effort to get help will be painful. They'll cry and scream, and you'll have to endure it. But if you stick to the plan, the harsh reality that follows will begin to sink in for your child, no matter how hard they try to make it on their own at first. Setting boundaries can help your kid stop using sooner. Boundaries are needed to get your child into rehab, and they are needed to maintain a healthy relationship with your child after rehab. Boundaries let your child know you mean business and that you aren't going to be pushed around and fall for the games anymore. Your seriousness imparts to them the seriousness of the situation. The important thing is that you set those boundaries out of love and not anger.

## Now, Not Later

If you're putting off enforcing boundaries, douse yourself with some cold, hard reality. The more you go back and forth yelling at your child and saying you've had it one minute, then turning around and letting them burst in the house at all hours and giving them money the next, you are letting the addiction grow stronger. Your child will learn to just ride out the temporary punishments and lectures and then turn up their palms for a handout once you've calmed down a bit. All the while, addiction wraps its coils more tightly around your child's neck.

There is a common saying within the Christian community that goes, "Let go and let God." Even if you aren't a Christian, the principle behind this saying applies to you now. The point behind the words is that sometimes you just have to step back and stop interfering in your life—or in this case, your child's life. The saying means to step back and let God do the work. Likewise, you need to step back and let reality take its course so that you can get your child to agree to rehab, where you step back once again and let the professionals take control.

So set your boundaries and then step back and let your child's life take its natural course under the effects of addiction. The only direction things can go is down, and your child will begin to realize they had it damn good before. If you let them know that they can have some of those benefits back again by going through recovery, you've just made an offer they can't refuse.

Don't forget that you're also setting these boundaries for yourself, too. You need to stop missing out on your own life due to your child's addiction. No more missing vacations. No more handing over money you really need to pay the bills. No more fighting with your spouse and blaming each other out of your own fear and unhappiness.

## Define Your Goals

You need set your boundaries with the end result in mind. By listing out your goals, you ensure that the boundaries you set actually work toward the things you want. Of course, your big goal is to get your son or daughter into rehab.

However, you can set smaller goals, too. For instance, one of your goals may be to stop letting your child disappear for a week, come home to sleep for three days, and then leave again. Set a boundary that curbs that habit. Make a rule that requires your child to be home for dinner. If they don't show, they will be turned away when they at last do show up looking for food and a soft bed. They will have to spend the night elsewhere. Then, if they come home for dinner the next day, they can stay that night. Relate back to the parents. Put a picture of how it will feel to come home home and take a shower and sit on the couch after a few days of being gone.

Set a goal to inhibit all the dangerous and maddening habits your child has developed because of addiction. Meeting all of those goals will help lead you toward the ultimate end goal of getting them to rehab.

By setting these boundaries, you not only curb the behaviors that have you up at night, biting your nails to nubs out of anxiety, but you also disrupt the addiction lifestyle. Your child likes getting high; that's why they turn to it again and again. They don't want to quit, but by setting boundaries that have real consequences, you interrupt the repetitive cycle and make their bad habits much harder to maintain.

## Types of Boundaries

There are two main types of boundaries: soft and hard.

A soft boundary is a gateway to setting hard boundaries.

It is a sort of test. You might implement a new, earlier curfew. You might tell your child they need to make a tangible effort to get a job within a certain amount of time or ask them to craft a resume that you can review.

If your child does these things, that's a very good sign. That suggests your child's habit isn't yet too serious. They will still need professional help so that it doesn't become serious, but those soft boundaries are great ways to make them take the necessary steps for shaking off the habit.

However, if your child's addiction is full-blown, I guarantee you they will not respond to those soft boundaries. Their mind is just so preoccupied with getting and using drugs that they'll hardly hear you ask them to come home an hour earlier or leave a resume on the counter for you to peruse. That doesn't mean you shouldn't ask. Soft boundaries are like homework assignments. If they pass, that's wonderful, but if they don't, those failed tasks give you fodder for setting the hard boundaries.

Hard boundaries are the no-nonsense, nonnegotiable rules with harsh consequences, so you shouldn't just spring them on your child. Test them with the soft boundaries, and then if you have to move to a hard boundary, you can list those failed soft boundaries as the reason for the hard-hitting blows.

A hard boundary is something like, "If you don't go to rehab, you can't live here anymore," or, "If you steal one more thing from this house, I will personally call the police and press charges against you."

You need to set hard boundaries for every aspect of your life that is affected by your child's habit. That means you need to set at least one personal, social, physical, emotional, and monetary boundary each.

A personal boundary prevents your child from constantly throwing your daily life into disarray. A personal boundary is forbidding your child to show up at your home high asking for money. Your child can no longer arrive at your home in the wee hours and expect to stay or receive any sort of help. If they get high under your roof, they're no longer welcome to stay there. If they are caught driving under the influence, they no longer have a car.

A social boundary addresses the common tendency for addicts to bad mouth you to others. There needs to be a consequence if you find out they've been telling teachers, other family members, or even friends that you're a bad parent. They will start to do this once you begin cracking down on their use. You don't deserve that disrespect, so make it known. Another social boundary might deal with your child's addicted friends. If a friend shows up at your house high or with drug paraphernalia, that friend is not allowed in your home again.

A physical boundary protects you from the violent rages of a serious addict. Many addicts become physically abusive toward those closest to them, especially when denied the things they want. Let your child know that you won't tolerate physical violence in your home. If they hit you, the police will be called and you will file charges.

An emotional boundary protects you from verbal abuse. When you don't give your child the money they asked for or you try to kick them out after they break a rule, they will most likely fly into a wide array of emotional tactics to try and pull as many of your heartstrings as possible in order to make you weaken. They will cry and plead. If that doesn't work, they will probably accuse you of cruelty and bad parenting. If that doesn't work, the string of cuss words and truly ugly sentiments will come tumbling out. You don't deserve to be berated this way. When the ugly words come out, the door gets slammed in their face.

A monetary boundary protects your checkbook and your livelihood. You're already going to have to spend a nice chunk of change getting insurance for treatment and helping support your child in the very beginning of recovery and aftercare; you don't need to deal with your child pawning your possessions, stealing your things, forging your checks, or snatching money from your wallet. They steal, you file charges or kick them out. Period.

## Putting Hard Boundaries in Action

A hard boundary should be an "If, Then" reaction. If your son steals another dime, then you file charges. If you daughter gets high in the house, then she'll be thrown out of it until she comes back clean and at a decent hour. There must always be a serious consequence to crossing the boundary.

Your child must understand that these boundaries are like your own personal laws. They must also understand that you will act as police, judge, and jury to enforce these laws. Otherwise, your child won't take them seriously. You must stand your ground. If you say it, you must mean it. This isn't like all those times before when you got fed up and yelled, "The next time you show up here high, you're out!" but you didn't enforce it the next day. These boundaries are not something you scream out in a fit of anger. You need to structure them logically and in a calm environment. You need to enforce them calmly and seriously. A verbal lashing has very little effect on someone whose brain is filled with the tiny voice of addiction constantly goading them to find more drugs. They'll hardly hear you unless you actually take action and stick by that action. Even if you enforce a boundary successfully once, if you're lenient the next time or forgive them the next day and reverse the consequences, your child learns that they can just ride out your anger and then get what they want a few hours later. That fixes nothing.

Remember that you are battling drugs, not your child. You're kicking cocaine out of your house. You're filing charges against heroin. Boundaries are not punishments like a swat on the butt or a week-long grounding. Boundaries are consequences for unacceptable behavior. It's not a slap on the wrist, it's a life-changing action—a change ultimately for the better.

## What Holds Parents Back

Many parents shy away from setting hard boundaries because of fear. They fear that if they kick their child out of their house, they'll never see them again. They fear that without a safe roof to get high under, their child will wind up on the streets, in a drug den, or turning to prostitution. They fear they will be left behind in their child's life and that their child won't turn to them anymore.

Many parents tell themselves it's unfair to set such harsh consequences because they blame themselves for the problems. They think they did something wrong as a parent; some even start to think they've passed on bad genes. All of this makes them reluctant to take charge.

Those fears and doubts can be hard to overcome if you simply see boundaries as punishing your child. That's not the case. Boundaries help your child. If you bend to your child's every whim, you're only feeding their addiction.

If your child wants to do hard drugs and dictate the course of their own life like an adult, then they need to start being treated like an adult. No more pampering. I see kids on a daily basis who have never been made to do anything. They don't even known how to do laundry or set an air conditioner on Auto for crying out loud!

Your child needs to grow up and face the consequences of their actions, or they're never going to learn anything. Speak to and treat them like an adult, and if they whine, remind them that they made the adult decision to take drugs, so you're going to treat them like the adult they clearly want to be.

## Conclusion

Enforce your rules with the severity of a puritan pastor. No leniency. You must be deaf to the pleading, the whining, and the ugly words. If they break the rules, no cash, no car, no friends, and no nice home to kick back in. Let them know that it can all stop if they just agree to go to rehab.

That's the key. Yes, enforcing the consequence will help wake your child up to the reality of their choices. It will make them see what life will be like if they continue down their chosen path. But you must provide a solution as well. They want things back to normal? Go to rehab. You've got it all planned out. Have that intervention before you start setting the boundaries. Make those consequences known if they refuse treatment at end of the intervention. That way, they've heard how great the facility is and they know what it will entail. Even if they reject it at first, trust me, it will start looking real good once you've made it clear you're sticking by your new laws.

If they go to treatment and then slip back into old habits during aftercare, those boundaries go right back in place. No exceptions.

The other main reason you need to set boundaries is because you deserve respect. I'll say it one more time: you deserve respect! I was awful to my parents when I was hooked on cocaine. I ran all over them, cursed them, and threw wild fits. My parents didn't deserve that treatment, and neither do you. You need to get back in control and reverse the authority back to yourself, the way it should be. Boundaries help you do that. If they respect you, they'll get respect in return. If they continue to act like a delinquent, they'll be treated as such.

Lastly, remember that you're doing this to get your baby back. Right now, they're a shell of their past selves, taken over and controlled by malignant spirit called drugs. The boundaries you're setting are not only barring you from the drugs, but are also working to tear a rift between drugs and your child. That rift will lead your child to treatment, and treatment is the only way to overcome the influence of drugs. Once it's overcome, you get your baby back. When you're feeling guilty, staring at your child's crying face as you shut the door behind them, keep that in mind to help you stay strong.

# CHAPTER 17:
# DATING HAZARDS

DATING IS SUPPOSED TO BE a fun, exciting, and fulfilling experience, but we all know that sometimes those expectations fall so flat you couldn't scrape them off the sidewalk with a high-end snow shovel—and that's without throwing drugs into the mix.

Dating while on drugs or early in recovery is a bad idea, period. However, dating after or even during recovery is something of an inevitability. As a result, recovering addicts are encouraged to learn how to properly approach the dating scene. That's why the unofficial "13th step" of AA is getting a significant other. However, trying to balance recovery and dating is a tricky and oftentimes dangerous thing, which is why most professionals recommend that a recovered addict waits a year to take that 13th step. I would argue that the time length isn't nearly as important as the stage of recovery at which your child starts to date—but more on that later. What I want to get across first is that newly recovered addicts are highly emotional people, so relationships can be either positive or negative triggers. If they meet the right person, it can be great. If they meet the wrong person, it can lead to disaster.

That's why I think it's important for you, the parents, to be aware of the dangers of dating and understand how to act preemptively to shut down a toxic relationship before it harms your child's life. But I also don't want you to fear your child dating, and the best way to curb fear is to gain understanding. So, I'm going to break down the most common types of relationships addicts become embroiled in before, during, and after rehab.

## Before Rehab

When I first started using, I was dating my high school sweetheart. She was a very good person, and too smart to put up with all of the crap that goes along with drugs. I hid it from her for a while. I knew she wouldn't like it, but I didn't stop because I thought I was the man. When my addiction became severe, around the age of 20, I couldn't hide the signs anymore, and I hurt her one too many times.

Many young addicts are lucky enough to have good, strong girlfriends and boyfriends beside them, but they're too fogged up and hazy to realize it. However, when their habit drives that positive influence away, it can lead to a faster, more dramatic downward spiral. The addict realizes they took their partner for granted, and the sadness and pain that comes along with that can heighten their drug use.

A good partner can often work as a sort of force field, pushing back against extreme, dangerous addictive behaviors. The addict won't want their partner to know what they're doing, so they will curb their behavior, make sure they don't use when they see them, and may not even feel the need to use when around them. However, even prince charming or a fairytale princess can't hold off the effects forever. Once they appear, they drive off the positive partner, which often causes the addict to seek comfort in another drug user.

If you put a rat in a cage with nothing but drugs, it will ingest them. But if you put a rat in a cage with two water bottles, another rat who hasn't tasted drugs, and a little pile of drugs in the corner, it won't have any reason to choose the drugs. A recovering addict needs a healthy social atmosphere to lead him away from the temptation of that little pile in the corner. The timing and circumstances of a relationship can lead him away from it or lead him back to it.

Two drug users who think they're in love and are constantly at each other's side will feed off each other. Two addicts equals double the drug use. Cocooned in their own little chrysalis they convince each other nothing is wrong or that their behavior is perfectly acceptable. They don't have to hide their use from each other, so they use more often. What they don't realize is that they're in love with the drugs, not each other. Their whole relationship is based around the desire to use; it's why they sought each other out. Their romantic activities involve getting and using drugs, and little else.

If your child gets into a relationship like this, be vocal about your opinion of the other person. Don't ban your child from seeing that other person or scream and yell about how that other kid is the enemy. That never works; it can actually drive the two addicts closer together. Talk to your child one-on-one in a calm but serious way. Make them look you in the eye while you list out all the reasons that boyfriend or girlfriend is bad for them. Above all, encourage safe sex, and if your child has track marks scarring his arms, remind him not to share needles with that girl either. Sadly, they still may not listen to you, but make your opinion known all the same. If they don't listen, bust your butt to get them into rehab and away from that person even faster.

## During Rehab

If your child was in a toxic relationship before entering rehab, they will use that person as a reason to complain about going.

"But I love her, she needs me."

"I can't be away from him that long."

They will pine over that partner, but not because they

really love them. That person has been so connected to drugs in their mind that leaving them symbolizes turning away from drugs. They miss drugs while going through treatment, so they think they miss the partner too.

Another problem that arises during rehab is that as the addict's body is weaned off the drugs, they experience a boost in libido. Many drugs are inhibitors that suppress sexual desire and can effect sexual performance. As those drugs are taken away, it appears that those sexual feelings come back full force. It is most noticeable in females, but that's probably just because young men have an insatiable sex drive all the time.

Don't believe me? The term "rehab babies" is a common one amongst the recovery community. A large number of women get pregnant in treatment facilities, which is just one reason why co-ed sober homes are a bad idea.

The cause isn't just a boost in libido, though. What I have found is that addicts in the process of banishing drugs from their life and assimilating back into society often fill the void with sex. When drugs are taken away, addicts can feel as though a large part of their identity has been lost. This loss of identity can lead to a strong desire for attention, love, and closeness, which leads to these rehab romances.

## After Rehab

When your child is at last allowed to leave the rehab facility, that fresh taste of freedom may drive them to act more impulsively. That's why a sober home is the next step, because it provides a structure that keeps the addict in check. That's also why I recommend encouraging your child to date while at the sober living home versus waiting until he moves out on his own. On his own in an apartment, he has a higher chance of crashing and burning. Sex and dating are two different things, and often an addict will hold off dating, but in the thrill of being free and out of recovery, they seek out sexual encounters and partners with the wrong attitude in mind. I recommend that addicts start dating toward the end of aftercare or during the outpatient level of care, while they are still under the confines of sober home rules, because the restrictions of the home (like following a curfew and not allowing anyone but residents inside) will make your child slow down and properly court a partner.

That courtship is important because it will allow your child time to understand their emotional state and what qualities they are actually seeking in a partner before they dive right in. If they have no boundaries forcing them to take their time, they can easily fall back into a bad relationship, either because they're trying to fill a void with sex or because they have a harmed self-image they're trying to boost with new affection.

After rehab, your child may still be pining for that toxic person, and the sober home sets rules that can help keep that person at bay. Your child should start searching for someone new to shoe-horn that other person from their mind. It's tough on addicts; I see this firsthand, how toxic relationships can sabotage sobriety so easily.

A sober home also provides the support of peers who can help open your child's eyes to a toxic situation or encourage a good one. Your child will also most likely need that support for courage. Many addicts don't even remember how to talk to and flirt with someone who isn't messed up on drugs. Those peers also provide comfort if a relationship doesn't work out. Without that encouragement, comfort, and support, many addicts relapse due to a breakup or by getting involved with the wrong person. From what I've seen, dating is the number one cause of relapse.

However, it can also be what gives your child the strength to continue recovery and stay away from drugs for good. A healthy relationship with someone who is not only compatible with your child but also a huge source of encouragement works to show your child how great a sober life can be.

It may take a while to find that person, though. So here are a few tips you may want to impart on your child.

1. They must remember to work on themselves. They need to treat themselves right; they don't need someone else to do it for them. If you're not okay with yourself, you can't make anyone else's life okay.
2. If they're trying to get back with that high school sweetheart, advise them to take it slow. That other person probably still remembers a lot more of the bad times than the good one that your child is dwelling on. They must be prepared to accept that that person doesn't want them back yet. Odds are that high school sweetheart moved on already. That's often hard on them, and they need accept that it's over. No stalking on social media; they need time to get over it. Rejection is often a trigger for using.
3. They need to start thinking about what they want and need in a partner. What's going to help them through this time? What kind of personality traits do they like? The only trait they were looking for before was someone to get high with, so they probably need to reevaluate what they actually like in a person.

## What Can I Do?

You are probably wondering how on earth you can help your child maintain a healthy dating life while they're off in a sober home or out on their own. While there isn't any miracle trick that will ensure your child actually takes your advice and avoids the wrong relationships, there are a few things you can do to encourage positive, healthy dating behavior.

1. Encourage safe sex. They may roll their eyes and say, "Yeah, yeah, sure," but if you include some condoms

in those goodie packages you send them, they'll be a lot more likely to use them than if they had to go out and get them themselves. Second, get your daughter birth control! Take her to the doctor yourself if you have to. It's better to get the shot or an insert so it's not something she has to keep up with daily.

2. Let them know that if they just want to have sex for the sake of having sex, that you aren't going to try and stop them (it's their choice), but tell them that if you see it starting to affect their recovery, you will step in. If dating begins to become obsessive or a substitute for drugs, point that out to them. They probably aren't aware of it, and having you bring it to light may help them readjust their course.
3. If their toxic ex is the mother or father of their child, encourage your son or daughter to focus on being a parent to their kid rather than trying to focus on the relationship with the ex. Not everything can or needs to be repaired. Try to make your child realize the best thing to do is take care of himself first. Don't let him sabotage his life using the kid as an excuse.
4. If they take up a new partner that you sense is trouble, remind your child of the old ex and all the problems that relationship caused. Let your child know the similarities you see between this new partner and the old one.
5. If you see your child throwing themselves into a new relationship in a short amount of time, encourage them to step back and focus on themselves for a while. Ask them why they feel the need to move so quickly; encourage them to discuss that with their therapist, as they may realize that eagerness for affection and attention is coming from loneliness or a lack of self-confidence that needs to be addressed.

6. Young recovering males usually need to learn how to have real confidence in themselves, not the feigned macho facades that can get them into trouble. That genuine self-confidence will prevent them from becoming possessive or smothering. Young recovering females are often just coming out of an abusive or obsessive relationship that has drained them of self-respect. They need to be encouraged to raise their standards to what they truly deserve so that they don't keep slipping back into harmful relationships.
7. Talk to them about your own relationships. Be open about what made your relationships stronger and what tore them apart. It is encouraging to your child to hear that they aren't alone in these struggles. If you and your spouse are divorced, be open about what lead to that. Not only will it provide your child with practical advice, but it will also help you assess your own life and relationships. If you are divorced, encourage your child to talk about that with their therapist as well. Divorce is never easy on children, and it could be a separate underlying issue that needs to be addressed.

## Conclusion

Talking openly about personal subjects like those above will strengthen your relationship with your child. Each time you give your daughter solid advice that she is able to apply to her own relationship, she will become more and more likely to turn to you in times of need. However convincing your kid something is wrong in her relationship is far easier said than done. Young adults are often blind to the issues. Opening their eyes is often just a hope and a prayer at the end of the day, but the best thing you can do as a parent is be there for them. None of these conversations will be easy, but take some solace in knowing that they *can* help, even if it's only in a minor way.

Try not to make things awkward. Sometimes the awkwardness will be unavoidable, but just keep the conversation moving. Try not to ask too many questions. Let them talk to you and provide advice on the questions they ask rather than drilling them about their life. They will tell you the details as they are ready to reveal them, and only then.

Dating is the number one thing I have seen lead to relapse. As awkward as it sounds, you must talk to your child about the subject and be aware of what's going on in her dating life. After all the hard work she put into treatment and all the hard work you put in to get her there, don't let a bad breakup or a bad influence come in and ruin it in the space of a few weeks. With a little time and some self-evaluation of standards and desired traits (which you can help them with), your child can meet someone who will enhance her recovery, not hamper it.

# CHAPTER 18:
# THE REALITIES OF RELAPSE

RELAPSE: THE DREADED WORD THAT no parent ever wants to hear. Well, get your fingers out of your ears because it must be discussed. Why? It happens. It takes years for an addict's brain to fully heal, especially if he or she used for an extended period of time. Rehab doesn't last years. That's why it's so important to find outpatient programs and sober homes that check in regularly to monitor all environmental and psychological aspects of patients' lives.

Relapse is an unfair thing. You've sacrificed your time and money to put your child through all the steps. You've felt the joy of seeing them clean and happy again. You've seen how hard they've worked to uncover new things about themselves and reverse their old, dangerous way of life. No one wants any of that to be snatched away.

What I want you to realize is that relapse isn't the end. If your child uses again, it's not as though you have to throw your hands up in surrender and become resigned to the fact that they will never get better.

Relapse doesn't destroy recovery, it just delays it. Yes, there will be new work to take on and old steps to rehash, but it's not the end if you handle it right.

That's what this chapter is about: noticing the signs of relapse, wrangling the situation back into control, and getting your child the necessary help to get back in that sweet spot again.

## Two Types of Relapse

Everyone relapses at different times for varying reasons, but there are really only two types of relapses: the crash and the slip.

The crash is the uglier of the two. Someone who experiences this sort of relapse doesn't just fall off the wagon, they overturn it in a ravine. They've been dwelling on using for some time, battling old desires. When they finally give in, they fall hard, indulging in the same levels of use they were into before rehab. This is extremely dangerous because they no longer have the same tolerance after being clean for an extended period of time. The old amounts can easily lead to overdose and death. Remember, that one "hotshot" is all that's needed for a fatal overdose. There is real danger is using just one more time.

A slip is hitting a bump on the road and accidentally sliding off the back of the wagon at low speed. It's easier to stand up without injury, brush yourself off, and hop back on. People who do this have also been entertaining the idea of using again, but only as a one-time test to see if they still like it (at least that's what they tell themselves). They aren't craving the old lifestyle, the old endless highs. It's more just a nagging curiosity, a pull of nostalgia of using just once. This is still dangerous, as any slip up can lead to a total fall out. However, people who fall prey to this sort of temptation use a small amount in a moment of weakness; it isn't a total plunge back into the lifestyle. Oftentimes, they will realize the high isn't for them anymore and isn't worth the trouble it causes. The drugs will continue to call to their body, which will never completely stop craving them, but they will take their new habits back up again and move on from it without serious incident. The relapse then becomes part of the recovery, if corrected quickly, because it puts some of those nagging curiosities to rest and helps them decide once and for all that the high isn't as desirable as their nostalgic brain would like them to think.

If you suspect your child has relapsed, you need to gage how serious of a fall it was. Have they only used once, or have they been sneaking around and getting high for a month already? Stage a new intervention and get the truth so you can begin to decide what level of care they need to be placed in.

## Why Can't They Just Quit for Good?

As a consultant, I've spoken with many young addicts who have relapsed. Ninety percent of them tell me they knew it was coming; it's rarely a spur of the moment decision. So why didn't they take precautions to stop it?

They try, but the thought of using grows and grows until it's a mental block that fills their whole head, pushing against the sides of their skull and building up pressure until they can't think of anything else. At first, they only contemplated using every now and then, but eventually the thoughts become continuous. They begin to convince themselves they can get away with using again. The urges block out all the training, and their mind never turns to their sober network (sponsors, peers, their psychologists, their parents). It is mental warfare, the good and bad angels clashing until the good angel begins to tire and weaken.

Every addict will face this struggle, but there are certain common things that can tip the scales in the fallen angel's favor.

1. From what I've seen, addicts who shoot up with needles have a harder time maintaining sobriety. Shooting dope directly into your veins can alter the body's regular function and makes drugs a necessity. The withdrawal symptoms are more severe and the cravings are more intense.

2. They may have a mental health issue that keeps grabbing them by the shoulders and forcing them to look back at drugs as a solution to ease the symptoms.
3. Similarly, there could be deep seeded trauma in their past that is unresolved. The flashbacks, nightmares, or general pain and uneasiness are enough to drive them back to drugs just to try and forget.
4. They can hold onto old resentments, whatever those might be. Maybe their life hasn't taken shape in the way they wanted it to, even now that their sober. Maybe the fact that their ex still won't take them back even after they've been clean a while makes them wonder why in the world they got sober in the first place.
5. Some people just love getting messed up. They love the feeling of the high. They love having fewer inhibitions. They love experiencing life through the lens of the drugs.
6. Drugs may provide comfort in the form of the familiar. Some addicts turn to drugs in times of stress or trouble to calm their nerves or forget their problems, and when a new stressor arises, thoughts of using begin to plague them.
7. Sometimes drugs are just something to do. Snorting cocaine is a way to liven things up and relieve the boredom and mundanity of everyday life.
8. If they went to rehab for the wrong reasons, a relapse is often inevitable. If they went just to please their parents or get leniency in a court case, they aren't likely to take the treatment seriously or implement the tools given to them in therapy.
9. An addict's environment can determine whether or not he or she will relapse. Going back to old hangouts or reconnecting with other, unreformed addicts can present too many opportunities to resist.

## Noticing the Signs

The best case scenario is that you're able to catch the signs before the relapse happens and prevent it. You may not be able to do so with a simple talk—further professional treatment may be required—but if you can prevent them from putting the drugs back in their system and risking overdose, that's a win.

Here are a few signs that your child may be contemplating using again:

1. A shift in attitude, whether it be mopey and depressed or anxious and on edge.
2. Lack of motivation. If you notice that your child seems less enthusiastic about continuing their new job, dating a new partner, or taking any sort of step to get their life back in order, they may be looking backward instead of forward.
3. Getting complacent with treatment. Speak up if you notice your son or daughter isn't going to AA or NA meetings on a regular basis. Ask them when the last time they talked to their sponsor was. If you have a sneaking suspicion it's been a while, but your child isn't fessing up, call the sponsor yourself.
4. Negative talk, whether it be putting down themselves or their sober network, or a sudden tendency to see the dark side of every scenario. All this suggests doubt in the process and thoughts of serious change.
5. Exaggerated positivity. If three months into sobriety your child gushes about how everything is hunky dory every time you ask how they're doing, but they never really give you any details, it could be a sign they're putting up a false front of over-the-top success to mask their backward-sliding behavior and thoughts. Recovery is never easy or full of constant sunshine

and rainbows, and if your child is acting like it is, they may be overcompensating to try and throw off suspicion.

6. Isolation. Withdrawing from social circles and retreating into your own thoughts is never a good idea for a recovering addict. When left alone without support, there is nothing to mute the calling of temptation.

If warning signs of potential relapse aren't caught, you will eventually begin to see the all-too-familiar signs of use. They'll change their routine, miss appointments or events, lose their job and lie about it, and begin to badger your for money.

You may not catch onto the early warning signs unless you have some sort of inside contact into your child's life, like a sober home manager. This is because addicts are very good at only letting you see what they want you to. If they aren't living with you, they'll be able to put their best face forward just for when they show up to meet you, hiding what's really going on in their life.

If your gut flip flops when your child asks you for some cash or to take them shopping, slow down and think things out. Don't overreact; your child may just honestly need a little extra cash for necessities. Maybe they were sick for a few days and missed some work, and they're paycheck is low. Weigh the circumstances, ask questions, and take your time on making a decision.

If multiple signs begin to pop up, that's when you take the reins again.

## How to Prevent Relapse

If you notice the warning signs, there are a few things you can do to prevent a full blown relapse or overdose.

Have drugs tests ready and use them. If your child is in a sober living home, they are already being tested. If they live with you, you'll need to do it yourself. You should also be checking their rooms and other property regularly. If they live with you, you're the new house manager.

Keep them busy with productive tasks if they seem to have too much downtime. Keep them active, but don't have them running around too crazy or they may get a bad case of what I call the "fuckits" and stop doing anything... except thinking about drugs.

Make sure they're being active in their recovery steps. Talk to their OP program leaders or their sober living home managers to make sure they're actively going to their therapy sessions, medical checkups, and support meetings.

One way to keep tabs on your child's activity without being overbearing is to know their routine. And if they don't have a routine, help them establish one. Structured days keep them busy forming good habits and staying away from the old ones.

If your child had a heroin addiction, you *need* to have a Narcan pen or nasal spray in your home in case of an overdose. Heroin is one of the hardest addictions to overcome, and it is also one of the most dangerous when it comes to deadly overdoses. In some areas, you can buy Narcan over the counter from places like CVS, but the over-the-counter versions aren't as strong. Ask your child's doctor for a prescription. Hopefully you won't ever have to use it, but it's a precaution that must be taken because the chances of an overdose are much higher during a relapse.

## Back to Square One?

If your child is at a sober home, a relapse is likely to be caught fairly quickly due to frequent testing and the level of accountability. If your child's test comes up positive at the sober home, ideally, the manager or staff will confront your child with their options and inform you of the relapse (make sure you get a release signed so that they can legally tell you these things). Oftentimes, these confrontations will lead to the addict owning up to the use because they don't want to lose their place at the home, their new freedom, their new job, or their new friends. That's why getting them to establish such ties is so important.

If your child is living with you, you'll know when a relapse has occurred if you're paying attention. During your child's stay, you will grow accustomed to seeing him sober, so if he slips up, you'll notice. You'll need to stage the intervention yourself again. Just follow the same steps as last time. The only difference is that there are multiple options for levels of treatment.

Your child doesn't necessarily have to start the process all over again. If they had a minor slip and are eager to get back to the new life they've created, there are a few inpatient treatment options that will allow them to get help without too much interruption of their new life.

If your child is honest and comes forward about their relapse with little or no prompting, and if they show a real desire to make things right again, the house manager may allow them to stay in the home under stricter rules, like an earlier curfew and a boost in the number of mandatory support group meetings they must attend each week. The manager may also recommend an outpatient program or an inpatient stabilization/refresher on treatment with renewed therapy and new strategies for dealing with the relapse.

If your child relapsed while still attending an outpatient program (OP) or intensive outpatient program (IOP), the clinical team there will assess whether your child needs to be sent to a higher level of care or if a simple boost in the frequency of outpatient care is needed. For instance, if your child was in a two day a week OP program, they might be bumped up to a three to five day a week IOP schedule.

An addict who has experienced a crash relapse and completely slipped back into their old ways will need more serious help. The same goes for any addict who, when caught (even if caught after just the first use) tries to deny their slip or minimize the gravity of the situation. If either of these things is the case, the addict will need to return to inpatient rehab treatment in what is called stabilization.

They usually won't need to stay for an extended period of time, like the first go-around. Just a few days or weeks will do. It's more of a refresher course that helps them get back a clear head in a stable environment and work through what caused their relapse.

If your child relapsed on hard drugs and was using for an extended period before being caught, they will need another medical detox before going back to rehab. You can do inpatient or outpatient. In South Florida, where I live, many rehab centers push for inpatient detox at their own affiliated facility, however, in my opinion, that isn't always necessary. The problem with this push is that not all cases are actually serious enough to warrant this stay, and many addicts have to lie about taking harder medications like benzos just to get admitted. Another problem is that some addicts will choose to go to inpatient instead of outpatient because they want to get some Suboxone pumped into them as a little bonus high. If your child's withdrawal is going to be very severe and painful, inpatient is probably the right choice, but if not, simply getting medically cleared and going straight to stabilization will do the trick. Regardless of which you choose, you want this detox to be a light taper. You don't what your child pumped full of detox drugs. There needs to be just enough to make your kid comfortable, not so much that he or she has to be detoxed off the detox meds.

After detox is complete, they can go back for their

refresher rehab course. Many centers will tell you that this stay must always last two weeks. Honestly, it's a myth that many places perpetuate to keep insurance money coming in. Yes, the worst cases of relapse will definitely need the two weeks, but not everyone does. The problem is that centers don't usually take the time to fully evaluate the situation, they just automatically stamp a two week period on every relapse client.

The problem is that two weeks is long enough to derail the life the addict has worked to rebuild while out of treatment. Addicts whose relapse is caught fairly quickly still have their new job. As part of the sober home's requirements, they've taken up responsibilities and started integrating back into society. If the center keeps them for two weeks without evaluating their situation or state of mind, they can potentially do more harm than good. Making the addict stay in a center for two weeks can make them miss meetings, miss a rent payment, and lose their job. When they get out of treatment, they're life is back in disarray.

Sometimes the full two weeks is necessary. If your child relapsed on heroin and disappeared from the sober home and their job for a few weeks, only to show up at your door late at night asking for money, those two weeks of stabilization are definitely needed, at the very least. If they just had one slip, but the severity of the one use was bad enough to need medical outpatient evaluation, they do need to go into detox and then treatment, but they should only have a few days' stay in detox, at most. That way, they can keep their new life in order. Many addicts don't want to lose what they've built for themselves, and that often drives them to throw themselves into the outpatient treatment with real enthusiasm and motivates them not to slip again.

The two week myth is something Oceans Medical Centers is seeking to change. If one of our past clients relapses, we take the time to gage the situation and the client's mindset to determine how long he or she needs to stay for stabilization. Relapse shouldn't signify the end of life as the client has come to know it. That's damaging. Many addicts are hard on themselves after a relapse because they feel like they can't ever get their life back, so they give up. Any opportunity to help them stay rooted in the progress they've already made should be taken while treating the relapse vigilantly.

## Conclusion

Relapse is not the end, no matter how long stabilization takes. You must make your child understand that, if they relapse. I have heard many addicts say things like, "Man I almost had a year, what the fuck?" after they slipped up. They beat themselves up, feeling hopeless and down, like they wasted their time. One way to combat this is to approach the incident with a calm, actionable attitude of "Let's do this. Let's get you what you need so you can get back to where you were." My dad was always good at this during my recovery, being the eternal optimist he is.

Learn from the relapse. After they've gotten sober again, you need to start asking questions. Ask them why they used and what made them miss using. Ask where they got the drugs and if they were with anybody when they used them. The answers will help the both of you pin down what behaviors need to change and which people and situations your child needs to distance themselves from.

Next evaluate your own actions, but leave the judgmental attitude out of it. Did you get a little too excited about their progress and become lax on some of your rules? Did you give them more money than they really needed? If the answer is yes, don't get mad at yourself, just make note of what needs to change. This is a process that must be practiced and is never perfect; mistakes are just part of the deal.

Relapse is a discouraging thing for all involved. Addicts

often berates themselves (if not initially, then after getting back into treatment) and feel like they threw away all of their work. This isn't true. The work they have put in is still there. They slid down the rungs of the ladder for a second, but the foundation is strong and they know how to make the climb. It won't take nearly as long to get back to the rung they were on. Encourage them to pick back up their recovery routines: get back to support groups regularly, call their sponsor immediately, and reconnect with their sober buddies.

For parents, relapse can bring back old heartbreaking memories. It's like a nightmarish déjà vu. But this isn't like the first time. You're prepared; you're battle worn. You have the armor and the sword ready, tucked away. Get them back out and fight for your child.

# CHAPTER 19:
# STICK IT TO THE STIGMA

YOU SEE PEOPLE TALK BEHIND their hands. You see your neighbor's blinds twitch when your child pulls in the drive. People are always going to talk about things that are none of their business. People are going to notice when the cute kid down the block who played on the high school football team starts running amuck. People are going to talk when the pretty girl next door starts to look ragged and peels out of the cul-de-sac at all hours of the night.

No matter what level of recovery your child is at, you will have to address the social stigma surrounding drugs. That's why using social stigma as an excuse to ignore the problem is just absurd. Drugs, if left to their own devices, leave a noticeable mark. You won't be able to hide it forever. Letting the fear of social judgements make you turn a blind eye and pray the problem fixes itself is only going to make matters worse.

For many parents, it's not so much about what others think than it is about coming to terms with the fact that the child that they once bragged about and felt so much pride and joy for has fallen from grace. It is difficult when talking about your child's life and activities makes you feel shame rather than pride. Some parents' solution, though, is just to not talk about their child anymore. Ignorance is bliss, right?

They take up the "Don't tell Grandma" attitude. When their bosses ask them how Johnny or Katie is doing, they quickly change the subject or act as if nothing has changed—

Johnny is still going to Yale and Katie is still a champion soccer player.

But what you need to realize, if the shame has started to eat at you, is that drugs cannot be contained. People will find out one way or another. And honestly, the gossip (about both you and your child) will be far worse if your kid isn't making any progress. Yes, there will be chatter when folks find out your son or daughter has been checked into rehab, but hey, that's a lot better than the gossip my mother had to deal with.

She found out about my arrest on the radio. My *Big Brother* win made the story top news. "*Big Brother* winner, Adam Jasinski, arrested for selling drugs." She knew she wasn't the only one who heard it, either. She knew she'd eventually be getting lots of curious phone calls, people casually asking about me under the pretense of having a casual chat. She knew family members would be dying to know if it was true.

So, she acted preemptively. She sent out a mass email to all of her contacts, not just family (talk about guts), acknowledged that it was true, and revealed the struggles I had been facing for years.

Your child's problem will come out one way or another. You have to decide how you're going to deal with the backlash.

## Cower or Stand Tall

You can try to minimize the severity of the problem or attempt to hide it all together. Or, you can acknowledge the problem and then move on to addressing it.

It's pretty obvious which one you're supposed to pick, but that doesn't always make it easy. Hiding sounds so tempting; it's much easier than facing the terrible truth. So let me lay out what will happen if you choose this route.

The influence of narcotics starts off minimal, usually. A slip in grades. A lack of interest in old hobbies. Keeping that under wraps isn't so bad, right? It's just a part of growing up. Well, sometimes it is, but the glazed look in their eye or their drunken entrances at two in the morning or that pipe you found in their drawer say otherwise. But at this stage, denial is so easy.

Then your child drops out of school. That's a little bit harder. Oh, but kids will be kids. Katie just wants to get out and see the world a little bit. She'll get her GED in a year or two. The uneasiness grows, but you shove it in a closet and try not to think about it, like my dad did with my mental health issues.

But the beast thrives in the dark of that closet and grows stronger away from prying eyes. Eventually, it outgrows its make-shift prison and becomes restless.

Your child starts acting wild. Katie causes a scene at a family get-together. Johnny starts hanging out with some shifty characters. Behind closed doors, you begin to get uneasy. You can no longer deny the seriousness, but you still don't want others to know. You decide to confront your child. Johnny tells you he just smokes a little pot to let loose with his friends. Katie acts offended that you think she has a problem; she's just acting her age. Sure she drinks a little; didn't you when you were her age?

You know the smell of pot; that's not what Johnny's smoking. Katie's constant flush and her erratic mood swings tell you she's doing more than just having a few fruity Smirnoffs with her girlfriends. But those minimizations give you an excuse. You have to believe them, right? Wrong.

The addict's minimization is bad enough; they're in denial about how bad their habit has become and don't see anything wrong with continuing it. To have the parents then minimize it, too, so that they don't have to deal with it or the social repercussions turns the brewing storm into a tropical hurricane. Your minimization is another affirmation to your child that what they're doing isn't so bad.

The beast grows stronger and breaks free of its bonds. Katie, the former homecoming queen, gets popped for stealing. Johnny gets caught up in his dealer's turf war and is arrested for possession. All that talk that Johnny's and Katie's parents tried so hard to avoid comes spilling in from all directions.

Let's look at the same scenario from a different angle. When Johnny talks of dropping out of school, his father confides in his close family about his worries of possible drug use. His brother tells him he ought to buy a home drug test; that's what a friend of his did when he thought his kid was using pot. The encouragement from the other family members pushes Johnny's dad to act faster, and he confirms Johnny's cocaine habit before Johnny goes completely off the rails.

When Katie has a minor car crash and her mother observes her dilated pupils and the smell of alcohol on her breath, she shares her worries with her best girlfriend. To her surprise, her girlfriend's niece got into some real trouble using club drugs. She recommends the treatment center that got her niece back on her feet.

The more people who know of the problem, the more people who may rally around you. You never know who's been there. Drug addiction is a major issue these days, and it's actually hard to find someone who doesn't at least know someone else who's dealt with the struggle themselves or with a loved one. In fact, one in ten homes is harboring the hardships of addiction. Having you share your problems may help someone else open up about their own. You also need to let the human resources department at your job know what's going on so there is more understanding if you need to head out of work suddenly to help your child. Sometimes HR can even help you find treatment for your child. Ask someone in HR if they have an Employees Assistance Program (EAP). Even if they won't directly get your child into a program, they can usually provide some resources for you.

Yes, if you're open about the situation, you will get some judgmental looks and whispers. There are always going to be assholes in the world. There are always going to be ignorant people who judge situations they know nothing about. But those sharp-tongued whispers and pitying looks are going to happen eventually. In fact, the stigma will be worse if you let things slide out of control. My mom understood this. She sent out that email so that people would know she had nothing to hide anymore. She acknowledged my problem and let everyone know that she was going to help me work through it. The gossip amongst her social circles was minimal compared to what it would have been if she'd tried to cover up my arrest and acted like nothing had happened.

If you're sitting around worrying that people might notice your child's strange behavior, I guarantee you they already have. It's like being a battered wife. Everyone knows she's being abused, but no one says anything to her face because she won't acknowledge it herself.

Speak up and share with those close to you. Yes, you may feel vulnerable, silly, scared, or ashamed, but you're feeling those things anyway. Why not seek support from others to help you through it?

If that's not enough to convince you, your child's wellbeing ought to be. Hiding the problem allows it to thrive. If your child knows you're ashamed of their use, they can use that as leverage. If you don't give them money, they'll threaten to go asking your friends and family for it. Not to mention the fact that you're embarrassed by them only further damages their self-esteem and drives them to use more.

If you don't tell Grandma or Aunt Janie that Katie's

using, Katie can easily manipulate them into giving her drug money. However, if you're making everyone aware of your child's habit, your child must face the repercussions of that from all sides. They'll know everyone's watching them. They'll find it much harder to obtain money. They'll also have a large support system working to help them get better if they say yes at the intervention.

The whispers will never stop, even when your child starts the recovery process, but they will hold far less sting if you can stand tall and face the problem without shame or fear. You didn't cause this, but you can help fix it.

## Understand Your Child's Social Pressures

Many young people start getting high to ease social anxieties or find social acceptance. If you think you're worried about social stigma and other people's opinions, think back to when you were a teen. The desire to be cool and fit in is enormous and daunting.

As social pressures squeeze them from all sides, they may turn to drugs to calm down, ease the awkwardness, and numb the loneliness.

You need to understand and address this to better help your child overcome the desire to use. You need to try your best to make your child realize that they ought to be concerned about themselves and what brings them joy rather than what others think. The truth is that people are just concerned with themselves; they don't really give a crap that you have pimples or an out-of-style shirt. The people who pick on others are those who are uncomfortable with themselves.

You've probably told your child this sort of thing already, and you can say it till the cows come home and they still may not believe you. However, the real key is just being there when your child feels rejected and awkward. You need an open relationship. You want your child to come to you when they feel this way, or you at least need to be able to recognize when they are feeling these pressures. If someone isn't there to lift them up, drugs will be.

You also need to be aware of how young people's social lives help them find drugs and other addicts. In the age of the internet and social media, finding likeminded peers takes a few clicks. If your child feels left out in their immediate circles, they can turn to online ones to meet up with people who share their interests. That's a great thing, unless the interests are getting high and finding drugs.

If your child becomes curious about drugs, they can overload on everything there is to know with just a few simple searches. Stumbling across the dark web where illegal items are sold is a lot easier than you think. Monitor your child's online use if you have suspicions. You don't have to stalk everything they do on there, just be aware. Check their search histories, scan their Facebook wall. A small invasion of privacy is worth saving their life.

Also keep a watchful eye on their social circles. If Johnny distances himself from his childhood buddies and starts hanging out with a new group that shows little respect for you and has a reputation for delinquency, you need to take note and start asking questions. If Katie drops her soccer teammates and starts hanging out with party girls who always come to pick her up an hour before her usual curfew, you need to toss privacy aside and start digging.

## Conclusion

Ignoring or covering up your child's changes in behavior just makes them think they're getting away with it. They think, "If no one's noticed, it must not be so bad." They won't realize how out of control things are getting if everyone around them just acts like everything's normal.

You need to realize that even small life changes like moving to a new school district or getting dumped by their first crush is a huge deal to a young adult. Be aware of your child's social activities and pressures. Be aware that the social stigma you fear is going to explode either way. It's better to ignore the gossip and think only of your child's recovery. You also have to accept that your child has changed. But don't feel shame, feel motivated. If you're really worried about bragging rights and feeling proud of your child, just think of what a huge accomplishment a successful recovery is. I can't tell you how elated my loved ones are over the book you're almost done reading.

This isn't about your social life; this is about saving your child's life. Letting people know isn't going to ruin anything. In fact, it can open new doors and provide you with the support you need. Don't try to keep things bottled up in the home; it's what goes on outside your walls that is usually the biggest influence in your child's use.

Stand tall and stare down those judgmental faces. You have nothing to be ashamed of unless you ignore your child's needs just to save a little face.

# CHAPTER 20: MY SECRETS TO QUALITY LIVING

Getting cleaned up and sent back out into society, freshly scrubbed and shining with enthusiasm, is the easy part of recovery. Maintaining the enthusiasm, motivation, and willpower to stay clean for the long haul is the truly difficult part. Every recovering addict needs to find their own rhythm and their own methods, but I want to share what has worked for me over the past seven-plus years, in the hopes that at least some of them work for you and your child. For me, the end of the process, when I was out from behind the veil of the treatment centers and prison walls, was the hardest part. But I figured it out, and now it's the area I specialize in.

I know that I never want to go back to where I was, and that desire has driven the course of my life and allowed me to discover the patterns and tips I'm going to share with you now. These are not just tips for addicts; they are tips for a quality life after being touched by the influence of drugs and mental illness. So, parents, I hope maybe you can find comfort and help in some of them. You may want to let your child read this chapter, too, when they get into aftercare, and let them hear it directly rather than you having to relay it to them secondhand.

## Secret #1: Faith

I credit my faith as the driving force behind my success. I read the Bible cover to cover multiple times while participating in *Big Brother*. Doing so gave me depth. Yes, I strayed from my faith before and after, and slipped up, but the beauty of faith is the forgiveness that comes with it, so long as you're willing to accept it. When I got my head clear again, all of the things I'd adsorbed while reading scripture came back.

I talk to God throughout every day, asking for help and giving Him thanks. I know I will never be perfect; I'll never achieve long-term sobriety on my own. God has walked me through the darkest of deserts, and each time, I've come out untouched. I now have life in abundance. God is the ultimate support group. He's always there, and he has more power to help than any person could ever hope to.

That's why I go to church and try to do what the scripture says is right at all times. Yes, I fail, but the key is trying. The trying keeps me on the right path.

I find encouragement in daily Bible emails using the Bible app on my phone. It gives me a chance to read scripture every day. I don't always have to take a ton of time each day to sit down and read a huge chunk of the Bible, so I use the app to help me remember to read a little bit each day. I put the app on my phone's front screen so that I see it regularly.

I humble myself daily. I remember my faults, accept them, face them, and seek to overcome them. I know I'm no better than anyone else, but I know that everyone deserves help. That's why I've dedicated my days to helping others who've experienced similar hardships.

To me, faith makes my new life possible. I feel the truth of God somewhere deep in my gut, and I thank Him every day for all that I have. I try not to take credit for my successes and get a big head. I do my best to give the credit to God.

My faith is something that I'm naturally very private about. My relationship with Jesus is a close bond between Him and me, and I struggle to be public about it, but I know it must be said because I think people ought to know the comfort and guidance it can bring. I believe in the power of prayer, and I hope that others can apply that power to their own life.

## Secret #2: Routines

Routines are a recovering addict's best friend. By repeating a productive, enjoyable schedule, good actions become habits. The schedule doesn't have to just consist of big things like going to work, going to the gym after work, and attending support group meetings, though all those things are vital. There will always be little moments of time that can be filled up with something productive, like always washing the dishes right after dinner. Adopting fun hobbies like reading before bed or going to a movie every Saturday part of a routine makes sure you're not just running around working all day. Just make sure your life isn't boring and that you're getting out of the house. You have to break up that old routine every now and then.

I work for myself, so my entire day is up to me to plan. I schedule my activities around my own basic routine, and I stick to it. I don't change my core schedule to please others. My recovery is about me, not anyone else. I put my healing first and a solid routine is at the core of my healing.

After I established a healthy routine, I would feel that something was off if I began to backslide from it. This allowed me to recognize the warning signs of relapse faster all on my own because that shift in schedule was jarring. A schedule is also a way to jump back into recovery. If I notice a break in routine, I can focus on getting back into it and restoring that much-needed balance. That focus helps to drive the tempting thoughts from a recovering addict's mind.

## Secret #3: Aware of Being Aware

My therapist taught me that I need to try and observe my life from above, if you will. To imagine my life as a walk through a valley of trails. Every decision or change will take me down a new path. One small decision today can take me down more treacherous paths in the future, down paths that eventually lead to the edge of a ravine.

That's why I am acutely aware of what I'm doing daily. I take time to evaluate how I'm feeling. If I'm feeling low and depression is looming, I can observe that change and then tell myself, "Okay, I'm bummed right now. I need to take a break and slow things down." Then I adjust my actions accordingly.

## Secret #4: Get Up and Wear Yourself Out

Because I am a bipolar maniac, I have to get out and get active to wear down that excess energy. If I don't come home at night feeling nicely tired, I start to get stir crazy and yearn for action. That usually leads to some bad behavior.

But I am now aware of that. That's why I don't take a lunch break in a traditional sense. My day is a constant "get up and go" situation, non-stop all day. I make sure to go to the gym before or after work, run errands, pay bills, etc. until five or six every night, and then I can shut down because I'm truly tired. I don't rush around so much on the weekends, but I still go out and do stuff around the house. I still get out and go somewhere I want to enjoy.

This is something I do because of my personal condition. Of course, working out is never a bad idea, but I make constant movement part of my daily routine, not just a weekly or every other day thing, because that's what I need to do. Someone with a different disorder may need to add something totally different to their routine. It's personal to everyone.

## Secret #5: Plugins

If I have too much downtime, or I start to feel anxious

or fidgety, I know that can lead me to trouble. That's why I have certain activities that I call "plugins." These are things that I plug into my schedule during free periods to kill time or distract my mind. Free time can pop up at any time. It's what you do in that time that makes the difference. If a meeting is canceled, and I'm near a library, I'll pop in for a book. If I'm near a TJ's, I'll stop by to check the clearance rack. The key is to do something productive and enjoyable during these periods instead of heading to an old haunt.

These plugins are a mixture of work and pleasure activities for me. For instance, I'll go to the beach, ride my dirt bike, treat myself to some new clothes, go to a kickboxing class, go grab a book from the store or the library, watch a life advancement video, do some online research on an idea that recently popped into my head, clean the house, wash my car, or do some laundry. There's any number of things that can serve as plugins. My list has grown over the years of discovering new things I like doing, things that I never tried out before or didn't give time to because I was too busy getting high.

The point is just to be proactive—nothing too complicated—to avoid that deadly downtime.

## Secret # 6: Reward Yourself (When It's Earned)

I take time to reward myself. But I don't just go spending willy-nilly. I plan ahead to treat myself when I can. That way, I don't break the bank and I have something to look forward to. Sometimes I buy concert tickets a month or two in advance or plan a trip to an amusement park.

Spur of the moment fun, like cutting out of work early and going to watch a football game at home on the couch is just filling a void, and it can lead to trouble. If you plan ahead for some clean, healthy fun, looking forward to it gives you motivation to keep working hard so you can afford the big event and enjoy your time off. When the day comes, it's far more rewarding than an impulse decision that can jeopardize your job or some other aspect of your life.

Figure out what you want and work toward it. That's a real accomplishment. At the moment, I have all types of toys that bring me joy, like motorcycles, dirt bikes, golf carts, and boats. But I didn't buy them all up at once on an impulsive trip through a display. I bought them one by one over time.

I would look every day for great deals on places like Craigslist, keeping my focus on my goal and getting a good idea of what I'd need to achieve it. Sometimes it took months before I found the right thing for the right price, but that period of driving steadily toward a goal is a huge part of the reward.

When I first sat down to write this book, I was looking for a new truck. I didn't have the money right then, but I had fun looking, and I knew I'd get it eventually. As I'm writing this chapter, the truck sits in my driveway.

## Secret # 7: Self-Spoil

Spoil yourself. This one sort of builds off #6. I'm not spending all my money on drugs anymore, which gives me a major boost in my income. I use that to invest in myself and enjoy the spoils of my hard work.

Doing the right thing is hard, tiring, and sometimes downright boring. You ought to be rewarded when you stick to it.

That doesn't mean blowing all your money. It means making a happy life for yourself and spoiling yourself with things that you don't really need but that bring you happiness. Nothing is better than a new pair of sneakers. Right?

## Secret #8: It's a Selfish Program

Recovery is a selfish program, meaning that you're getting sober for yourself and no one else. To achieve sobriety, you have to jump right into the process and embrace it. You have to power through the steps by yourself, ultimately, so you need to be doing it for you.

The only way to take care of others is by getting yourself right first. And no one can do everything for you. I used to have my mom or girlfriend do everything I could possibly prod them into. That manipulation got me nowhere, and I realized I needed to be self-sufficient if I ever wanted to truly accomplish anything. If you aren't prioritizing your own life and you aren't being your best, you can't help others, as all the support groups teach. You are the person with the most interest and investment in your wellbeing, so don't neglect yourself.

## Secret #9: Forget the Word "Drugs"

Life is not all about drugs, contrary to what I once felt. When drugs are calling the shots, they make everything about them, and it's hard for an addict to see anything else. I still spend a lot of time with people trying to get off drugs, through my work. This helps me keep the hardships and issues of addiction at the forefront of my mind so that I never lose sight of what I've come from or where I could slide back into if I'm not careful. However, I don't let that rule my life or my conversations. It's simply about awareness now. But instead of glorifying drugs and the war stories of my past, I talk to recovering addicts about dreams, new ideas, laughs, and funny experiences. I want those young people to know that there really is a great life out there that doesn't revolve around drugs.

## Secret #10: Labels

For years, I thought that I would never be anything but an addict, that I'd never have nice things or healthy relationships. I worried I'd never be an honest, fulfilled person.

It is easy to get stuck in a rut like this when drugs are still dictating every aspect of life. However, jail snapped me out of it. It doesn't always take something so drastic, but sometimes it does take something that serious to open an addict's eyes.

Don't keep treating yourself like you're still an addict. Don't put other people's labels on yourself. While in active addiction 20+ years ago, I got mixed up in credit card fraud, and I was nervous for years afterward every time I used a card, feeling like I was doing something wrong. If you've turned away from those old habits, don't keep smacking yourself over the head with them.

Similarly, if you are suffering from a mental illness, get rid of that "insane" label you're putting on yourself. I once read somewhere, "If you are thinking properly enough to observe your behavior and think that you're insane, you're not insane." Quit calling yourself that.

Use new labels to redefine and describe your sober self, like successful, fun, loving, and professional.

## Secret #11: Keep Social

I used to think I knew everything. No one could convince me otherwise. A solo mission through life is never going to work. Yes, recovery is about you, but you need others by your side, helping you.

I finally let God take control of my life because I realized that I had obviously screwed things up for myself when I was at the helm. I've surrounded myself with a network of people all willing to stand behind me and give me a push when I need it. My friends are caring. I surround myself with people who have the kind of life that I want, so that they stand out as an encouraging example of what I can achieve. (Thanks, Jarod!)

When I have a problem or feel stuck in life, I first give it to God. Then, I lean on my friends who have endured those same pitfalls and my professional team who know better than me.

I once heard that you must spend your life in three parts. One third of your time is spent around people better than you. One third is spent around equals. The final third is spent helping others less fortunate than you.

The healthier the people you are around, the healthier you will be. Surround yourself with people you want to be like. It keeps you from going backward and instead pushes you forward.

## Secret #12: Mentors—Get One (or a Few)

To surround yourself with people better than you, seek out mentors in different areas of life. For instance, I have a mentors I turn to for business advice and ones I turn to for spiritual advice. Before, I used to be jealous of those better than me. Now I want to know them.

I actually lost touch with my old AA sponsor (who was like a mentor to me) when I was in jail, but that's normal. As life shifts, your mentors shift to match.

Your relationship with your mentor doesn't have to be someone you see face-to-face all the time. You just need a conversation with someone who can provide advice and solace. My mom is one of my mentors, in business and in life.

This is a huge advantage that can mean the difference between success and failure. You need to have one person who acts as a pedestal, raising you higher. They will guide you and genuinely care for you.

All successful people had help, and once they've achieved that success, the best ones will look backward to help others reach that same goal. A mentor is a winner who will coach you to be a champion, too.

For instance, one of my best friends became a real estate mogul at an early age. I could bounce ideas off of him, and I just enjoyed listening everything he had to say because he was doing something I wanted to do.

The key to picking the right mentor is finding someone who's doing life exactly the way you want to, and then align yourself with them. Bad mentors do exist and should be avoided at all costs. I had a drug dealer role model who taught me how to best rerock cocaine. A bad mentor shapes a life just as a good one does. A mentor sets you on a path, so find someone whose path you want to follow.

Once you've found them, be their friend, feel their friendship in return, and emulate the best of what they do. Nothing is holding me back from achieving the same things as my mentors. I was damn good at being a drug addict, so why can't I be damn good in an area that actually grants me success?

## Secret #13: Speak Your Thoughts

The power of manifestation is real; I've experienced it. There is just something inherently powerful about the spoken word. That's all manifestation is, speaking things that you want aloud. Speak and ye shall have.

Saying things aloud is also a good way to prioritize and consider your goals. Sometimes things sound totally different when you speak them out than they did bottled up in your head.

## Secret #14: Do What You Can with What You Have

For a long time, I would always need something to start something, saying, "I can't do this because I need _____." I wouldn't do the laundry, because I'd run out of detergent. I wouldn't mop, because I needed to get soap. I wouldn't go after a life goal, because I felt I needed something first: money, backing, etc.

Now, I do what I can with what I have at the moment. I ask a neighbor for some soap, or I sweep the floor and plan to get soap on my next trip out. I sort the laundry that night so that I have to go out and get detergent the next morning. If I want to start a business, I'll save those ideas and do research until I have the necessary capital; I don't just let the idea die out or dismiss it as impossible.

There is always something there to start off with, you just have to actively look for it, and then get your butt in gear and do it. There is always something you can do to advance your plan, even if you can't finish it right away. Don't just walk away from it. Small steps today are strides tomorrow.

## Secret #15: Dream Big

Drugs robbed me of dreams I had when I was a child. They made me give up on forming new dreams. But those days are behind me now. Recovery is the perfect time to start dreaming again.

My dad has always told me, "Shoot for the top; there is more there." He's right. There's never any harm in aiming high; the best things are always on the top shelf.

I dreamed of writing a book for years, and once I really started to act on that dream, doing what I could each day with what time and resources I had, I got closer and closer to that top shelf where my freshly printed book lies. Now I'm writing one of the final chapters!

Everyone has the right to dream big; it's others who shoot you down, for their own selfish reasons. You don't have to broadcast your dreams, but keep on dreaming. Get those mental gears turning, and you'll find out that you like yourself and what you can dream up.

Even if not all those dreams don't come true, it's the act of dreaming that keeps us truly alive. Who cares if a few fall through? I guarantee others will come to fruition, and there's no better feeling in the world.

## Secret #16: Keep Confident

For too long I thought I was a failure. I labeled myself a scumbag drug addict, and I used that label to justify my behaviors. I never thought I would make $1,000 a week; I wasn't worth it in my mind. I had to step back and realize that I am worthy of good things and I deserve a good life.

Thinking I didn't deserve a good life held me back. Building confidence in myself took time, years, but once I began to experience new belief in myself and witnessed the results that confidence had on my life, it became contagious. Building confidence is necessary to get rid of debilitating fear. Walk tall. Head up and shoulder's back. Life is not easy, and if you don't go through it with confidence, you won't make it at all. Be confident that you will have a good day and that you will stay sober. . It's like a WWE wrestling match, good guy pitted against bad guy. They each try to gain momentum until one pushes farther and ends up the victor. You either progress or regress; by staying confident, you push yourself forward and use that momentum to head in a positive direction. Once the boulder starts rolling down that hill, it becomes easier to push it.

## Secret #17: Ditch Distractions

When I got high, I would find any way to waste my day. I

never did anything productive—never had the motivation to. Of course, if someone called asking to hang out, I was out the door.

I had no focus, only distractions, and I let that pattern continue until I lost everything I previously had. I had to learn that there is always going to be a TV show on or a friend to sit around with killing time, but there is a time and place for that sort of thing.

Take the time to turn down distractions and tune in to priorities. I know what needs to get done each day, and that comes first, not giving people rides or swinging by my boy's house to smoke some weed. Keep up with your good habits and don't get distracted.

## Secret #18: Slow Your Roll

My mania keeps my life in a cycle of endless "go, go, go" if I let it. I have learned that I need to take breaks and step away from things, take time to reflect. That time of reflection helps me think up better solutions and keeps me from burning out. Obsessing over things doesn't help anyone; you can only focus on one thing continuously for so long. Whether it's a partner or a job or a hobby, take a break when you need it, and think about something else for a little while.

I have found that meditation really helps combat my disorder. It allows me to slow down and ground myself, and to expend extra superfluous, distracting thoughts.

## Secret #19: Practice What You Preach

I practice the "reap what you sow" principal. The Bible says it, and I have heard it since I was a kid, but I never thought it amounted to anything real. But now I know it to be fact. If you do good now, you get good later. You have the choice to sway that bitch Karma in your favor.

My wrongs and debts have been paid back, and now I focus on sowing positive, healthy things. If you put that out into the universe, it will come flying back like a well-thrown boomerang.

## Secret #20: Invest in Yourself

I invest in myself. I read a ton of books each year in a quest for knowledge that will make me a better person. Every solid career requires a continuation of education, and I have decided to make one of my careers improving myself. So, I continue to gather information from masters like Wayne Dyer, Tony Robbins, and Jesus Christ.

Whether it's a new self-help book, classes, or a golf lessons, I regularly seek out new knowledge to fill the void left by drugs, keep me occupied, and give me renewed satisfaction. You never know what you're really good at until you try a bunch of new things.

## Secret #21: Momentum

For every new thing you try, take the time and effort to build up momentum. Send that snowball rolling. Momentum brings motivation, and motivation brings victories. Learn the basics, start moving toward improvement, learn how to get better, and let the victories roll in. It takes some butt-kicking effort in the beginning, but once things get going, it's really not much work at all because the momentum takes hold.

## Secret #22: Time Will Turn Things Around

My addiction, mental illness, and my embarrassment over my situation had me shackled for a long time. However, I realized that dwelling on my arrest and letting it rule me wasn't going to get me anywhere. So, little by little, I turned my circumstances into a positive thing, while getting my life back on solid ground. A few steps in the right direction today are strides next week.

My past is actually a blessing in the consultation field I'm currently in. I have an education on the subject of addiction, mental health, and how the system works that you can't really pay for.

Be strong, be patient, be positive, and you can turn any bad situation upside down. Things don't change in a day. I didn't get out of jail a completely changed person, shouting, "Look at me! I made it! I'm clean!" I took my time; put in the work over days, months, and years; studied hard; and turned things around big time.

## Secret #23: Tune In

My aunt used to always say, "God shines down a spotlight. You're either in it, out of it, or half in and half out. Get all in, and see what happens."

There are positive, productive frequencies out in the universe. That spotlight is the frequency. When you see something work, go with it. When you recognize your gut urging you to do something, do it. Tune into that radio station broadcasting the life of your choice, and live by what it says.

If there's too much static in the form of distractions and negative influences, adjust the dial until it produces quality music.

## Secret #24: Qualifying Questions/Think Things Through

I ask myself quality questions. You have to challenge yourself and be aware of your faults, strengths, actions, and inactions.

Here are some questions that I ask myself regularly:

Is this the right time to make this move?

Am I really going to let this situation affect me?

What will I get out of going there?

Know yourself, ask yourself questions, and think things through in order to make rational decisions. This practice puts the brakes on impulse actions and impulsive words that you can't take back. Even this little pre-assessment of any decision can help you avoid a poor or even fatal one.

## Secret #25: Forget About Fear

I am the first to tell myself I can't do something. If something is hard, I'll catch myself asking, "Why bother?"

This is a self-destructive habit. Do not doubt yourself until you try. Poor self-talk and "stinkin' thinkin"get me nowhere; I've put them in the past. I use an "I can and I will" mentality.

When you're wallowing in the lows of a bad situation, it's hard at first, but it's worth the effort. Now, I am not afraid to try anything so long as I've taken the time to evaluate whether my motivations behind it are pure.

Quit drugs; don't quit on yourself. Overcome doubt and worry. It can't get as bad as it was so long as you make the effort to do positive things, so what is there to be afraid of?

## Secret #26: Self-Sabotage

Back in my days of addiction and manic behavior, I was the king of setting myself up for failure just at the moment I was about to have a big success. Case in point, right when I won a huge pot of money, I turned back to old vices and blew most of it on partying and drugs, eventually landing myself in jail.

This sort of self-sabotage is common among drug addicts. They will end up wandering into someplace they ought not be, reach out to an old friend who is still using, or for some unknown reason just reach for the old substance out of impulse.

To combat this, the addict must identify the inner blocks or unbroken habits that are leading to drug use, and eradicate them. Know the signs of self-sabotage, pick up on the markers of those bad habits, and cut them off at the root instead of acting upon them.

I have developed an intuition, or a sixth sense, about right and wrong actions. I feel it when I walk into the wrong place or come across the wrong people. I let that instinct guide my situations.

Start reading people and looking for their motivations. Everyone wants something, and sometimes the people you're around are wanting something negative from you. If you can pick up on that, you can extricate yourself from a bad scenario. If what that person wants is something positive that aligns with your personal goals, that person is a great one to hang around.

Addicts' instincts become fine-tuned to help them read places and people because they are seeking each other out and trying to avoid detection. If they can turn those instincts around and use them to find positive influences and environments, they have a better chance of avoiding relapse.

## Secret #27: Pick Your Partner

When looking for a life partner, if you have a go-getter attitude in your life and you want the best, seek out someone who believes in your ability to succeed and supports you on the way to that success.

My relationship isn't 100%; nobody's totally is. Don't let your personal life with a partner adversely affect your actions. That person needs to validate your life. They need to be a comfort at the end of a hard day. Yes, there will be issues, but they shouldn't overwhelm everything else.

## Secret #28: What's Your Talent?

Figure out your personal assets. While I was using, I was never clear-minded enough to evaluate myself. I never knew the positive skills I naturally possessed. Now that I've taken the time to test and observe my strengths, I know that I'm good with people. I'm a talker, I'm compassionate, and both those things make me great at finding new talent.

Everyone ought to take time to learn about themselves. When something comes easy, it's a natural asset. Focus on and fine-tune those areas.

## Secret #29: Validation and Naysayers

Addicts are always seeking validation, especially early in recovery. At that point, they aren't very confident. They've seen what their decisions about drugs did to their life, and now they worry they will mess up again by making a wrong decision. Sometimes it gets so bad that they need validation and approval for every little thing they do, like getting a new haircut or buying a new pair of clothes that is different from their regular style. No one should need validation for those sorts of things. You need to be self-assured that you look good, that you're doing good.

When I started doing well again and making larger decisions in business, I would get a lot of naysayers asking me, "Do you really want to do this?" or "Can you really afford that?" or "Maybe you should slow down."

If a non-addict working part-time on construction sites decides to start his own construction business, he gets slaps on the back and lots of encouragement. If a former addict wants to do the same thing, he gets skeptical looks from the people closest to him. Sometimes people close to an addict have a hard time letting go of those old worries. They'll say, "Maybe you should wait and do that until you have a little more money," or "Are you sure you can handle that much responsibility?"

What I came to realize is that no one really knows my motivations or my vision. I'm self-assured in my decisions. If I feel it's right in my gut, I go for it no matter what others say. I have confidence in my own judgment, and that keeps me from allowing others to intimidate me into backing down from something I really want to do. Former addicts need to learn to have confidence in their decisions, big or small.

## Secret #30: Small Wins

Not every decision I make is a complete success. I mess up sometimes. I'm not a robot. However, the difference between a small step backward and a total failure is picking yourself up and keeping your life moving forward.

If you do that, you'll start winning. I know I did. It feels good, even just a small win. And you can always turn those small wins into big ones. Some wins for recovering addicts might simply be getting their license back or getting off probation. If they can build off the momentum of those simpler wins, they can achieve larger goals, like being able to move to a better neighborhood and find a better job.

## Secret #31: Speak Up and Ask Questions

Ask for what you want. Ask for help. I used to have a deep fear of rejection, but now, the more no's I get during my search for a goal, I know that that just means I'm closer to getting a yes. I just learned to use that same persistence that helped me track down the best deals for drugs to relentlessly hunt down productive things.

## Secret #32: Instant Nothing

My desire for instant gratification helped fuel my drug

habit. I wanted a quick fix for the issues that came along with my bipolar disorder. I wanted a quick fix to help me forget things and have a good time.

I had to learn the value of patience, to make myself slow down, think things through, and take the right steps to get what I want, and not give up just because something is taking longer than I want it to.

## Secret #33: Tackle the Scary Stuff First

I used to build up walls of fear that held me back from doing things. It turns out, though, that the things I was scared of doing were usually some of the easiest things I ever did.

Now, I wake up and make sure that I do the things that are worrying me and kept me up the night before first. That way, they're out of the way and can't bother me anymore. Before, I would have turned to drugs as an easy out from facing the tasks I needed but was afraid to do. Now I face them head on and attack them first, and the rest of the day is much easier, like pedaling downhill.

## Secret #34: You Don't Know It All

I used to think I knew everything. I thought I knew that drugs couldn't really harm me. I thought I knew that I was doing perfectly fine in life. In fact, I thought I was living an enviable life of fun and indulgence. Well, I was wrong, and I had to learn that I'm not right about everything. No one is, and thinking that way will get you high again real fast.

## Secret #35: The Big Picture

Focus on the big picture. In order to keep moving forward in life and in recovery, you can't let little hang ups stop you in your tracks. No matter how hard it is sometimes, I work to prioritize everything I have to do in my day and in my life, and if one little, unimportant thing goes wrong, I can't let myself dwell on it.

## Secret #36: Follow Through

I have made it a priority to actually follow through on things. During the height of my mania and drug use, I would start out determined to finish some project or accomplish some task, but then I would crash, turning away from all the good things I was doing. Now, I make sure I complete even the smallest tasks once I start them. I actually use a gift card all the way through. I finish my vitamin bottles. Just little things like that keep me in the habit of finishing what I start.

## Secret #37: Keep a Wishlist

I always thought keeping a wish list was total bullshit. I never believed that just writing things you wanted down and keeping the list near you would actually help any of those wishes manifest, but I was wrong. This month, my girl made me one to hang on my wall, and I actually crossed off three of those things in just one month.

It's as simple as putting a picture of the house you want to buy on the mirror or any place where you will look at it every day.

## Secret #38: Blueprints

If you want something, there's probably no need to come up with some brand new, convoluted scheme to get it. For most things in life, there is already a basic blueprint. Others have gone before and gotten the same things, and you can achieve them, too, just by following those actions and ways of thinking. There's no reason to reinvent the wheel when you can just use the blueprint that's already there. You'll get further faster.

## Secret #39: Self-Image ... Project a Positive One (Killer Self-Image)

I create my reality from my beliefs. If you believe you are a no-good drug addict, your reality will be that of a drug addict. If you believe you're a hard worker who will earn plenty of money, then that will become your reality.

Build an image of yourself that you're in love with. I had to move away from the junkie image of myself that I had come to hate, and form an idea of what I actually wanted to be. Once I had that vision and believed I could achieve it, I was able to make a plan of action about how to make it reality. When you change your inner beliefs about yourself, your outside life will change to match them.

## Secret #40: Feelings, We All Have Them

Most addicts use drugs as a way to mask or escape their feelings. Well, feelings are real and must be faced, good or bad. I learned to be the boss of how I felt. I take time to process my feelings as they come, and then if they are bad, I put them aside and let them pass. If they're good, I take the time to actually enjoy them.

## Secret #41: Rome Wasn't Built in a Day

All recovering addicts need to understand that it is going to take time to feel 100% again and build the life they really want. The key is to get up and do your absolute best every single day; no half-assing it anymore. If you do that, it will still take time, but you will be able to chart noticeable progress that will encourage you to keep reaching for the end goal.

## Secret #42: Appreciate Failures

Appreciate failure. Life is full of good and bad circumstances, and you need to learn that and accept it. All circumstances are temporary. The important thing to know is that the more you fail the more you will succeed. Why? Because a failed attempt is still an attempt. Only when you don't make an effort to try do you truly miss out on success. Again, the more no's you get, the closer you are to a yes.

## Secret #43: Faith First

My final tip for you is to have faith. Have faith in God and in yourself. Believe in your decisions. Believe you are meant for great things. Be faithful to others, and keep your word. If you do all of that, you really can't fail.

# CHAPTER 21: SOLUTIONS AND REALITIES FOR PARENTS

NOW THAT WE'VE COVERED ALL of the technical, essential steps of getting help for your child, it's time to put the focus back on you as the parent. I want to discuss the harsher realities of what you will experience and feel throughout the whole process, and perhaps even long after your child exits rehab, if you don't do something about them.

Some of the things I'm about to say may be tough to swallow, but they are realities that must be faced, and I hope to provide you with solutions for overcoming them and letting them go. Nowhere in this chapter will I be telling you how to be a parent or accusing you of doing things wrong. I don't know your individual story. I don't know your child's specific situation. Every family and every addict is different, but chances are you've experienced at least one of the things I'm going to list here because these are situations that I have either dealt with in my own life or seen occur in the lives of the hundreds of kids I've worked with over the years. I hope by laying out everything, you can find a solution for the things you're struggling with buried somewhere within.

The whole process of addiction, rehab, and sobriety is an enormous undertaking that overwhelms everything like a tidal wave, crashing into your home and leaving you to scrounge through the leftover wreckage and put it all back together. Hopefully you're insured!

This book in your hand was designed to help you tread lightly through the mess, proceed cautiously and with purpose, and hopefully minimize the damage. It is meant to help you make sound decisions backed by solid solutions instead of letting your feelings fling you around without direction.

After you've done your part and begun guiding your child through to an independent life, it's time to rebuild. This chapter seeks to help you do that.

## It Starts with Acceptance

I said it at the very beginning of this book, and I'll say it again because I know that so many parents struggle hard with this. If you walk around with blinders on about the severity of your child's issue, it's an open invitation to stumble through life, wreaking havoc, unable to see the full picture and all of the things around you. This blind stumbling leaves your home a wreck, emotionally and financially. Denial is an open invitation to death. This isn't a problem you can ignore. The sooner an addict gets help, the better shot he or she has at sobriety. You can't blame yourself for your kid's addiction, but you have to take responsibility for getting her help because she isn't going to do it herself.

My parents blamed themselves and each other for my issues for a long time. It's easy to get pulled down and give up, but you can't let that happen. You have to accept the sour lemons you've been dealt, take them in your hands, and make lemonade by rolling, cutting, and squeezing the sour aspects of your child's situation and expertly transforming them into something good. Sure, life didn't turn out as you planned. That star athlete son may never go pro. You may not be getting a wedding or grandkids any time soon. Well, no one gets everything they want in life. Make new dreams and chase them.

## Slow Down and Think

As more problems arise due to your child's addiction, the feelings of anger, doubt, and desperation pile on top of each other. When you feel those waves of emotion, slow down and use your intuition and the knowledge you've gained in this book to make the right decision about how to move forward through your child's recovery.

Take the time to be thorough in your research of facilities. Prepare before you make your move and stage and intervention. Quit trying to outsmart your child and the drugs that are ruling them, and instead work toward providing solid solutions that guide your child in the right direction.

Practice taking time to chill out and process your thoughts and emotions as they well up, so that you can carry emotion from the right side of your brain, where it first appears, to the left side of your brain where you can approach it logically and use it to come up with a solution.

## Hold onto Rationality

When a child is in danger, a parent rarely thinks rationally. It's a natural impulse to want to just jump in and yank your child out of harm's way. However, this isn't as simple as pushing your child out from in front of a moving car or snatching them back from a low railing. This is more like springing them from an enemy prison camp. You have to think strategically; you can't go in guns blazing.

I have seen the strongest, most dominant people make tragically terrible decision when dealing with a drug-addled child. You can't let that happen to you. If you need to, when you slow down and develop a strategy, base it not around saving your child but around defeating drugs. By defeating drugs you save your child, and by looking at it from the perspective of attacking drugs rather than jumping in and rescuing your child, you may find it easier to cool down and strategize a coherent, effective plan.

## Put Your Best Face Forward

When faced with a dire situation and an oblivious child who refuses to see the destruction all around them, it's very easy go off the handle and do or say something you'll regret. When addressing your child, all actions and words should be good natured, even when discussing tough subjects. That does not mean coddling or pacifying them; that only supports their addiction. What I mean is that you must handle all conversations about their use with a calm and even, at times, lighthearted nature.

When you discuss your child's use and try to make them see the damage they're causing, you have to speak in a rational, calm, but serious tone. Blowing up and yelling only causes strife and actions you'll regret. It also ensures that your child won't listen, which means they'll just keep on with their unacceptable behaviors and cross more boundaries while you're busy feeling guilty and worrying about your outburst.

Keep it serious when it's serious, and joke when it's over, but never act out of vengeance or pain. You need to make your child understand your pain, but lashing out with it teaches nothing.

## Stop Being a Victim

Your child's addiction is not your fault. I've said it many times. Don't let that self-blame allow you to pick up a "poor me," "why me" mentality. If you let the blame rest solely on yourself, it's easy to feel overwhelmed, and then you find yourself using your kid's addiction as an excuse. Johnny's cocaine habit is why you can't pay the bills. Katie's pill popping is behind your poor performance at work. Dealing with these issues is hard, but it must be done. Don't let your child and their issue become a scapegoat for everything that isn't perfect in your life. If you don't rise up and be the strong one in this scenario, it's never going to get better. Your child is in the grip of drugs, you're not.

If you're going to quit something as a parent, quit the blame game. Don't quit trying. Don't blame your spouse, either. Your husband isn't to blame just because he let your daughter have the car. Your wife isn't to blame because she "spoiled" your son as a kid. It's the drugs' fault. Playing the blame game and putting everything off on yourself or your loved ones just allows the abuse to keep on raging. Be a team with your spouse and those closest to your child, and take control of the situation.

## There's Nothing Tough about Love

When you're setting those consequences in preparation for the intervention, don't think of it as tough love. That concept doesn't really make sense to me. Not paying your nineteen-year-old's bills isn't tough love. That's just life. If they are old enough to go out and buy drugs for themselves and con people out of money, they're old enough to face life as an adult. Why do we feel the need to allow legal adults to leach off their parents until they're twenty-six? If they are no longer minors, you owe your children love and emotional support, that's it. You don't owe them money or a place to stay or free groceries.

Many times parents have a hard time differentiating what's necessary to provide and what's too much. You don't owe them a car, an allowance, or a cellphone. Sure, if they're applying themselves in life and doing good and you want to give those things to them as a reward, that's great. But you don't *owe* them that stuff just because they're your child, even when they're minors. They're going to have to learn to grow up and live on their own eventually, so why not get a start now? That's not tough love. That's reality.

When the influence of drugs and alcohol makes it impossible for you to communicate with your child with mutual respect, it's time to break contact. That's not a lack of love. In fact, it's a way to show love. As we discussed previously, forcing them to face reality and make it on their own can stimulate the realization that they need to get drugs out of their life in order to survive.

If your child is a minor, you probably shouldn't kick them out of the house, but there are other ways to make them face reality. If they want their favorite foods from the grocery store, they've got to cough up the money. They have plenty, right? That's how they get those drugs. From now on, you're just getting what *you* want from the store.

Quit doing their laundry. Quit cleaning their room. Quit packing their lunches. These are things that they can easily be doing themselves. Make them take responsibility. The key is to make them realize that if they let drugs drive their actions, you're getting out of the car. Therefore, they aren't going to have nice things or get to do everything they want when they want.

Other family members may not agree with you kicking you twenty-year-old out of the house or forcing your sixteen-year-old to pay for her own special groceries. You may be judged and called a bad parent. So what? Your child's life is in danger; you need them to wake up, and other people's opinions be damned.

Still, it's nice to have the support of your family, so be vocal and open with them about why you're doing what you're doing. Lay out your plans before you implement them and ask for support in carrying them out. If you come to them for help and explain your reasoning, you have a better chance of them understanding your choices and helping you implement the changes.

## Giving vs. Earning

Part of the myth of tough love springs from the inability to differentiate between giving and earning when it comes to presenting a child with things. Every parent struggles with this because you want to give your child the world, as you should. However, that doesn't mean they should be given every little thing they want.

My parents spoiled me in many ways, but they still made me earn things I wanted. In my line of work, I see many kids who automatically expect things they don't deserve. Things that they squander and don't appreciate.

Giving your child the things they want isn't a bad thing when done in moderation, but when drugs become involved, it's all about the bare necessities. No more handouts. No more expecting Mommy and Daddy to take care of everything. If they want something, they have to earn it in some way. They have to learn something, take a positive step, and show you respect, or else they don't get anything. Money and things can't buy love. They may whine and scream, but that won't get them what they want. If you hold strong, eventually they will realize that they actually have to make the effort and do what you're asking, first.

## Could-a, Should-a, Would-a

I don't want to hear, "If I was a better parent ...," "If I had done this or that ..." Get over it. That sort of thinking isn't doing anyone any good.

The damage is done. Make peace with the past, because you can't change a damn thing about it. What you can do is learn from it. Beating yourself up takes time away from making a plan and holds you back from fixing things. Take those old mistakes and craft new actions that will create a better tomorrow.

## Don't Let Your Kid Kill You

Your child on drugs is a danger, not just to themselves but to you. When the drugs start talking, they will make it all your fault. When you don't give them what they want, they'll call you a bad parent and tell you that you did this to them. The drugs do this because they want something from you. They want to guilt you into giving your child money or allowing them to leave the house late at night. Drugs have no soul or conscience, they just have a need for more.

Fueled by the single-minded determination of an addict, your child will not stop. They will lie and steal and con and manipulate you until you're physically ill, if you let them. Don't let it get to that point. You're the parent; you don't follow their orders.

## Throw Away the Band-Aids

Whenever you clean up after the consequences of your child's use, you're slapping a Band-Aid on it. When you bail Johnny out of jail and pay his fines because he said he was sorry, you're not curing anything. Sure, the fines are gone and Johnny's out of jail, but he has learned nothing. Addicted children need to be forced to handle their own messes. Live and learn is the best cure. Let them patch up their own issues. Sure, you can steer them right and instruct them, but they have to be the ones to take action. If they never learn for themselves, nothing ever really changes.

## Codependence

Codependency, often referred to as the "relationship addiction," is when a person dedicates their life entirely to caring for a mentally ill or addicted person. A codependent person becomes so overwhelmed with helping out the afflicted loved one that they learn to put aside their own emotions, needs, wants, and responsibilities to care for the other person. They become withdrawn, lose self-esteem, and are constantly covering for the ill person.

I was my mother's addiction. If I needed anything at all, she was there with it. She was the world's best mom, but when I became addicted, that took on a serious downside. Her love for me and her need to believe everything I said allowed me to play her many, many times over. When I screwed up, she mopped up the mess. However, codependency does not help cure the addict, it only destroys the codependent.

Take care of yourself. Don't let your needs entirely fall by the wayside because of your child's condition. You can only help them when you're at your best. Be a mentor and a leader, not an enabler. Don't worry about being overbearing or a micromanager.

Now, of course your child needs your help, but they don't need money or a place to crash after a binge. You need to help them see the light. You need to help get them into rehab. After they get out, you may want to help them get on their feet, but you don't need to follow behind them handing over everything they ask for and fixing all the bad decisions they make. If you feel you are struggling with codependency, there are many sites online that provide "lessons" on how to deal with it.

It's a fine line trying to figure out when to help and when to step back. Sometimes you feel that you're damned if you do and damned if you don't, but through trial and error, you can find the right balance. Before you make a decision about whether to step in or not, think about what it will cost you and if it will actually help to set your child straight.

## Don't Confuse Help with Control

Some parents exert strong control over every aspect of their child's life. Sometimes, such a tight grip can be a reason why the child acts out and uses in the first place.

Kids need to be kids, and kids need to grow up. My mom wants to be in control of everything at all times. I knew this, and I used it to my advantage. I knew I could get away with all kinds of things and do just about whatever I wanted, and screw the consequences, because I knew she'd come along behind me and take control of the situation for me.

Doing things for your kid just to make life a little easier and get things done quicker doesn't actually help. Your child needs to develop skills that allow them to engage in life's hardships and feel the satisfaction of seeing their efforts produce results. Step back and make them either reap the consequences or take the reins and steer themselves out of harm's way.

## Don't Transfer Your Hopes and Dreams onto Your Kid

This is a hard one because it seems to just be human nature. You want those you love to love what you love, but you can't force someone to love something. You want the best for your kid, so you imagine him or her doing all the things you wished you had done or that you once did.

However, this sort of pressure can be toxic. Your child can feel that they aren't doing well enough if they don't do the exact things you'd like to see them do. They can feel unwanted, a failure.

Talk to your kid about their likes, and be aware of the motives behind your desires for your child's accomplishments.

## You Cannot Force a Way of Thought

If your kid is gay, he's gay. If he likes rap music, he likes rap music. You can't force anything on anyone. Trying to do so just drives a wedge between the two of you.

Your way is not the only way. You are not God. You do not have absolute authority over another human being. Try to understand why they have certain opinions or why they've chosen to dress and act a certain way, and accept them for who they are.

## Project What You Want

In the previous chapter, I talked about the power of thinking things into being. It sounds odd, but it really can work.

Envision a sober child. Imagine what that would be like. Imagine how you'd feel. Imagine what you think they might be doing. Picture them in rehab, working toward that happy goal. By thinking positively on a regular basis and focusing hard on what you want, you can manifest those thoughts into reality.

## The Healing Process

The only person you can ever change is yourself. This should come as an encouragement because it means that you can take control of your own healing. You can overcome the anxieties and the pressures that have plagued you through your child's addiction.

Healing begins with dropping the "poor me" attitude. Invest in the power of prayer and give up your worries to God. Part of directing your own healing is seeking out help. Attend groups like Al-Anon and learn how others are dealing with the same issues. Find support in others who have been in the same situations and have come out okay. Find a mentor whom you can confide in and whose example you can follow. That mentor should be someone who came out the other end of the same tunnel you're in, with a sober child and a healthy, repaired family life.

## Reestablish Trust

Addiction can wear down your ability to trust yourself and others. But that's no way to live. You need to repair that damage. Start trusting your gut and acting on its prodding. Trust that you are making the right decisions because you are educating yourself on the best courses of action. Trust your partner to work with you. Trust the process; it's worked countless times before. Still, don't be naïve and trust blindly. Think things through. Understand the realities. Yes, the process has been proven to work, but only if all the effort possible is put in. It's been known to fail plenty of times, too. But that doesn't mean you shouldn't trust it; it just means you need to be aware of all the avenues. Trust yourself to use the system to your advantage.

## Moving Forward with Your Child

Just because your child has completed rehab doesn't mean he's out of the woods. Maintaining a strong bond with you is going to be a key factor in maintaining sobriety, especially if your child is still a teen. A strong parental relationship is one of the best protective and preventative factors for kids. Reading this book means you're past the preventative stage, but these preventative methods are just as effective at *keeping* your child clean. And, who knows, maybe you have another child. Implementing family dinner nights, checking in with your younger children once or twice a day, paying attention to who your children hang out with, and having serious conversations about the realities of use and abuse can both help keep your recovering child from slipping backward and prevent your other child from falling into the same mistakes. An absent parent is no parent. It's all about creating a safe, honest household that acts like a sanctuary where your child can shed stress and speak freely. Listen to your children and let them know that their opinions are important to you. Lastly, your home, though a place of comfort and relaxation, should have clear cut rules and consequences for unacceptable behavior. The rules should always be enforced in the same manner every time they are broken. Structure, mutual respect, and investment in your child's day-to-day lives makes your home a shield against drugs.

## Be Cool

If you're going to survive this process, you need to hold onto your sense of humor. See the good inside each failure; I promise you there's some there. Keep calm, engage your child, and keep smiling, and you will emerge a better parent and a greater human being for your troubles.

# CONCLUSION

Well, here we are. In a few short pages, you will reach the end of this book, but "The End" in my book doesn't mean the end of the story. It doesn't mean closing the cover and setting it aside. "The End" in this book means taking action.

You're an educated parent now; the kind who can take charge with authority and confidence. You know what you need to do. Now do it!

Approach your child. Establish that new rapport. Ask the hard questions. Impart understanding and help, not judgement. Stay strong through the tantrums and administer a drug test. Know for sure. Gather your team. Stage your intervention. Find the right rehab and get your child into treatment. Find a quality sober home. Whatever you do, wherever you are in this process, *don't stop.*

The first step is education, the second is action. Yes, reading about taking action is always easier than doing it, but look at your child. Now that you know that your son or daughter is suffering, that he or she truly cannot stop the addiction alone, can you really do nothing? I don't think you can. Don't put it off, either. Every hit, smoke, or tweak is a gamble that brings your child one step closer to disaster. The time is now.

You *can* do this. I don't care how you handled things before. I don't care if you unwittingly enabled your child. I don't care if you yelled and screamed out of fear and frustration. And you shouldn't either. All that matters is what you do now. Don't wallow in your mistakes; learn from them. Your child needs you, and now you have the tools to help. Keep this book close. The beauty of a book is that it can be opened again and again, and the knowledge it imparts is always right where you last left it. Don't put this one away on a shelf to gather dust. Bring it back out as you reach each step. If you have specific questions about your child's personal situation and needs, please, go beyond the book and contact the person behind the words. I am more than happy to help in any way I can. You can find my contact information in the appendix.

If you stay strong, create boundaries, and take the proper action, things *will* change. Imagine, you look at that microwave clock and feel the soft warmth of happiness building in your gut, not the clenching fist of fear. It's almost noon, not midnight, and your son should be here any minute. Right on time, you hear his car pull in the drive. When he walks through the door, he smiles like he used to. His eyes are clear. He's pursuing his dreams again, and he tells you about them over lunch. Is everything perfect in his world? No, but that's life, and he's really living it again.

That image is not far-fetched. It's entirely achievable. But it all starts with you. It starts with a single, purposeful action.

# APPENDIX A:
# SAMPLE PRE-ASSESSMENT

Full Name:

DOB:

Phone Number:

Insurance:

Member ID:

Subscriber:

Subscriber DOB:

Where Are You Coming From? (State/Treatment/etc.):

Why Are You Leaving the Facility You're Currently At?

Date of Last Use:

Drugs Used:

Length of Time Used:

Most Recent Treatment?

Any Legal Issues?

Do You Have a Legal Guardian?

Have You Been Hospitalized? If so, Was It A State Hospital?

Other Notes:

# APPENDIX B:
# COMPREHENSIVE DRUG CHART

Alcohol is an intoxicating substance made from the fermentation of sugar, starch, and yeast. Consumption of it depresses the central nervous system. Alcohol is quickly absorbed and affects the body's neurotransmitters, resulting in enhanced or depressed sensations and moods. It can be highly addictive, and dependence occurs with regular use and quickly deteriorates the body, especially the liver. It comes in wine, beer, and hard liquor. Signs are impaired functions, slurred speech, and a bad hangover. Alcohol can be detected by a breathalyzer, which as relatively inexpensive. I recommend getting one just to be sure, and let your kid know you're not playing games when it comes to drinking, especially while driving. Alcohol can also be tested with dipsticks for urine and in the blood up to 48 hours after consumption.

Benzos. Below are the most popular. They mostly all have the same effects and can be dangerous in high doses. Many of the below are prescribed after tragic loss to ease severe anxiety and can be manipulated out of medical professionals by addicts. Benzos will be detected in the system for up to three days after consumption.

-*Alprazolam* is a prescription medication used to treat anxiety and panic disorders. It can also be used to treat depression or pre-menstrual syndrome and may be highly habit-forming. This medication decreases levels of abnormal excitement in the brain.

-*Xanax* is the name brand of the generic drug alprazolam, which is a benzodiazepine. It is primarily used to prevent anxiety and panic attacks, as well as anxiety caused by depression in some patients, by altering the chemicals in the brain. The effects of Xanax addiction can be devastating. Withdrawal can be fatal. Xanax comes in a variety of milligrams; the most common are the "bars, zannys, or totem poles," which are white and cost around $5-10 a piece on the street. Heavily slurred speech difficulty standing and loss of memory are common symptoms.

-*Valium* is used to treat anxiety, seizures, and muscle spasms. It can be habit-forming, so it should not be taken for an extended period of time. It's a small, round, blue pill, and the name brand will have a V cut into of the middle.

-*Klonopin*, the brand name for clonazepam, is used to control certain types of seizures caused by epilepsy. It decreases abnormal electrical activity in the brain. Klonopin is also prescribed to treat panic attacks because it relieves anxiety.

-*Lorazepam* is an anti-anxiety medication that works by slowing brain activity. Often marketed under the names Ativan and Temesta, lorazepam is also helpful in treating insomnia, epilepsy, and nausea caused by cancer treatments. This drug can be habit-forming.

-*Ativan* is a brand name for lorazepam, which is used in the treatment of anxiety, epilepsy, IBS, and several other conditions. Low doses have sedative effects, whereas high doses can be hypnotic. It decreases activity in the brain for relaxation. Other variations are Diazepam and Clonazepam.

# Sleep Meds

-*Ambien* is a brand name of the drug zolpidem. It is commonly used as a short-term treatment for insomnia, and it can also be used to treat certain brain disorders. Ambien effectively initiates sleep, but does not effectively maintain sleep. It is used by many who abuse uppers like cocaine and meth to achieve sleep. Many times fatalities happen due to the deadly mixture with alcohol and the uppers.

-*Nembutal* is a brand name for pentobarbital sodium, which is a part of the group of barbiturate drugs. This medication is primarily used for the purpose of insomnia treatment for short-term relief. It can also be used as a sedative before surgery.

-*Rohypnol* is used to treat patients in a pre-surgery situation and to treat insomnia. It can be used to reduce muscle tension, to induce sedation, to reduce anxiety, and to prevent convulsions. Rohyphnol causes partial amnesia. This is what is widely known as "roofies," a date rape drug often slipped in a drink or food.

**Amphetamines** have a detection window of about three days in the blood and urine.

Amphetamines are psychoactive drugs that stimulate the central nervous system. They increase the release of dopamine and norepinephrine in the brain while inhibiting reuptake. Amphetamines are prescribed for several conditions, but they are also abused illegally.

-*Methamphetamine* is a stimulant that is highly addictive and has a high potential for widespread abuse. Methamphetamine is referred to as speed, ice, crank, glass, meth, and crystal. It looks like shards of broken glass and has a strong chemical smell. It can cost upwards of $100 a gram and is most often homemade in rural parts of the country. It was popularized by bikers years ago. It destroys the body fast and ruins the teeth because it is commonly smoked, but it can be sniffed, ingested, or injected. Meth keeps you wide awake for days. People are known to stay awake for weeks at a time, and the effects are dangerous. It is a powerful stimulant that speeds up the central nervous system and the effects can last from 6-12 hours depending on the method of use. This stimulation of the central nervous system results in a short-lived euphoric feeling and an increased heart and breathing rate, among other effects.

-*Adderall* is a medication that is given to treat symptoms of attention deficit hyperactivity disorder. Adderall can be habit-forming and is usually given in conjunction with therapy or other treatment. It comes in tablet form. It is usually taken by mouth but is sometimes snorted. It is commonly used by students who are cramming in school work. It is obtained by prescription but commonly sold for $5-10 a pill, depending on the milligram. Noticeable signs are dilated pupils, no sleep, hyper focused, and on edge behavior.

-*Dexedrine* is a brand name of the drug dextroamphetamine, which produces feelings of wakefulness, focus, decreased fatigue, and decreased appetite. It is commonly used to treat ADHD and narcolepsy, and it may be used to treat obesity and certain types of depression.

-*Dextroamphetamine* is used to increase alertness and focus, as well as to reduce appetite and fatigue. This drug makes up approximately 75% of the ADHD treatment Adderall. It also treats narcolepsy, treatment-resistant depression, and exogenous obesity.

-*Desoxyn* is a brand name for methamphetamine hydrochloride. It is a stimulant drug that causes appetite suppression and is sometimes used to treat obesity in patients who have had unsuccessful outcomes with other treatments. Desoxyn is also used to treat ADHD.

-*Dextrostat* is a brand name for dextroamphetamine, which is a stimulant used in the treatment of ADHD. It can increase blood pressure and depress the respiratory system while altering the brain's natural chemicals. This amphetamine has high potential for dependence and abuse.

-*Concerta* is a branded version of methylphenidate. This medication is used to treat the symptoms of ADHD. It is sometimes used to treat narcolepsy. It is part of the central nervous system stimulant drug family. It's available in chewable, pill, and liquid form.

Opiates and prescription pain killers all have similar signs of use such as pin point pupils, itching and scratching, nodding out, groggy voice, and severe withdrawal signs. The stronger the opiate, the faster the rate of dependency and the harder it is to quit. Many start with mild forms of the prescribed pain meds and gradually work up to harder versions as their tolerance increases or due to the lack of availability of the lighter versions. Can be tested for in the system for up to three days on average. Some opiates metabolize faster and can be in and out of the body in as little as 24 hours.

-*Heroin* is an addictive recreational drug known to induce feelings of intense relaxation and euphoria. It is an opioid derived from morphine, which is derived from the opium, poppy. Heroin can be injected, smoked, snorted, or taken orally. It is called by a bunch of street names like "boy, tar, but most commonly dope." Withdrawal is terrible from opiates and referred to as "dope sick." It comes in caps which look like the clear gel caps that supplements come in and in stamped wax paper packets with a variety of brand logos on it. Heroin is now often cut with harder more lethal synthetic opiates making the overdose rate skyrocket as of late. The cost for a bag of dope can be a little as $5, which makes it more appealing to those hooked on much more costly pain medications. Many start off sniffing heroin but quickly that escalates to IV use, as the majority of those who use heroin choose to shoot up.

-*Morphine* is an opiate analgesic classified as a narcotic. The drug is derived from opium and used to relieve severe pain. It impairs mental and physical functions, which can result in a euphoric feeling and decreased hunger, among other effects. Most commonly used in hospital and medical emergencies.

-*Fentanyl* is a potent narcotic analgesic that is used to treat severe or breakthrough pain. It is approximately 50 times more potent than heroin. It is often used in operating rooms, in intensive care units, and for treatment of cancer pain. It has made its way to the streets and is used as cut for heroin, as it is imported from foreign countries such as China and Mexico to make the dope stronger.

-*Duragesic* is an opiate analgesic applied as a skin patch. It is a brand of fentanyl patches, which are used to treat chronic and severe pain that does not lessen considerably with other narcotics. The medication can be habit forming.

-*Actiq* is the brand name for fentanyl citrate, which is a narcotic used for the treatment of pain. This particular narcotic is used primarily for cancer patients who experience pain that is not relieved by other types of medications. It can be found cut into heroin on the street and is way, way more potent than heroin. It often results in overdose fatalities.

-*Tussionex* is a prescription medication that contains a combination of hydrocodone and chlorpheniramine. The hydrocodone suppresses coughing, while the other active ingredient serves as an antihistamine. It is used to relieve symptoms of colds and the flu. It is what is called "syrup, lean, or squiggy" by many rappers and hip hop artists. Often, this is what they are drinking in the Styrofoam cups, sometimes mixed with sprite or other beverages to make it more of a drink than just the thick cough syrup. It costs upwards of $100 a bottle depending on the strength. It comes in red purple and yellow colors.

-*Codeine* is a prescription pain reliever that is classified as an opiate analgesic. This narcotic suppresses coughing, and it alters the body's perception of pain by mimicking natural endorphins. It is taken in pill or liquid form (similar to Tussionex). Codeine is often found in Tylenol. Codeine is often prescribed after removal of wisdom teeth. They are white pills with a 5 on them. Be cautious; just because it says Tylenol does not mean it is safe.

-*Percocet* is an analgesic that contains a combination of acetaminophen and oxycodon, used in the management and relief of moderate to severe pain. Percocet is typically used to deal with non-chronic pain. The drug is usually not used for breakthrough pain. Percodan is a mixture of aspirin and oxycodone. The aspirin reduces inflammation while the oxycodone serves as an opiate analgesic. This drug is used to relieve moderate to severe pain, and it can be habit-forming. Referred to as "percs," or in the case of the 10mg yellow pills, "bananas." They go for upwards of $10 a pill.

-*Vicodin* is a mixture of acetaminophen and hydrocodone. This pharmaceutical pain reliever is classified as a narcotic, as hydrocodone is an opioid analgesic. Vicodin depresses the central nervous system and impairs mental and physical functions. These are the lower-end strength of opiates, and Vicodin abuse was made popular by Brett Farve years back. On the street they cost approximately $5 a pill.

-*Roxanol*, also known as rectal morphine, is an opiate analgesic that is used to relieve moderate to severe pain. This medication comes in suppository form that must be inserted into the rectum. This drug can be habit-forming.

-*Roxicondone* is an opium-derived drug commonly used to treat patients that suffer from moderate to severe pain. This drug is commonly used in formulations with other drugs, such as acetaminophen or ibuprofen, to create brand name pharmaceuticals. Known as "Roxies or blues," the 30 mg pills were at the root of the pill mill epidemic around 2008. These are what I got busted selling and are highly potent for such a small pill. They are sniffed, smoked, ingested, and injected after broken down. They cost at least $15 each.

-*Ryzolt* is a brand name for tramadol, which is a prescription pain reliever. It is classified as an opiate agonist. Ryzolt is taken as a pill and mimics the effects of natural endorphins to change the body's perception of pain.

-*Tramadol* is a member of the opiate agonist drug family. Its primary use is pain relief, and it is administered in tablet form. Tramadol can be habit-forming. Tramadol dosage should be gradually decreased; abruptly stopping tramadol therapy can have unpleasant side effects. It is also called Ultram.

-*Norco* is a pharmaceutical-grade pain reliever that contains hydrocodone and acetaminophen. This medication is classified as a narcotic and is used to treat moderate to severe pain. The acetaminophen boosts the effects of the hydrocodone, which is an opioid analgesic.

-*Opium* is a street drug that is eaten, injected, or smoked. It is highly addictive and users quickly develop a tolerance for it. It has analgesic effects and severe withdrawal symptoms, including nausea and chills. This version of pain meds has recently gained popularity. Other similar pain medication names to watch out for are Lorcet, Lortab, Dilaudid (very popular because it can be in and out of your system in 24 hours, making it easy to avoid detection in drug screens), Hydrocodone, Biocodone, Hycodan, Hydromorphone, Demerol, Darvon, Darvocet, Hydrococet, and Dextropropoxyphene.

-*Oxycodone* is a medication prescribed to reduce and control pain. It is a narcotic that can be addictive. An overdose of oxycodone can be fatal. Oxycodone is a class B drug, meaning that it may be safe for use during pregnancy. OxyContin is the brand name for oxycodone. Side effects include fatigue, dizziness, and fainting. It is available as a liquid, tablet, extended-release tablet, and capsule. Known as Oxys, these pills are at the root of the opiate epidemic. Oxys come in a variety of sizes, and smart addicts learned to peel off the time-release coating when the drug hit the market so they could get high faster. The most common dosages are 20, 40, and 80 mg. The 80 mg pills, referred to as 80's, are the most potent. They are green and can cost well over $50 for one pill.

Cocaine, whether in powder or rock form has the same signs of use: heightened speech, sleeplessness, weight loss, loss of appetite, heightened heart rate, dilated pupils, and an obsession for more. Once you start, it's hard to stop. It's commonly used with alcohol and associated with partying because it counteracts the intoxication properties, letting you drink like a fish and not get drunk. It is bad for your heart and health and, as most drugs, will not be detected in the body after 72 hours from last use.

Cocaine is a stimulant drug and is very addictive. The three routes of administration for cocaine are snorting, injecting, and smoking. It stimulates the brain by releasing dopamine, which causes the user to feel pleasure. Cocaine is a party drug which leads to dependence after regular use. It comes in small baggies and is sold in denominations of $20–40 dollar bags. The common breakdowns are a 1/16th of an ounce and 8balls (1/8th of an ounce). Then it goes to quarter ounces and half ounces. The more you buy, the cheaper it gets. A 7ball nowadays is around $200. Powder cocaine is cut with many substances like creatine, inositol, and lidocaine (enhances the numbing effect).

Crack cocaine is freebase cocaine. It produces an immediate high and is considered a highly addictive stimulant. Crack cocaine's effects include psychological effects like intense feelings of euphoria, increased energy, insomnia, paranoia, and more. Crack is cooked with baking soda to make what's referred to on the streets as "hard," whereas powder coke is called soft. Crack is almost always smokes in a crack pipe stem or glass dick. You will find Chore Boy, which looks like a copper brillo pad, used as a filter to melt the crack onto, then it's lit and smoked. The high is so intense, you get what's called an ear ringer, where your ears literally ring after hitting the crack pipe. Crack is popular because it's stronger and cheaper. It's usually sold for as low as $5 sized rocks and up, mostly broken down in $20 denominations.

## Designer Drugs

-*Bath Salts/Flakka* are cathinones, meaning man-made drugs that mimic cathinone, a stimulant found in the East African and Sourthern Arabian khat plant. The leaves can be chewed for mild stimulant effects, but the synthetic versions are much stronger and very dangerous because they are strong psychoactive (mind-altering) substances that meant to copy the effects of illegal drugs. They are marketed as "bath salts," but are in no way related to bath products like Epsom salts. Bath salts cheap substitutes for drugs like methamphetamine and cocaine. A lot of times so-called Molly (MDMA) pills actually contain synthetic cathinones instead. Bath salts usually look like white or brown crystal-like powders sold baggies or foil packages. Some other street names stamped on the labels are "plant food," "jewelry cleaner," or "phone screen cleaner." They are easily accessible online and even in drug paraphernalia stores. Some brand names are Flakka, Bloom, Cloud Nine, Lunar, Wave, Vanilla Sky, White Lightning, and Scarface. They can be swallowed, snorted, smoked, or injected. Bath salts and other variants are hard to test for because their chemical compositions are constantly changing, as dealers try to to make them legal each time they get banned. Many confirmation toxicology labs will be able to test for just one element of the compounds, and the labs are constantly updating their machines to test for these new designer drugs. Bath salts are very dangerous; many say it feels similar to what meth is like after being up for a week. People are zombie-like and out of their minds, taking off clothes and acting very erratic.

-*Huffing* is the act of inhaling a chemical vapor through the mouth or nose. These can be classified as volatile solvents, gases, aerosol sprays, and nitrites. The effects of inhalants range from an alcohol-like intoxication and intense euphoria to vivid hallucinations. People will huff gasoline, air freshener, even the Freon from air conditioner. Noticeable signs of huffing is a red ring around the mouth and a chemical smell.

-*Dextromethorphan* (DXM) is widely used in over-the-counter cough syrups. It works by affecting the part of the brain that controls coughing. DXM is part of the antitussive family of drugs. It can cause dizziness and stomach discomfort. It's called "robo trippin'" from the brand name Robitussin, which has dextromethorphan as an ingredient. A high level of this drug is needed to feel the high, so if you see whole packs of empty cough medicine in the trash, you know they are abusing this.

-*Kratom* is a tropical evergreen tree plant named Mitragyna speciosa Korth (commonly known as kratom, also ketum. Kratom has properties similar to opiates and other stimulants. It is also known as kava. If you come up positive for this in rehab, it will be considered a relapse. Kratom costs $5–20 dollars, depending on if you by the tea, the herb, or buy it in a kava bar. Some people take it for managing chronic pain, for treating opioid withdrawal symptoms, or — more recently — for recreational purposes. However, as of 2013, no clinical trials had been conducted on kratom to test its health effects, and there are no approved medical uses. Onset of the effects typically begins within five to ten minutes and lasts two to five hours.

Marijuana, also called cannabis, is a psychoactive drug that is most often smoked. The chemical compound tetrahydrocannabinol, commonly referred to as THC, is the major psychoactive element of cannabis. Marijuana is controversially used to treat some common medical conditions. Marijuana is very socially accepted these days and praised by pop culture. It can be smoked in the flower form which comes in a bud, and lesser potent strains will be a mix of buds and shake (shake is lower quality pot and looks like oregano). The weed nowadays is so fine-tuned that the THC content, the element that gets you high, is upwards of 30% in the grown flower form. Other new methods to get high on THC are edibles, which are in the forms of gummies, brownies, etc. There are oils that are smoked and look like e-cigarette juice, and wax called dabbing. The oil has a concentration of THC upwards of 80%. Marijuana is not believed to be addictive or have withdrawal symptoms, but as I said in the book, it can be the gateway for first time drug users to harder drugs. The CBD element in marijuana is what is believed to have the healing and medical properties that have an assortment of benefits. The CBD can be obtained separate from the marijuana and extracted from the hemp plant, and it can be more of a novelty to young kids because it is available in retail shops and at gas stations. Marijuana stores itself in the fatty cells and can be in your system for an average of 28 days or more. The buds, or flower version, are rolled up in cigars or rolling papers or smoked out of glass bowls, bongs, or dry herb vaporizers. The wax is also smoked out of electronic devices along with the oil.

-*Hashish*, often referred to as hash, is a product of the cannabis plant. Prepared from marijuana buds, hash is commonly burned and inhaled. The effects are often many times more potent than those of unprocessed marijuana buds. Hash looks like tar or clay and is, for the most part, harder to come by. Flower marijuana is sold in denominations similar to cocaine, most commonly in grams, which average $20–40. The weed around today is not the stuff from the 60s. It's potent and has a strong odor. The wax and oils may be a bit pricier due to the concentration. Many states are going forward with medical laws, recreational use laws, and decriminalization. Check your individual states laws.

## Hallucinogens

-*LSD* is the abbreviation for lysergic acid diethylamide. LSD, or acid as it is usually called, is a drug that causes several psychological effects including hallucinations. It isn't addictive and is commonly taken orally, via things like sugar cubes or blotter paper. Its effects are called trippin', and there can be bad trips as well as good. The high lasts for several hours, and dilated pupils and blank stares are common symptoms. It's not possible to overdose, or so I am told, but many people feel super human or get a dangerous feeling that they can fly and end up dead from jumping off a ledge. This is the real concern with the hallucinogens. A hit of acid can cost as little as $5, and it's enough to get you really, really fucked up. Some acid on blotter paper will have a design on the sheet and users will refer to it as that design, like "Mad Hatters" or "Bart Simpsons." Gel tabs look like little squares of plastic and are similar to the little 1/2"x1/2" paper hits. Somehow LSD and other hallucinogens are more available to teens than adults. I could find acid everywhere when I was 17 but came across it rarely after I was 21. Teens usually trip in groups and plan it as an event. I am not sure there are any drug tests to test for LSD, but many say they see trails when high and often have flashbacks years after use.

-*Mushrooms*, often called Magic Mushrooms, are a specific strain of fungi that contain the hallucinogens psilocybin. It causes a distortion of the senses, which can be pleasurable or terrifying, when the mushroom is consumed whole or brewed into tea. The high lasts about half as long as LSD and is milder. An eighth of an ounce of "shrooms" goes for upwards of $25.

-*Peyote* is a drug found in a small, spineless cactus. After eating peyote, the user experiences dream-like hallucinations. The active ingredient in peyote is mescaline, and the effect varies from person to person. Indigenous Americans often used peyote for rituals.

-*Mescaline* is a naturally occurring psychedelic drug found in the peyote cactus. Mescaline visually distorts the user's vision. It does not cause hallucinations, and tolerance is built with continued use. Mescaline is illegal in the United States.

-*PCP* is the abbreviation for phencyclidine, an addictive drug with anesthetic, sedative, and hallucinogenic effects. It is a white powder that can be dissolved in water or alcohol. PCP can be smoked, snorted, injected, or taken orally. "Sherman sticks" were popular when I was younger. They were cigarettes dipped in PCP and, as I was told, embalming fluid. PCP smells like straight chemicals. I remember coming home all fucked up one night, and my mom said, "Let me smell your breath." It stunk like cleaner because I was taking bong hit of this shit. It makes people crazy, and they sometimes strip naked. When I bought it, it came in wax paper packets like heroin and seemed to me like tea leaves or oregano soaked in the powerful liquid. It was around $5 a packet back in 1996, but I have not heard much about the use of it lately. It can be tested for up to three days in the urine and blood.

## Club Drugs

-*Ecstasy* is the street name for the drug MDMA. MDMA is a synthetic psychoactive drug that induces feelings of euphoria, increased energy, and emotional warmth in the user. It is taken orally as a capsule or tablet. Known as E or, nowadays, Molly, it is a popular substitute for LSD. When I was a kid there was no ecstasy. As I understand, MDMA is the pure version of Molly; it comes in capsules. The ecstasy tablets' effects are either dopey or speedy based on what they are cut with and can be named things like Rolex or Green Marshmallows and stamped with a logo on the pill. Rolling is what some call the high, and effects are similar to LSD. Molly goes hand in hand with electronic music, as it makes the music enjoyable. Many people open up and see the "big picture" when on E. A dose costs around $20, and one or two pills is enough to be high for hours.

-*Ketamine* was originally developed as a general anesthetic, Ketamine is a form of PCP. Ketamine causes its user to dissociate from his surroundings and himself. In controlled forms, the drug is also used as an anesthetic for humans and animals. Known as K, Special K, or Kitty, it comes in either as cooked powder that is sniffed or in "licks," which are IV vials that are injected. The liquid form can also be cooked in a microwave, or baked in the oven to evaporate the water leaving the powder left over on the plate. It's scrapped up and sniffed and is usually jarred up in little brown or clear vials. If you do too much, you go into what's called a K Hole where some have an out-of-body experience, and your feet feel like you have on cement shoes. Oddly enough, you look sober for the most part on ketamine. The high lasts for 20 to 30 minutes, and the hangover is not so bad. A lick of K can cost $100, and a gram will got for around $60.

-*GHB*, which is short for gamma hydroxybutyrate, is a pharmacological substance that was approved to treat narcolepsy. The odorless powder or liquid is affects the brain's GABA receptors and depresses the central nervous system, causing intoxication. G will completely fuck you up. The name brand was Verve when I was younger, and using too much is very easy to do. It is also used as a date rape drug. If you use too much, you will puke, black out, take off your clothes, and urinate and/or defecate on yourself. It was initially used by body builders to get deep sleep to heal the muscles faster. A bottle of G is a few hundred dollars and is popular to combine with other club drugs to add to the high.

-*Quaalude* is a sedative drug that was once prescribed for insomnia and as a muscle relaxant. It gained popularity in the 1960s and 1970s as a recreational drug and is currently a drug that cannot be prescribed by physicians. Methaqualone is the generic term for Quaaludes. It was initially marketed as a non-habit-forming substitute for barbiturates, but it has slightly different properties and ultimately had a high rate of abuse. This sedative-hypnotic drug can cause euphoric feelings and sleepiness. Ludes are rare and have been out of production for many years.

-*Nitrous Oxide* is inhaled in and is a party drug. It comes in big tanks, like the ones used in race cars, is pumped into balloons. There are also what's called "whip its." Nitrous oxide is what's put in whipped cream containers to make the product shoot out. So if your whipped cream is not working in the fridge, odds are your kid inhaled it. It makes your head buzz and makes you laugh. It lasts only a matter of minutes. Whip its are sold in novelty stores for about $20. They are small, portable canisters of gas that are cracked open. A balloon is placed on the opening, and once it is full, the gas is sucked from the balloon.

## Common Prescriptions that, though less powerful than illegal drugs, have been abused.

-*Soma* is the brand name for the drug carisoprodol, which is a muscle relaxant. It is used as treatment for acute back pain. Dependency and side effects of this drug are controversial and have caused concern in some countries.

-*Ritalin* is one of the trade names for the stimulant methylphenidate. It is commonly used for the treatment of attention deficit hyperactivity disorder and the sleep disorder, narcolepsy. Ritalin is available in tablet, capsule, and liquid form.

-*Steroids* are a class of drugs used to stimulate certain functions in the body. Steroids are prescribed medicinally to stimulate cell production or a patient's appetite. When combined with hormones, steroids can be used as a contraceptive. The most popular is testosterone, known as TEST, but there are a number of other varieties. Some come in pill form, but most commonly it's used by injection. So if you find the needles, which are a different kind than those used for IV drugs, you will also find a vial along with it for the most part. Steroids can stunt growth, cause violent mood swings, cause skin to break out, cause the scrotum to shrink, and of course noticeable rapid muscle development is a sure sign. The real mood swings come when someone stops taking the steroids, or "juice" as it is called. This is when they start losing their muscle, and they become tired and on edge. A "cycle" of steroids costs upwards of $80.

## Prescription Drugs currently used for those dealing with addiction and dependence.

-*Methadone* is a narcotic analgesic that is prescribed to help patients with withdrawal symptoms from illegal drug use or to deal with severe pain. This medication can be habit-forming and may be prescribed in decreasing amounts to alleviate additional withdrawal.

-*Buprenorphine* is a drug that causes effects similar to methadone and heroin. When given at low doses, it can help individuals addicted to opioids avoid withdrawal symptoms. The drug is available as a tablet that's placed under the tongue.

-*Suboxone* is an FDA-approved drug used to supplement additional detox treatments for pain killer addictions. It contains buprenorphine and naloxone. When used under the supervision of a physician, this medicine can help an individual overcome an opioid dependence.

-*Subutex* is a brand name version of buprenorphine that is used to treat an opioid addiction. It, itself, is an opioid and can be addictive. It must be taken as directed to avoid the risk of serious injury or death, so it should be used with caution under observation.

-*Naltrexone* is an opioid receptor antagonist used in medication-assisted treatment of alcohol or drug abuse. Naltrexone comes in tablet form or in an extended-release injection form and acts blocks the effects of opioids.

-*ReVia* is classified as an opiate antagonist. Also known as naltrexone, this drug is used to help people avoid drinking and using drugs once they have achieved sobriety. It is available in tablet form and is often prescribed in combination with counseling.

-*Vivitrol* is another name for a naltrexone injection. It is prescribed along with counseling for addiction. It reduces the urge to drink or use drugs. It cannot be taken together with drugs or alcohol.

-*Orlaam* is a narcotic analgesic that is prescribed as part of a recovery because it helps prevent withdrawal symptoms. It is usually given as a detox drug in gradually decreasing doses until the patient is drug-free.

-*Clonidine* is an antihypertensive used in the treatment of high blood pressure, ADHD, dysmenorrhea, and other conditions. It relaxes blood vessels and decreases the heart rate. Clonidine comes in tablet form and is often combined with other medications. This medication is commonly prescribed in drug treatment programs for one reason or another.

-*Depade* is an addiction-recovery medication to help prevent relapse. This drug is an opiate antagonist, which means it works in the brain to prevent opiate effects and reduce the desire to take opiates.

-*Acamprosate* helps recovering alcoholics stay sober by maintaining the chemical balance of the brain. Acamprosate must be combined with therapy and complete abstinence from alcohol to remain effective. There is also evidence that acamprosate protects against neuron death caused by alcohol withdrawal.

-*Antabuse* is a brand name of the drug disulfiram, which prevents the breakdown of dopamine. It is used to treat severe, continued alcoholism by causing sensitivity to alcohol. Antabuse is also a possible treatment for cocaine dependence.

-*Chlordiazepoxide* is used to treat the effects of alcohol withdrawal as well as the symptoms of irritable bowel syndrome. It must be taken regularly to work correctly, but it can be habit-forming. Chloridiazepoxide should not be taken for more than four months.

-*Librium* is a brand name for chlordiazepoxide, which is used to treat the symptoms of alcohol withdrawal and IBS. It reduces anxiety and agitation by depressing the central nervous system. Librium is classified as a benzodiazepine and can be habit-forming.

-*Halcion* is a brand name for triazolam, which is a benzodiazepine. This medication is generally used as a short-term treatment for insomnia. It acts as a sedative and hypnotic, and it has a calming effect on the mind and body.

-*Campral* is a brand name for acamprosate, a medicine given to alcoholics to help them avoid drinking again. While it does not prevent withdrawal symptoms, it does help the brain function normally again.

-*Phenobarbital*, also known as Luminal, is a barbiturate. It is commonly used as an anticonvulsant to treat seizures. It can also be used to treat acute withdrawal from benzodiazepines, which can cause tremors and seizures. Pentobarbital works by slowing the brain and nervous system activity. It is used to treat insomnia for short-term relief, and has been used for sedation before surgery and as a treatment for seizures in an emergency. Luminal is a brand name of the drug.

-*Gabapentin*, brand name Neurontin, is referred to as johnnies. When 10-plus pills are consumed at the same time, it causes a high. The nickname "johnnies" refers to mixing gabapentin with Red Bull to enhance the high. This drug is approved by the Food and Drug Administration to treat epilepsy and shingles pain. It is also unofficially prescribed for depression, migraine, fibromyalgia and bipolar disorder, or as an alternative to opioid pain medication. However it is being abused because it isn't being properly regulated or regularly tested for because it wasn't thought to be have much potential for abuse. This is because gabapentin only creates a dependency when taken with other drugs, such as opioids, muscle relaxants, and anxiety medications like Valium and Xanax. When combined, it creates an extra euphoric effect. It can also act as a powerful sedative, so meth and heroin users will take it to mellow out before they tweak or start cutting drugs. Side effects include dizziness, fatigue, weight gain, inability to control muscles, drowsiness, and nervousness.

# APPENDIX C:
# EXTRAS

Want Extra Information, Resources, and Articles?

Check out my website for blog posts and videos on prevention, rehab, and recovery: www.Adamjasinski.org

**Want to Get in Touch with Me?**


| | |
|---|---|
| Address: | PO Box 2016 |
| | Delray Beach, FL 33483 |
| Phone: | 561.806.1001 |
| Email: | Adam@AdamJasinski.org |

# BIBLIOGRAPHY

About Emotional Brain Training. *Emotional Brain Training.* Retrieved from http://www.ebtgroups.com/about.

Emotional Brain Training. *Compassion Point Counseling Services.* Retrieved from http://www.compasspointcounseling.net/treatment-types/emotional-brain-training/.

Gad, Ron N. Psychodynamic Therapy. *Good Therapy.* Retrieved from http://www.goodtherapy.org/learn-about-therapy/types/psychodynamic.

Historical Data: The birth of AA and its growth in the US and Canada. *Alcoholics Anonymous.* Retrieved from http://www.aa.org/pages/en_US/historical-data-the-birth- of-aa-and-its-growth-in-the-uscanada.

Martin, B. (2016). In-Depth: Cognitive Behavioral Therapy. *Psych Central.* Retrieved from https://psychcentral.com/lib/in-depth-cognitive-behavioral-therapy/.

Sheff, David (2013). *Clean: Overcoming addiction and ending America's greatest tragedy.* Boston: Eamon Dolan/Houghton Mifflin Harcourt.

Therapy. *Mental Health America.* Retrieved from http://www.mentalhealthamerica.net/therapy.